Mark Twain

In Nevada

Journalism 1862- 1864

The Archive of American Journalism

Lincoln Steffens

Henry Stanley

Theodore Roosevelt

Richard Harding Davis

Ida Tarbell

Ray Stannard Baker

Nellie Bly

H.L. Mencken

Ambrose Bierce

Stephen Crane

Jack London

Mark Twain

Ernest Hemingway

Mark Twain

In Nevada

Journalism 1862 - 1864

Edited and with an Introduction by Tom Streissguth

The Archive, LLC
St. Paul, Minnesota
2016

Note on Sources

All articles are complete and unabridged, with headlines, subheads and formatting that match those of the original publication. Note that minor edits have been made to correct obsolete spelling and punctuation. Students and researchers: these are "public domain" texts that can be freely copied, reproduced and distributed without permission or cost. Please credit The Archive of American Journalism as your source.

The Archive LLC
9269 Troon Court
Woodbury, MN 55125.

Article selection and original Introduction Copyright ©2015 by Tom Streissguth. All articles contained within this volume, as well as original works of Jack London, Ernest Hemingway, Richard Harding Davis, Ambrose Bierce and other major American authors, are now freely available at www.historicjournalism.com

Cover Image: Las Vegas, from the Carol Highsmith Archive, Library of Congress

Library of Congress Control Number: 2015944398
ISBN: 978-0-9907137-0-8
Printed in the United States of America

Acknowledgments

For their encouragement and suggestions, sincere thanks to Mark Lerner, Gordon Hagert, Pier Gustafson, Phil Gapp, Jonathan Peacock, John Hatch, Marian Streissguth and our original founding supporters: *William F. Zeman, Phil Gapp, Walter Crowley, Adele Streissguth, Richard Prosser, Abhilash Sarhadi, James McGrath Morris.*

Contents

Introduction — xiv

Another Innocent Man Killed
Virginia City Territorial Enterprise/September 16, 1862 — 1

Local Column: A Gale
Virginia City Territorial Enterprise/October 1, 1862 — 2

Petrified Man
Virginia City Territorial Enterprise/October 4, 1862 — 5

[No Title]
Virginia City Territorial Enterprise/October 13, 1862 — 6

The Spanish Mine
Virginia City Territorial Enterprise/October, 1862 — 6

Silver Bricks
Virginia City Territorial Enterprise/November 1, 1862 — 8

Letter from Carson City
Virginia City Territorial Enterprise/c. December 12, 1862 — 9

The Pah-Utes
Virginia City Territorial Enterprise/c. December 13, 1862 — 12

A Big Thing in Washoe City
Virginia City Territorial Enterprise/c. December 24, 1862 — 13

The Illustrious Departed
Virginia City Territorial Enterprise/December 28, 1862 — 15

Local Column
Virginia City Territorial Enterprise/c. c. December 30, 1862 — 16

Local Column
Virginia City Territorial Enterprise/January 1, 1863   18

Sulphur Deposit
Virginia City Territorial Enterprise/c. January 1, 1863   19

Unfortunate Thief
Virginia City Territorial Enterprise/January 8, 1863   20

Local Column
Virginia City Territorial Enterprise/January 10, 1863   21

Local Column
Virginia City Territorial Enterprise/c. January 11, 1863   24

Territorial Sweets
Virginia City Territorial Enterprise/c. January 22, 1863   25

The Spanish
Virginia City Territorial Enterprise/c. February 12, 1863   25

Letter from Carson
Virginia City Territorial Enterprise/February 3, 1863   27

Letter from Carson
Virginia City Territorial Enterprise/February 8, 1863   30

Local Column
Virginia City Territorial Enterprise/c. February 17, 1863   34

Silver Bars--How Assayed
Virginia City Territorial Enterprise/c. February 17, 1863   35

Ye Sentimental Law Student
Virginia City Territorial Enterprise/February 19, 1863   38

Local Column
Virginia City Territorial Enterprise/February 25, 1863   40

Reportorial
Virginia City Territorial Enterprise/February 26, 1863   *43*

Local Column
Virginia City Territorial Enterprise/c. March 1, 1863   *44*

A Sunday in Carson
Virginia City Territorial Enterprise/c. March 3, 1863   *44*

City Marshall Perry
Virginia City Territorial Enterprise/March 4, 1863   *45*

Champagne With the Board of Brokers
Virginia City Territorial Enterprise/March 7, 1863   *48*

Examination of Teachers
Virginia City Territorial Enterprise/c. April 1, 1863   *49*

Local Column
Virginia City Territorial Enterprise/April 3, 1863   *51*

Advice to the Unreliable on Church Going
Virginia City Territorial Enterprise/April 12, 1863   *53*

Horrible Affair
Virginia City Territorial Enterprise/c. April 16, 1863   *54*

Local Column
Virginia City Territorial Enterprise/c. April 19, 1863   *55*

Letter from Mark Twain
Virginia City Territorial Enterprise/c. May 19, 1863   *55*

Letter from Mark Twain--All About Fashions
Virginia City Territorial Enterprise/c. June 21, 1863   *58*

Mark Twain's Letter--Home Again
San Francisco Daily Morning Call/July 9, 1863   *61*

Mark Twain's Letter
San Francisco Daily Call/July 15, 1863 — *64*

Mark Twain's Letter
San Francisco Daily Call/July 18, 1863 — *68*

Mark Twain's Letter
San Francisco Daily Call/July 23, 1863 — *69*

Mark Twain's Letter
San Francisco Daily Call/July 30, 1863 — *73*

Dispatches by the State Line
San Francisco Daily Call/August 2, 1863 — *74*

A Duel Prevented
Virginia City Enterprise/August 2, 1863 — *75*

An Apology Repudiated
Virginia City Enterprise/August 4, 1863 — *76*

Mark Twain's Letter--Fire Matters
San Francisco Daily Call/August 6, 1863 — *77*

Mark Twain's Letter
San Francisco Daily Call/August 13, 1863 — *81*

Letter From Mark Twain
Virginia City Enterprise/August 19, 1863 — *84*

Letter From Mark Twain--Steamboat Springs Hotel
Virginia City Enterprise/August 25, 1863 — *87*

Local Column
Virginia City Enterprise/August 27, 1863 — *91*

Dispatches By the State Line
San Francisco Daily Call/August 29, 1863 — *94*

Mark Twain's Letter
San Francisco Daily Call/August 30, 1863   95

Dispatches by the State Line
San Francisco Daily Call/September 3, 1863   99

Mark Twain's Letter
San Francisco Daily Call/September 3, 1863   100

Bigler vs. Tahoe
Virginia City Enterprise/c. September, 1863   101

Letter from Mark Twain
Virginia City Enterprise/September 17, 1863   102

How to Cure a Cold
The Golden Era/September 20, 1863   106

First Annual Fair of the Washoe
Agricultural, Mining and Mechanical Society
Virginia City Enterprise/c. October 20, 1863   111

A Bloody Massacre Near Carson
Virginia City Enterprise/October 28, 1863   116

I Take it All Back
Virginia City Enterprise/October 29, 1863   118

Letter from Mark Twain
Virginia City Enterprise/c. November 8, 1863   118

Letter from Mark Twain
Virginia City Enterprise/November 17, 1863   121

Mark Twain on Artemus Ward, "The Wild Humorist of the Plains"
Virginia City Enterprise/November 27, 1863   123

Review of "Ingomar the Barbarian"
The Golden Erae/November 29, 1863   123

A Tide of Eloquence
Virginia City Enterprise/c. December 1, 1863   *125*

Dispatches by the State Line--Death, Robbery
San Francisco Daily Call/December 2, 1863   *126*

Letter from Mark Twain
Virginia City Enterprise/c. December 6, 1863   *126*

Letter from Mark Twain
Virginia City Enterprise/c. December 13, 1863   *129*

Dispatches by the State Line
San Francisco Daily Call/December 11, 1863   *133*

Nevada State Constitutional Convention
Virginia City Enterprise/c. December 14, 1863   *133*

Local Column
Virginia City Enterprise/c. December 25, 1863   *141*

Christmas Presents
Virginia City Enterprise, December 29, 1863   *141*

The Bolters in Convention
Virginia City Enterprise/December 30, 1863   *142*

A Gorgeous Swindle
Virginia City Enterprise/December 30, 1863   *147*

Letter from Mark Twain--Politics
Virginia City Enterprise/c. January 11, 1864   *149*

Legislative Proceedings
Virginia City Enterprise/c. January 13, 1864   *152*

Legislative Proceedings
Virginia City Enterprise/c. January 14, 1864   *153*

Legislative Proceedings--House, Third Day
Virginia City Enterprise/c. January 15, 1864 — *156*

Legislative Proceedings--House, Fourth Day
Virginia City Enterprise/c. January 16, 1864 — *157*

Letter from Mark Twain--Miss Clapp's School
Virginia City Enterprise/c. January 19, 1864 — *158*

Legislative Proceedings--House, Ninth Day
Virginia City Enterprise/c. January 21, 1864 — *162*

Legislative Proceedings--Tenth Day
Virginia City Enterprise/c. January 22, 1864 — *162*

Legislative Proceedings--House, Sixteenth Day
Virginia City Enterprise/c. January 28, 1864 — *164*

Legislative Proceedings--House, Seventeenth Day
Virginia City Enterprise/c. January 29, 1864 — *165*

Letter from Dayton
Virginia City Enterprise/c. February 1, 1864 — *166*

Doings in Nevada
New York Sunday Mercury/February 7, 1864 — *167*

Letter from Carson City--Concerning Notaries
Virginia City Territorial Enterprise/February 9, 1864 — *171*

Letter from Mark Twain
Virginia City Enterprise/February 12, 1864 — *175*

Legislative Proceedings--House, Twenty-Eighth Day
Virginia City Enterprise/c. February 9, 1864 — *179*

Legislative Proceedings--House, Twenty-Ninth Day
Virginia City Enterprise/February 10, 1864 — *180*

Legislative Proceedings--Tuesday Afternoon
Virginia City Enterprise/c. February 11, 1864   *181*

Legislative Proceedings--House, Thirty-First Day
Virginia City Enterprise/c. February 12, 1864   *181*

Legislative Proceedings--Friday Afternoon
Virginia City Enterprise/c. February 13, 1864   *183*

Legislative Proceedings--Saturday Afternoon
Virginia City Enterprise/c. February 14, 1864   *184*

Letter from Mark Twain
Virginia City Territorial Enterprise/c. February 14, 1864   *184*

Legislative Proceedings--House, Thirty-Fifth Day
Virginia City Enterprise/c. February 16, 1864   *187*

The Removal of the Capital
Virginia City Enterprise/February 16, 1864   *188*

Legislative Proceedings--House, Thirty-Sixth Day
Virginia City Enterprise/c. February 17, 1864   *191*

Legislative Proceedings--House, Thirty-Seventh Day
Virginia City Enterprise/c. February 18, 1864   *193*

Legislative Proceedings--House, Thirty-Eighth Day
Virginia City Enterprise/c. February 19, 1864   *196*

Legislative Proceedings--House, Thirty-Ninth Day
Virginia City Enterprise/c. February 20, 1864   *197*

Legislative Proceedings--House, Fortieth Day
Virginia City Enterprise/c. February 21, 1864   *199*

Frightful Accident to Dan DeQuille
Virginia City Enterprise/April 20, 1864   *202*

Letter from Mark Twain
Virginia City Enterprise/April 28, 1864   *204*

Washoe. "Information Wanted"
Virginia City Enterprise/May 1, 1864   *207*

Personal Correspondence
Virginia City Enterprise/May 24, 1864   *211*

"Miscegenation"
Virginia City Enterprise/May 24, 1864   *216*

"Mark Twain" in the Metropolis
Virginia City Enterprise/c. June 17, 1864   *216*

A Notable Conundrum
The Californian/October 1, 1864   *219*

Concerning the Answer to that Conundrum
The Californian/October 8, 1864   *221*

Still Further Concerning that Conundrum
The Californian/October 15, 1864   *225*

Whereas
The Californian/October 22, 1864   *229*

A Touching Story of George Washington's Boyhood
The Californian/October 29, 1864   *233*

Daniel in the Lion's Den--And Out Again All Right
The Californian/November 5, 1864   *237*

A Full and Reliable Account
The Californian/November 19, 1864   *242*

Works by Mark Twain   *248*
Sources/Internet Sites   *250*
Further Reading   *250*

Introduction

After joining a volunteer Confederate militia at the outbreak of the Civil War, Samuel Clemens quickly discovered he had little aptitude for military life, and only a very brief opportunity to hone his skills. Upon hearing the rumor of an approaching Union squadron, the Marion Rangers promptly agreed to disband, after just two weeks in the field. In the same fateful spring of 1861, Clemens' brother Orion had been appointed secretary of the new western territory of Nevada. With arrest for his desertion of the Southern cause a distinct possibility, and no other promising vocation at hand, Clemens climbed aboard a westbound stagecoach at St. Joseph, Missouri on July 26. The brothers endured 21 long days on the trails heading over the Great Plains and the Rocky Mountains, and through the Great Salt Lake and Great Basin deserts, before finally arriving in Carson City, Nevada Territory.

Although he was drawn by the legendary riches given up by the nearby Comstock silver mine, Clemens soon found buying claims and digging for silver-bearing ore to be an uncertain proposition. But he also made the acquaintance of Joseph Goodman, a 24-year-old New York-born emigrant employed by *The Golden Era*, an esteemed San Francisco literary paper. The friends exchanged letters, with Clemens describing in entertaining detail his long string of failures in the silver-mining line. After purchasing with his partner Denis McCarthy the *Virginia City Territorial Enterprise*, a struggling news sheet based in a bustling Nevada mining town, Goodman found himself in need of a reporter. His leading literary fixture, Dan DeQuille, was on leave, and in Goodman's opinion, Clemens would do as a temporary.

In late September, 1862, Samuel Clemens walked 130 miles over sagebrush plains and through rock-strewn valleys, from the Aurora mining district to the busy streets of Virginia City, to take up journalism. Goodman's instructions to his new reporter were short and direct: Clemens was to walk the streeets and ask questions. The ordinary events of mining town life--the street fights, murders, highway robberies, stock scams, hotel balls, the arrival of hay wagons and pack trains--were to be magnified into "breaking news" and dramatic bulletins. When news was short, *Enterprise* writers had liberty to vary their repertoire: scientific hoaxes, lampoons, poetry, exaggeration and satire were given free reign alongside the eye-glazing reports from the San Francisco broker's exchange and the Nevada territorial legislature.

Clemens wandered Virginia City for five hours, finding nothing to his interest, and returned to the *Enterprise* office in some frustration. Goodman directed his reporter's attention to the arrival of commercial hay wagons, which carried news and rumors along the remote trails leading to Virginia City from all points. Finding nothing more than a single wretched specimen in the street, Clemens turned to an enhanced reality, transforming the mundane fact into a spectacular fable. Hay wagons by the dozen began tumbling through the streets, alerting the citizens to fascinating and terrifying events beyond the city limits. By the end of the day, Samuel Clemens had found his true calling.

These were not his first published writings; as a teenager Clemens wrote fillers for the *Hannibal Western Union,* run by Orion Clemens out of the front parlor of the brothers' boyhood home, and for papers in Keokuk and Muscatine, Iowa. The writing profession had never struck Clemens as a particularly worthy career, but William Barstow, the business manager of the *Enterprise,* was so taken with Clemens' work that he offered the rookie a permanent position as a local reporter at a salary of $25 a week. Facing a serious lack of funds, and finding writing an amusing way to pass the time, Clemens negotiated, and then accepted.

"I took the position of local editor with joy, because there was a salary of forty dollars a week attached to it and I judged that that was all of thirty-nine dollars more than I was worth, and I had always wanted a position that paid in the opposite proportion of value to amount of work."

Clemens discovered that news came on its own, and without much prompting, through his own network of barroom friends and street acquaintances. He gained some local renown as a writer and talker, and his reputation grew along with that of the *Enterprise.* In the 18 months after investing in the paper, Goodman had transformed it from small-town wallpaper stock into one of the most successful dailies between Chicago and the west coast. Housed in a handsome stone building on C Street, Virginia City's main drag, the *Enterprise* had five editors, a steam-driven press and an in-house cook, and was netting a clean profit of $1,000 a day.

On the return of Dan De Quille, Clemens took the more experienced man for a mentor. De Quille specialized in improbable hoaxes, done up in all seriousness and written well enough to be accepted for reprinting in much larger papers across the country. The De Quille influence soon made itself apparent.

On October 4, 1862, Clemens reported on the discovery of a prospector's body in the nearby desert ("Petrified Man"). It was not an unusual event, but in this case the lonely, undiscovered corpse had been hardened into limestone by a slowly dripping stream of mineral-bearing water; reasonable estimates put the age of the rare human fossil at approximately one century. The Virginia City coroner G.T. Sewall, according to the account, had immediately summoned a jury of inquest and headed into the desert, where onlookers, frustrated in their efforts to pry the body loose, had proposed dynamiting it. Sewell had adamantly refused, insisting for the sake of decorum and scientific inquiry that the body must be preserved intact.

It was the custom of major newspapers to reprint interesting dispatches from the distant territories, sent via telegraph, and much to the embarrassment of the real G.T. Sewall, "Petrified Man" appeared in several California dailies. Samuel Clemens had perpetrated his first public hoax, and made the first of several local enemies.

The young reporter had found there was no lack of genuine events to spur his writing. The Ophir, Spanish and Mexican mines worked noisily around the clock in the surrounding desert hillsides. Stock scams proliferated, while in the streets, brothels and barrooms a crowd of rowdy, hard-working men with a few dollars to spare clamored noisily for amusement. The circumstances gave rise to violent incidents, all great fodder for an imaginative reporter who didn't feel too strictly bound by the simple facts. Clemens also had a chance to further his education in the often-questionable business practices of local mining companies. In this racket, partners could form a joint-stock corporation about as easily as they could buy a round of drinks. Ore samples used to support their claims were "salted" with melted-down coins, and gaily printed stock certificates were sold to gullible investors seeking the chance at real money from the reputedly vast silver fortune waiting underground.

Clemens soon was in possession of a library of his own certificates, turned over to him in the expectation that his articles would give a prominent voice to the boastful claims. But he didn't quite have the presence of mind or the talent to personally profit from these scams; he simply couldn't navigate the sudden rises and drops in exchange prices, and with all his connections couldn't seem to maneuver himself into the right place, with the right mining stock, at the right time. Although in almost all cases the paper eventually proved worthless, he was gaining valuable experience in a vital skill: the manipulation of public opinion.

In February 1863, under an innocuous dispatch sent while on assignment to the territorial legislature in Carson City, Clemens signed his name "Mark Twain." According to men who knew him, the name came from a familiar local phrase, much used by Mr. Clemens himself in local saloons, to order two drinks, on credit. On the investigation of later biographers, the origin ascribed by the author himself--as a pseudonym used by a riverboat captain named Isaiah Sellars--turned out to be yet another imaginative hoax.

As "Mark Twain," the *Enterprise* reporter found himself at greater liberty to create a distinctive voice and journalistic personality. The reputation of Mark Twain began to spread beyond the environs of Virginia City, most importantly to the home of *The Golden Era*, the *Daily Morning Call* and other leading papers. In September, 1863, Twain left for a visit to San Francisco and the offices of the *Era*, where his contributions were beginning to draw attention.

On his return to Virginia City and the *Enterprise*, Twain felt surefooted enough to perpetrate "A Bloody Massacre Near Carson," another grand hoax. This was a shocking tale of a local prospector left broke and enraged enough by the underhanded practices of a San Francisco water company to murder his entire family, then cut his own throat. The vivid details distressed more delicate readers, who could not get past the blood to understand Twain's real purpose: to satirize the financial manipulations of cheating capitalists in Virginia City as well as San Francisco. Very few saw the humor, however, and Twain's subsequent retraction ("I Take it All Back") and apology did little to assuage shocked sensibilities. The resulting scandal drove Twain down to Carson City, where he dutifully sent up a series of numbingly detailed reports on the doings of the territorial legislautre.

Mark Twain never did quite take newspaper reporting seriously. He may have realized that subtle exaggeration did not always sit well with the readers, but he simply could not resist a cutting jibe when a good one suggested itself. Commenting on the activity of a local charity drive, he tossed in the following convoluted joke:

> "The reason the Flour Sack was not taken from Dayton to Carson was because it was stated that the money raised at the Sanitary Fund Fancy Dress ball, recently held in Carson for the St. Louis Fair, had been diverted from its original course, and was being sent to aid a Miscegenation Society somewhere in the East, and it was feared the proceeds of the sack might be similarly disposed of."

The implication that charitable funds were being dishonestly diverted, along with a throwaway reference to racial mixing, caused an indignant detonation among the ladies who organized the campaign. Their husbands protested violently; Twain apologized privately, claiming he had sought to withdraw the article before publication. He then dug himself in a little deeper by claiming that a rival newspaper, the *Virginia City Union*, had reneged on its own charitable pledge. Threats, challenges, and insults were freely exchanged in the two papers until Twain was moved to pick up a gun and begin target practice for the expected showdown with James Laird, the *Union*'s gravely insulted publisher. Although the confrontation was headed off at the last minute, Twain had offended some respectable citizens as well as the law against dueling: there was, comically, an ordinance against "sending a challenge" in Virginia City.

There was no clear path out of his difficult situation, and so on May 29, 1864, Twain boarded a stagecoach headed west over the Sierra Nevada to San Francisco. His brief association with the *Enterprise* and the silver-mining country turned out to be a stroke of elusive good luck; over the course of the Civil War the *Enterprise* developed the highest circulation of any daily between San Francisco and Chicago, and Twain's articles appeared with regularity in the *New York Sunday Mercury*, the *San Francisco Daily Morning Call* and *The Golden Era*. Under the name Mark Twain, the formerly luckless Samuel Clemens was gaining a nationwide audience for his unique combination of keen observation, sardonic wit, and common-sense philosophy.

—Tom Streissguth
July, 2015

Post-Script and Notice to Readers

The editor pays his cordial respects to Mr. Twain's admirable liberality in the matter of capitalization, and his favoring of certain common nouns with the decorum of capitals, however, he takes some exception to the original text in the matter of orthograpy and punctuation, and holds hyphens, dashes, commas and semicolons to be entirely at his (the editor's) mercy.

In Nevada

Journalism 1862- 1864

THE DAILY TERRITORIAL ENTERPRISE

Is published every morning, Sundays excepted.

—BY—

GOODMAN & McCARTHY,

J. T. GOODMAN, ... D. E. McCARTHY.

PUBLICATION OFFICE,

A STREET, ... VIRGINIA CITY

TERMS OF SUBSCRIPTION:

ONE YEAR, in advance............................$16 00
SIX MONTHS....................................... 10 00
THREE MONTHS..................................... 6 00

Subscribers in VIRGINIA CITY, SILVER CITY, GOLD HILL, DAYTON, and CARSON CITY, will be Served by the Carriers at Fifty Cents per Week.

ADVERTISING

DONE AT REASONABLE RATES.

Enterprise Job Printing Office

As we have the finest assortment in the Territory, of

PLAIN AND FANCY TYPE, BORDERS,

etc. etc., and employ none but good workmen, we are prepared to execute, in the best style and at reasonable prices,

EVERY DESCRIPTION OF JOB WORK

— SUCH AS —

Visiting Cards,	Ball Tickets,	Certificates of Stock,
Wedding Cards,	Bill-Heads,	Real Estate Deeds,
Business Cards,	Circulars,	Mining Deeds,
Justices' Blanks,	Programmes,	Posters, etc.

GOODMAN & McCARTHY.

Virginia City Territorial Enterprise
September 16, 1862

Another Innocent Man Killed

    A man named Samuel L. Franklin was shot by another named Peyton, between the hours of nine and ten o'clock on Sunday evening last. Peyton drew his pistol to shoot a man named Wooley, but Wooley caught his arm, and in the scuffle that ensued the pistol was discharged, almost instantly killing Franklin, who was seated in a chair reading a newspaper. The ball struck the unfortunate man near the navel, passed through his body and lodged under the skin to the left of the spine, causing death in about ten minutes.

    Mr. Franklin was a native of Baltimore, Md., and had been in the Territory about four months. He had been in Humboldt part of this time and had reached this place but about four weeks before the accident resulting in his death. He was a man of remarkably fine personal appearance and but about 27 years of age. On his person was found letters from his mother begging of him to return to her at her home in the States, and mourning over the "long absence" of her "dear boy."

    The following evidence was giving before the Coroner's jury:

    JAMES H. WOOLEY. Being duly sworn said the affair occurred on C street at Mr. McCoy's saloon, somewhere near 9 o'clock; between the hours of nine and ten o'clock. I had met Peyton at Mac's saloon, the first thing that occurred between him and me was when Mr. Williams came into the house and wanted me to take a drink with him, I did and this man Peyton was sitting in a chair. On standing up, he said to me when I was about to sit down "you are such a good-natured cuss I want you to take a drink with me."

    "Well" said I, "Yes, I will take a drink with you." He then commenced talking with me in a slanging manner, and I took it for a long time in good sport, he called me an "ill bred, low-bred pup." I then turned around and said to him, "I am as well bred a gentleman as you are, sir." He then stood at the corner of the counter; he jumped back, put his hand in his side pocket and drew his pistol; I then started for him and caught his pistol hand by the wrist. I struck his hand down towards the floor to prevent his hitting me or anybody else, I held his hand between my legs when the pistol went off while between my legs, shooting a person immediately behind me, the person was Mr. Franklin.

Mr. W. STAFFORD, being sworn, said: He was in the saloon at the time the shooting occurred; they (Peyton and Wooley) came up to the bar and took a drink together and stood joking together; I saw Peyton step back toward the back end of the saloon; I saw him draw his pistol; he drew it from his side pocket, cocked it and presented it at Wooley. Wooley jumped and seized his arm, when a scuffle ensued; Mr. Williams ran up to them, and at the moment the pistol was discharged the man Franklin was sitting in a chair.

A number of other witnesses were examined, the tenor of whose evidence was the same as that given above. A verdict was given and in accordance with the facts as above shown, Peyton was committed by a Coroner's warrant to the custody of the Sheriff to await the action of the Grand Jury which will be in session on Monday next, and is now lodged in the county jail.

Persons who were acquainted with the deceased speak in the highest terms of him. He was no drinker or frequenter of saloons, and merely went into the one in which he met his death on account of the chilliness of the night, while awaiting the return of a friend with whom he had been talking some time in the street, and who recollected some business it was necessary for him to attend to on B street. Deceased was well known and had many friends in San Francisco. His funeral took place yesterday afternoon at 4 o'clock. The expenses of the funeral were paid by a subscription raised among our citizens.

Virginia City Territorial Enterprise
October 1, 1862

Local Column

A Gale

About 7 o'clock Tuesday evening (Sept. 30th) a sudden blast of wind picked up a shooting gallery, two lodging houses and a drug store from their tall wooden stilts and set them down again some ten or twelve feet back of their original location, with such a degree of roughness as to jostle their insides into a sort of chaos. There were many guests in the lodging houses at the time of the accident, but it is pleasant to reflect that they seized their carpet sacks and vacated the premises with an alacrity suited to the occasion. No one hurt.

The Indian Troubles on the Overland Route

Twelve or fifteen emigrant wagons arrived here on Monday evening, and all but five moved on towards California yesterday. One of the five wagons which will remain in the city is in charge of a man from Story County, Iowa, who started across the plains on the 5th of May last, in company with a large train composed principally of emigrants from his own section. From him we learn the following particulars:

When in the vicinity of Raft River, this side of Fort Hall, the train was attacked in broad daylight by a large body of Snake Indians. The emigrants, taken entirely by surprise—for they had apprehended no trouble—made but a feeble resistance, and retreated, with a loss of six men and one woman of their party. The Indians also captured the teams belonging to thirteen wagons, together with a large number of loose cattle and horses. The names of those killed in the affray are as follows: Charles Bulwinkle, from New York; William Moats, Geo. Adams and Elizabeth Adams, and three others whose names our informant had forgotten.

The survivors were overtaken on the afternoon by a train numbering 111 wagons, which brought them through to Humboldt. They occasionally discovered the dead bodies of emigrants by the roadside; at one time twelve corpses were found, at another four, and at another two—all minus their scalps. They also saw the wrecks of many wagons destroyed by the Indians. Shortly after the sufferers by the fight recorded above had joined the large train, it was also fired into in the night by a party of Snake Indians, but the latter, finding themselves pretty warmly received, drew off without taking a scalp.

About a week before these events transpired, a party of emigrants numbering 40 persons was attacked near City Rocks by the same tribe of uncivilized pirates. Five young ladies were carried off, and, it is thought, women and children in all to the number of fifteen. All the men were killed except one, who made his escape and arrived at Humboldt about the 20th of September.

This train was called the "Methodist Train," which was not altogether inappropriate, since the whole party knelt down and began to pray as soon as the attack was commenced. Every train which has passed over that portion of the route in the vicinity of City Rocks since the 1st of August has had trouble with the Indians. When our informant left Humboldt several wagons had just arrived whose sides and covers had been transformed into magnified nutmeg-graters by Indian bullets. The Snakes corralled the train, when a fight ensued, which lasted forty-eight hours. The whites cut their way out, finally, and escaped. We could not learn the number of killed and wounded at this battle.

More Indian Troubles

Mr. L. F. Yates, who arrived in this city a few days since from Pike's Peak, has given us the following particulars of a fight his train had on the 8th of last August, about one and a-half miles this side of the junction of the Lander's Cut-off and Fort Bridger roads. Their train consisted of 15 wagons and 40 men, with a number of women and children. The train was attacked while passing along a ravine by a party of Indians being concealed in among a thick growth of poplar bushes.

When the attack commenced, most of the front wagons were some 80 rods in advance. They formed in corral, and intrenched behind their wagons, refused the slightest aid to those who were struggling with the savages in the rear. The party thus left to fight their way through the ambushed Indians numbered but nine men, and there were but four guns with which to maintain the battle. Five of the nine were killed and one wounded.

The names of the killed are as follows: Parmelee, James Steele, James A. Hart, Rufus C. Mitchell, from Central City, Colorado Territory, and McMahan, residence unknown; the name of the man wounded is Frank Lyman. He was shot through the lungs—recovered. The thirty-one men who were hidden snugly behind their wagons, with a single honorable exception, refused to render the slightest assistance to those who were fighting for their lives and the lives of their families so near them. Although they had 27 guns they refused to lend a single gun, when at one time four men went to ask assistance. The cowards all clung to their arms, and lay trembling behind their wagons.

A man named Perry, or Berry, was the only one who had sufficient courage to attempt to render his struggling friends any assistance. He was shot in the face before reaching the rear wagons, and was carried back to the corral. The fight lasted nearly two hours, and some seven or eight Indians were killed, as at various times they charged out of the bushes on their ponies. Several Indian horses were killed, and at length the few left alive fought through to where their thirty heroic friends (?) were corraled, leaving the killed and two wagons in possession of the Indians. Thirty bigger cowards and meaner men than those above mentioned never crossed the plains; we are certain that every man of them left the States for fear of being drafted into the army.

Virginia City Territorial Enterprise
October 4, 1862

Petrified Man

A petrified man was found some time ago in the mountains south of Gravelly Ford. Every limb and feature of the stony mummy was perfect, not even excepting the left leg, which had evidently been a wooden one during the lifetime of the owner—which lifetime, by the way, came to a close about a century ago, in the opinion of a savant who has examined the defunct.

The body was in a sitting posture, and leaning against a huge mass of croppings; the attitude was pensive, the right thumb resting against the side of the nose; the left thumb partially supported the chin, the forefinger pressing the inner corner of the left eye and drawing it partly open; the right eye was closed, and the fingers of the right hand spread apart.

This strange freak of nature created a profound sensation in the vicinity, and our informant states that by request, Justice Sewell or Sowell, of Humboldt City, at once proceeded to the spot and held an inquest on the body. The verdict of the jury was that "deceased came to his death from protracted exposure," etc. The people of the neighborhood volunteered to bury the poor unfortunate, and were even anxious to do so; but it was discovered, when they attempted to remove him, that the water which had dripped upon him for ages from the crag above, had coursed down his back and deposited a limestone sediment under him which had glued him to the bed rock upon which he sat, as with a cement of adamant, and Judge S. refused to allow the charitable citizens to blast him from his position.

The opinion expressed by His Honor that such a course would be little less than sacrilege, was eminently just and proper. Everybody goes to see the stone man, as many as three hundred having visited the hardened creature during the past five or six weeks.

Virginia City Territorial Enterprise
October 13, 1862

[No Title]

William Young of Long Valley arrived in Virginia, lately, with a drove of cattle, sold the same, and put the proceeds in his saddlebags and the saddlebags on his horse. He then adjourned to the dance house, and having partaken of the sinful pleasures of that place, he came back and found that somebody had carried off saddlebags, money and all, during his absence. The fact of his leaving the horse and saddlebags lying around loose in the street at night is sufficient proof of Young's confidence in the honesty of our citizens, and the fact that the thief didn't take the horse also when he took the money, is sufficient proof that that confidence was not entirely misplaced.

Virginia City Territorial Enterprise
October, 1862

The Spanish Mine

This comprises one hundred feet of the great Comstock lead, and is situated in the midst of the Ophir claims. We visited it yesterday, in company with Mr. Kingman, Assistant Superintendent, and our impression is that stout-legged people with an affinity to darkness may spend an hour or so there very comfortably.

A confused sense of being buried alive, and a vague consciousness of stony dampness, and huge timbers, and tortuous caverns, and bottomless holes with endless ropes hanging down into them, and narrow ladders climbing in a short twilight through the colossal lattice work and suddenly perishing in midnight, and workmen poking about in the gloom with twinkling candles—is all, or nearly all that remains to us of our experience in the Spanish mine.

The Comstock Mine

Yet, for the information of those who may wish to go down and see how things are conducted in the realms beyond the jurisdiction of daylight, we are willing to tell a portion of what we know about it. Entering the Spanish tunnel in A street, you grope along by candle light for two hundred and fifty feet—but you need not count your steps—keep on going until you come to a horse. This horse works a whim used for hoisting ore from the infernal regions below, and from long service in the dark, his coat has turned to a beautiful black color.

You are now upon the confines of the ledge, and from this point several drifts branch out to different portions of the mine. Without stopping to admire these gloomy grottoes you descend a ladder and halt upon a landing where you are fenced in with an open-work labyrinth of timbers some eighteen inches square, extending in front of you and behind you, and far away above you and below you, until they are lost in darkness.

These timbers are framed in squares or "stations," five feet each way, one above another, and so neatly put together that there is not room for the insertion of a knife-blade where they intersect. You are apt to wonder where the forest around you came from, and how they managed to get it into that hole, and what sums of money it must have cost, and so forth and so on, and you wind up with a confused notion that the man who designed it all had a shining talent for saw mills on a large scale. He could build the frame-work beautifully at any rate.

Whereupon, you desist from further speculation, and waltz down a very narrow winding staircase, and the further you squirm down it the dizzier you get and the more those open timber squares seem to whiz by you, until you feel as if you are falling through a well-ventilated shot-tower with the windows all open.

Finally, after you have gone down ninety-four feet, you touch bottom again and find yourself in the midst of the saw mill yet, with the regular accomplishments of workmen, and windlasses, and glimmering candles, et cetera, as usual.

Now you can stoop and dodge about under the "stations," and get your clothes dirty, and drip hot candle grease all over your hands, and find out how they take those timbers and commence at the top of the mine, and build them together like mighty window sashes all the way down to the bottom of it; and if, after coming down that tipsy staircase, you can by any possibility make out to understand it, then you can render the information useful above ground by building the third story of your house to suit you first, and continuing its erection wrong end foremost until you wind up with the cellar.

You will also find out that at this depth the lead is forty-six feet wide, with its sides walled and weather boarded as compactly and substantially as those of a jail. And here and there in little recesses, the walls of the lead are laid bare, showing the blue silver lines traced upon the white quartz, after the fashion of variegated marble—this, in places, you know, while others, where the ore is richer, the blue predominates and the white is scarcely perceptible.

From these various recesses a swarm of workmen are constantly conveying wheel-barrow loads of quartz to the windlasses, of all shades of value, from that worth $75 to that worth $3,000 per ton—and if you should chance to be in better luck than we were, you may happen to stumble on a small specimen worth a dollar and a half a pound. Such things have occurred in the Spanish mine before now.

However, as we were saying, you are now one hundred and seventy feet under the ground, and you can move about and see how the ore is quarried and moved from one place to another, and how systematically the great mine is arranged and worked altogether, and how unsystematically the Mexicans used to carry on business down there—and you may get into a bucket, if you please, and extend your visit to the confines of purgatory—so to speak—if you feel anxious to do so; but as this would afford you nothing more than a glance at the bottom of a drain shaft, you could better employ your time and talents in climbing that cork screw and seeking daylight again.

And before leaving the mouth of the tunnel, you would do well to visit the office of Mr. Beckwith, the superintendent, where you can see a small cabinet of specimens from the mine which has been pronounced by scientific travelers to be one of the richest collections of the kind in the world. We shall have occasion to speak of the steam hoisting apparatus now in process of erection by the Spanish Company at an early day.

Virginia City Territorial Enterprise
November 1, 1862

Silver Bricks

The citizens of Virginia City propose to send to the Sanitary Commission the sum of $20,000 in silver bricks. The shipment will be made in solid silver bricks, stamped with an appropriate inscription, and will prove the biggest advertisement for Nevada Territory that ingenious brains have yet conceived. These silver bricks will be curiously examined and commented on by many a man in New York who would forget in fifteen minutes after he heard it, the fact that $20,000 in gold coin or Treasury notes had been sent from the unknown land of Nevada.

Building Lots

Hundreds of building lots have lately been staked off east of town by speculative peg-drivers. We shouldn't wonder if there was money in these lots. This city would not stop growing should it try. It's bound to go ahead, and we must have some place to spread.

The Petrified Man

Mr. Herr Weisnicht has just arrived in Virginia City from the Humboldt mines and regions beyond. He brings with him the head and one foot of the petrified man, lately found in the mountains near Gravelly Ford. A skillful assayer has analyzed a small portion of dirt found under the nail of the great toe and pronounces the man to have been a native of the Kingdom of New Jersey. As a trace of "speculation" is still discernible in the left eye, it is thought the man was on his way to what is now the Washoe mining region for the purpose of locating the Comstock. The remains brought in are to be seen in a neat glass case in the third story of the Library Building, where they have been temporarily placed by Mr. Weisnicht for the inspection of the curious, and where they may be examined by anyone who will take the trouble to visit them.

Virginia City Territorial Enterprise
c. December 12, 1862

Letter from Carson City

EDITORS ENTERPRISE: Ormsby heads the world on the turnip question. The vegetable upon which I base this boast, was grown in the turnip garden of Mr. S. D. Fairchild, back here towards King's Canyon—in the suburbs—say about eight squares from the plaza. Mr. Fairchild left it at the branch of the ENTERPRISE office in Carson, a day or two since. The monster was accurately surveyed, with the following result: circumference, forty inches; weight, a fraction over eighteen pounds.

Col. Williams, of the House, who says I mutilate his eloquence, addressed a note to me this morning, to the effect that I had given his constituents wrong impressions concerning him, and nothing but blood would satisfy him. I sent him that turnip on a hand barrow, requesting him to extract from it a sufficient quantity of blood to restore his equilibrium—which I regarded as a very excellent joke. Col. Williams ate it (raw) during the usual prayer by the chaplain. To sum up: eighteen pounds of raw turnip is sufficient for an ordinary lunch—Col. Williams had his feet on his desk at the time—he beamed—wherefore, I think his satisfaction was complete.

Carson also boasts the only pork-packing establishment in Nevada Territory. Mr. George T. Davis is the proprietor thereof, and he has already killed and packed two hundred and fifty fine hogs this winter. This will be cheering news to the young lady who told me the other evening that she "loved pork."

The pleasantest affair of the season, perhaps, although not the most gorgeous, was the "candy-pull" at the White House, a few nights ago. The candy had not finished cooking at nine o'clock, so they concluded to dance awhile. They always dance here when they have time. I have noticed it frequently. I think it is a way they have. They got a couple of able-bodied fiddlers and went at it.

They opened with the dance called the plain quadrille, which is very simple and easy, and is performed in this wise: All you have to do is to stand up in the middle of the floor, being careful to get your lady on your right hand side, and yourself on the left hand side of your lady. Then you are all right, you know. When you hear a blast of music like unto the rush of many waters, you lay your hand on your stomach and bow to the lady of your choice, then you turn around and bow to the fiddlers.

The first order is, "First couple fore and aft"—or words to that effect. This is very easy. You have only to march straight across the house—keeping out of the way of the advancing couple, who very seldom know where they are going to—and when you get over, if you find your partner there, swing her; if you don't, hunt her up—for it is very handy to have a partner in these plain quadrilles.

The next order is, "Ladies change." This is an exceedingly difficult figure, and requires great presence of mind; because, on account of shaking hands with the lobby members so much, and from the force of human nature also, you are morally certain to offer your right, when the chances are that your left hand is wanted. This has a tendency to mix things.

At this point order and regularity cease—the dancers get excited—the musicians become insane—turmoil and confusion ensue—chaos comes again! Put your trust in Providence and stick to your partner. Several of these engaging and beautiful plain quadrilles were danced during the evening, and we might have enjoyed several more, but the rostrum broke down and spilt the musicians.

I was exceedingly delighted with the waltz, and also with the polka. These differ in name, but there the difference ceases—the dances are precisely the same. You have only to spin around with frightful velocity and steer clear of the furniture. This has a charming and bewildering effect. You catch glimpses of a confused and whirling multitude of people, and above them a row of distracted fiddlers extending entirely around the room. The waltz and the polka are very exhilarating—to use a mild term—amazingly exhilarating.

Nothing occurred to mar the joyousness of the occasion. The party was very select except myself and Col. Williams; the candy was not burned; the Governor sat down on a hot stove and got up again with great presence of mind; the dancing was roomy and hilarious, and fun went to waste. Henceforward my principles are fixed. I am a stern and unwavering advocate of "candy-pulls."

There was a slight conflagration in Mr. Helm's office yesterday morning—at least I was told so by my friend, the reporter for the Virginia Union, who is not very reliable. He also stated that no damage was done; but I don't put much confidence in what he says.

The ladies have not smiled much on this Legislature, so far. Thirty-two of our loveliest visited the halls night before last, though, which is an encouraging symptom. I cannot conscientiously say they smiled, however, for the Revenue bill was before the House. This cheerful subject is calculated to produce inward jollity, but the same is not apt to blossom into smiles on the surface. The ladies were well pleased with the night session, though—they enjoyed it exceedingly—in many respects it was much superior to a funeral.

The Revenue bill was finished up last night, and in the name and at the request of the members, I invite all the ladies in town to call again, at any time, either day or night session. That Revenue bill was one of those nonsensical general public concerns that we are not used to; but the fun will be resumed right away, now that we are back on our regular toll roads again.

I went down to Empire City yesterday to see the Eagle Fire Company try their new engine (by the way, you have, so far, neglected to mention either the machine or the company in your paper). They first threw an inch and a quarter stream over Dutch Nick's hotel, and then a three-quarter inch stream over the liberty pole. This brought cheers from the multitude (there were many ladies there from neighboring cities). The boys grew excited and ambitious. Several ladies passed by, wearing the new fashioned light-house bonnets.

The Eagles, in their madness, attempted to throw a half-inch stream over those bonnets. They puffed their cheeks and strained every nerve; there was a moment of painful suspense, as the pearly column went towering toward the clouds—then a long, loud, reverberating shout, as it bent gracefully and went over, without touching a feather! But the engine broke.

If McCluskey, of the Delta Saloon, could send me a reporter's cobbler—an unusually long one—I think it would relieve my cold.

Virginia City Territorial Enterprise
December 13, 1862

The Pah-Utes

Ah, well—it is touching to see these knotty and rugged old pioneers—who have beheld Nevada in her infancy, and toiled through her virgin sands unmolested by toll-keepers; and prospected her unsmiling hills, and knocked at the doors of her sealed treasure vaults; and camped with her horned-toads, and tarantulas and lizards, under her inhospitable sage brush; and smoked the same pipe; and imbibed lightning out of the same bottle; and eaten their regular bacon and beans from the same pot; and lain down to their rest under the same blanket—happy, and lousy and contented—yea, happier and lousier and more contented than they are this day, or may be in the days that are to come; it is touching, I say, to see these weather-beaten and blasted old patriarchs banding together like a decaying tribe, for the sake of the privations they have undergone, and the dangers they have met—to rehearse the deeds of the hoary past, and rescue its traditions from oblivion!

The Pah-Ute Association will become a high and honorable order in the land—its certificate of membership a patent of nobility. I extend unto the fraternity the right hand of a poor but honest half-breed, and say God speed your sacred enterprise.

Virginia City Territorial Enterprise
December 23, 1862

A Big Thing in Washoe City

Or, The Grand Bull Driver's Convention

On the last night of the session, Hon. Thomas Hannah announced that a Grand Bull Drivers' Convention would assemble in Washoe City, on the 22d, to receive Hon. Jim Sturtevant and the other members of the Washoe delegation. I journeyed to the place yesterday to see that the ovation was properly conducted. I traveled per stage. The Unreliable of the Union went also for the purpose of distorting the facts.

The weather was delightful. It snowed the entire day. The wind blew such a hurricane that the coach drifted sideways from one toll road to another, and sometimes utterly refused to mind her helm. It is a fearful thing to be at sea in a stagecoach. We were anxious to get to Washoe by four o'clock, but luck was against us: we were delayed by stress of weather; we were hindered by the bad condition of the various toll roads; we finally broke the after spring of the wagon, and had to lay up for repairs. Therefore we only reached Washoe at dusk.

Messrs. Lovejoy, Howard, Winters, Sturtevant, and Speaker Mills had left Carson ahead of us, and we found them in the city. They had not beaten us much, however, as I could perceive by their upright walk and untangled conversation. At 6 P.M., the Carson City Brass Band, followed by the Committee of Arrangements, and the Chairman of the Convention, and the delegation, and the invited guests, and the citizens generally, and the hurricane, marched up one of the most principal streets, and filed in imposing procession into Foulke's Hall.

The delegation, and the guests, and the band, were provided with comfortable seats near the Chairman's desk, and the constituency occupied the body-pews. The delegation and the guests stood up and formed a semicircle, and Mr. Gregory introduced them one at a time to the constituency. Mr. Gregory did this with much grace and dignity, albeit he affected to stammer and gasp, and hesitate, and look colicky, and miscall the names, and miscall them again by way of correcting himself, and grab desperately at invisible things in the air—all with a charming pretense of being scared.

The Hon. John K. Lovejoy arose in his place and blew his horn. He made honorable mention of the Legislature and the Committee on Internal Improvements. He told how the fountains of their great deep were broken up, and they rained forty days and forty nights, and brought on a flood of toll roads over the whole land. He explained to them that the more toll roads there were, the more competition there would be, and the roads would be good, and tolls moderate in consequence.

Mr. Speaker Mills responded to the numerous calls for him, and spoke so well in praise of the Washoe delegation that I was constrained to believe that there really was some merit in the deceased.

Hon. Theodore Winters next addressed the people. He said he went to the Legislature with but one solitary object in view—the securing to this Territory of an incorporation law. How he had succeeded, the people themselves could tell. . . .

The Chairman, Mr. Gaston, introduced Colonel Howard, and that gentleman addressed the people in his peculiarly grave and dignified manner. The constituency gave way to successive cataracts of laughter, which was singularly out of keeping with the stern seriousness of the speaker's bearing. He spoke about ten minutes, and then took his seat, in spite of the express wish of the audience that he should go on.

Hon. Jim Sturtevant next addressed the citizens, extemporaneously. He made use of the very thunder which I meant to launch at the populace. Owing to this unfortunate circumstance, I was forced to keep up an intelligent silence during the session of the convention....

After this the assemblage broke up and adjourned to take something to drink. At nine o'clock the band again summoned the public to Foulke's Hall, and I proceeded to that place. I found the Unreliable there, and George Hepperly. I had requested Mr. Hepperly, as a personal favor, to treat the Unreliable with distinguished consideration and I am proud and happy to acknowledge he had done so. He had him in charge of two constables.

The Hall had been cleared of the greater part of its benches, and the ball was ready to commence. The citizens had assembled in force, and the sexes were pretty equally represented in the proportion of one lady to several gentlemen. The night was so infernally inclement—so to speak—that it was impossible for ladies who lived at any considerable distance to attend. However, those that were there appeared in every quadrille, and with exemplary industry. I did not observe any wallflowers—the climate of Washoe appears to be unsuited to that kind of vegetation.

In accordance with the customs of the country, they indulged in the plain quadrille at this ball. And notwithstanding the vicissitudes which I have seen that wonderful national dance pass through, I solemnly affirm that they sprung some more new figures on me last night. However, the ball was a very pleasant affair. We could muster four sets and still have a vast surplusage of gentlemen, but the strictest economy had to be observed in order to make the ladies hold out.

The supper and the champagne were excellent and abundant, and I offer no word of blame against anybody for eating and drinking pretty freely. If I were to blame anybody, I would commence with the Unreliable—for he drank until he lost all sense of etiquette. I actually found myself in bed with him with my boots on.

However, as I said before, I cannot blame the cuss; it was a convivial occasion, and his little shortcomings ought to be overlooked. When I went to bed this morning, Mr. Lovejoy, arrayed in fiery red night clothes, was dancing the war dance of his tribe (he is President of the Paiute Association) around a spittoon and Colonel Howard, dressed in a similar manner, was trying to convince him that he was a humbug. A suspicion crossed my mind that they were partially intoxicated, but I could not be sure about it on account of everything appearing to turn around so. I left Washoe City this morning at nine o'clock, fully persuaded that I would like to go back there again when the next convention meets.

Virginia City Territorial Enterprise
December 28, 1862

The Illustrious Departed

Old Dan is gone, that good old soul, we ne'er shall see him more—for some time. He left for Carson yesterday, to be duly stamped and shipped to America, by way of the United States Overland Mail. As the stage was on the point of weighing anchor, the senior editor dashed wildly into Wasserman's and captured a national flag, which he cast about Dan's person to the tune of three rousing cheers from the bystanders. So, with the gorgeous drapery floating behind him, our kind and genial hero passed from our sight; and if fervent prayers from us, who seldom pray, can avail, his journey will be as safe and happy as though ministering angels watched over him.

Dan has gone to the States for his health, and his family. He worked himself down in creating big strikes in the mines and keeping all the mills in this district going, whether their owners were willing or not. These herculean labors gradually undermined his health, but he went bravely on, and we are proud to say that as far as these things were concerned, he never gave up—the miners never did, and never could have conquered him.

He fell under a scarcity of pack-trains and hay wagons. These had been the bulwark of the local column; his confidence in them was like unto that which men have in four aces; murders, robberies, fires, distinguished arrivals were creatures of chance, which might or might not occur at any moment; but the pack-trains and the hay-wagons were certain, predestined, immutable! When these failed last week, he said "Et tu Brute," and gave us his pen. His constitution suddenly warped, split and went under, and Daniel succumbed.

We have a saving hope, though, that his trip across the Plains, through eighteen hundred miles of cheerful hay stacks, will so restore our loved and lost to his ancient health and energy, that when he returns next fall he will be able to run our five hundred mills as easily as he used to keep five-score moving. Dan is gone, but he departed in a blaze of glory, the like of which hath hardly been seen upon this earth since the blameless Elijah went up in his fiery chariot.

Virginia City Territorial Enterprise
c. December 30, 1862

Local Column

OUR STOCK REMARKS.—Owing to the fact that our stock reporter attended a wedding last evening, our report of transactions in that branch of robbery and speculation is not quite as complete and satisfactory as usual this morning. About eleven o'clock last night the aforesaid remarker pulled himself upstairs by the banisters, and stumbling over the stove, deposited the following notes on our table, with the remark: "S(hic)am, just laberate this, w(hic)ill, yer?"

We said we would, but we couldn't. If any of our readers think they can, we shall be pleased to see the translation. Here are the notes: "Stocks brisk, and Ophir has taken this woman for your wedded wife. Some few transactions have occurred in rings and lace veils, and at figures tall, graceful and charming. There was some inquiry late in the day for parties who would take them for better or for worse but there were few offers. There seems to be some depression in this stock. We mentioned yesterday that our Father which art in heaven. Quotations of lost reference, and now I lay me down to sleep," &c., &c., &c.

BOARD OF EDUCATION.—In accordance with a law passed at the late session of the legislature, a Board of Education is to be organized in each of the several counties. The Storey County Board will be composed of seven members, apportioned as follows: four from Virginia, two from Gold Hill, and one from Flowery. The Chairman of the Board will be County School Superintendent. These officers will have power to issue bonds sufficient to defray the expenses of the schools, from the 1st of January until the 1st of November; to establish schools of all grades, engage and examine teachers, etc.

The election for the Board of Education will be held next Monday, at the Court House, in Virginia; at the post office in Gold Hill, and at the house of I. W. Knox, in Flowery, the polls to be open from 8 o'clock in the morning until 6 in the evening. The Board will meet and organize on the Monday following their election.

BLOWN DOWN.—At sunset yesterday, the wind commenced blowing after a fashion to which a typhoon is mere nonsense, and in a short time the face of heaven was obscured by vast clouds of dust all spangled over with lumber, and shingles, and dogs and things. There was no particular harm in that, but the breeze soon began to work damage of a serious nature.

Thomas Moore's new frame house on the east side of C street, above the Court House, was blown down, and the fire-wall front of a one-story brick building higher up the street was also thrown to the ground. The latter house was occupied as a store by Mr. Heldman, and owned by Mr. Felton. The storm was very severe for a while, and we shall not be surprised to hear of further destruction having been caused by it. The damage resulting to Mr. Heldman's grocery store amounts to $2,200.

AT HOME.—Judge Brumfield's nightmare—the Storey County delegation—have straggled in, one at a time, until they are all at home once more. Messrs. Mills, Mitchell, Meagher and Minneer returned several days ago, and we had the pleasure of meeting Mr. Davenport, also, yesterday. We do not know how long the latter gentleman has been here, but we offer him the unlimited freedom of the city, anyhow. Justice to a good representative is justice, you know, whether it be tardy or otherwise.

THE SCHOOL.—Mr. Mellvile's school will open again next Monday, and in the meantime the new furniture is being put up in the school house. The Virginia Cadets (a company composed of Mr. Mellvile's larger pupils) will appear in public on New Year's Day, the weather permitting, armed and equipped as the law directs. The boys were pretty proficient in their military exercises when we saw them last, and they have probably not deteriorated since then.

SAD ACCIDENT.—We learn from Messrs. Hatch &. Bro., who do a heavy business in the way of supplying this market with vegetables, that the rigorous weather accompanying the late storm was so severe on the mountains as to cause a loss of life in several instances. Two sacks of sweet potatoes were frozen to death on the summit, this side of Strawberry. The verdict rendered by the coroner's jury was strictly in accordance with the facts.

THRILLING ROMANCE.—On our first page, today, will be found the opening chapters of a thrilling tale, entitled "An Act to amend and supplemental to an Act to provide for Assessing and Collecting County and Territorial Revenue." This admirable story was written especially for the columns of this paper by several distinguished authors. We have secured a few more productions of the same kind, at great expense, and we design publishing them in their regular order. Our readers will agree with us that it will redound considerably to their advantage to read and preserve these documents.

FIRE, ALMOST.—The roof of the New York Restaurant took fire from the stovepipe, yesterday morning, and but for the timely discovery of the fact, a serious conflagration would have ensued, as the restaurant is situated in a nest of frame houses, which would have burned like tinder. As it was, nothing but a few shingles were damaged.

PRIVATE PARTY.—The members of Engine Co. No. 2, with a number of invited guests, are to have a little social dance at La Plata Hall, this evening. They have made every arrangement for having a pleasant time of it, and we hope they may succeed to the very fullest extent of their wishes.

Virginia City Territorial Enterprise
January 1, 1863

Local Column

MORE GHOSTS—Are we to be scared to death every time we venture into the street? May we be allowed to go quietly about our business, or are we to be assailed at every corner by fearful apparitions?

As we were plodding home at the ghostly hour last night, thinking about the haunted house humbug, we were suddenly riveted to the pavement in a paroxysm of terror by that blue and yellow phantom who watches over the destinies of the shooting gallery, this side of the International. Seen in daylight, placidly reclining against his board in the doorway, with his blue coat, and his yellow pants, and his high boots, and his fancy hat, just lifted from his head, he is rather an engaging youth than otherwise; but at dead of night, when he pops out his pallid face at you by candle light, and stares vacantly upon you with his uplifted hat and the eternal civility of his changeless brow, and the ghostliness of his general appearance heightened by that gravestone inscription over his stomach, "today shooting for chickens here," you are apt to think of spectres starting up from behind tombstones, and you weaken accordingly—the cold chills creep over you—your hair stands on end—you reverse your front, and with all possible alacrity, you change your base.

NEW YEAR's DAY—Now is the accepted time to make your regular annual good resolutions. Next week you can begin paving hell with them as usual. Yesterday, everybody smoked his last cigar, took his last drink, and swore his last oath. Today, we are a pious and exemplary community. Thirty days from now, we shall have cast our reformation to the winds and gone to cutting our ancient shortcomings considerably shorter than ever. We shall also reflect pleasantly upon how we did the same old thing last year about this time.

However, go in, community. New Year's is a harmless annual institution, of no particular use to anybody save as a scapegoat for promiscuous drunks, and friendly calls, and humbug resolutions, and we wish you to enjoy it with a looseness suited to the greatness of the occasion.

Virginia City Territorial Enterprise
c. January 1, 1863

Sulphur Deposit

L. Dow Huntsman, who reached Carson on Monday from Humboldt County, brought to the office several specimens of pure sulphur with him, which had been taken from a small mountain of that material, situated about twenty miles west of Unionville. That locality may be in close proximity to the lake which burneth with fire and brimstone, and it may not. Yet we are of the opinion that this item will change the destination of a good many moderate Christians who are now preparing to emigrate to Humboldt. However, it will give the regulars a better chance than they generally have in mining regions.

Virginia City Territorial Enterprise
January 6, 1863

Local Column

FREE FIGHT—A beautiful and ably conducted free fight came off in C street yesterday afternoon, but as nobody was killed or mortally wounded in a manner sufficiently fatal to cause death, no particular interest attaches to the matter, and we shall not publish the details. We pine for murder—these fist fights are of no consequence to anybody.

Humboldt stocks are plenty in the market, at figures which we have no doubt are low for the claims. The want of buyers is probably attributable to the indefinite knowledge of these claims. There are unquestionably many valuable ledges in the district offered at exceedingly low prices.

The old friends and acquaintances of Jno. D. Kinney (who came to Nevada Territory with Chief Justice Turner, and who returned to the States last March), will be gratified to learn that that sterling patriot is now a captain in the Seventh Ohio Cavalry.

Milstead, who murdered a man named Varney some time ago, near Ragtown, in Humboldt County, will be hung in Dayton next Friday.

James Leconey, W. H. Barstow, Jas. Phelan and John A. Collins were elected members of the Board of Education at Virginia.

Virginia City Territorial Enterprise
January 8, 1863

Unfortunate Thief

We have been suffering from the seven years' itch for many months. It is probably the most aggravating disease in the world. It is contagious. That man has commenced a career of suffering which is frightful to contemplate; there is no cure for the distemper—it must run its course; there is no respite for its victim, and but little alleviation of its torments to be hoped for; the unfortunate's only resource is to bathe in sulphur and molasses and let his finger nails grow. Further advice is unnecessary—instinct will prompt him to scratch.

Virginia City Territorial Enterprise
January 10, 1863

Local Column

THE SANITARY BALL—The Sanitary Ball at La Plata Hall on Thursday night was a very marked success, and proved beyond the shadow of a doubt the correctness of our theory, that ladies never fail in undertakings of this kind. If there had been about two dozen more people there, the house would have been crowded—as it was, there was room enough on the floor for the dancers, without trespassing on their neighbors' corns. Several of those long, trailing dresses, even, were under fire in the thickest of the fight for six hours, and came out as free from rips and rents as they were when they went in.

Not all of them, though. We recollect a circumstance in point. We had just finished executing one of those inscrutable figures of the plain quadrille; we were feeling unusually comfortable, because we had gone through the performance as well as anybody could have done it, except that we had wandered a little toward the last; in fact we had wandered out of our own and into somebody else's set—but that was a matter of small consequence, as the new locality was as good as the old one, and we were used to that sort of thing anyhow.

We were feeling comfortable, and we had assumed an attitude—we have a sort of talent for posturing—a pensive attitude, copied from the Colossus of Rhodes—when the ladies were ordered to the centre. Two of them got there, and the other two moved off gallantly, but they failed to make the connection. They suddenly broached to under full headway, and there was a sound of parting canvas. Their dresses were anchored under our boots, you know. It was unfortunate, but it could not be helped.

Those two beautiful pink dresses let go amidships, and remained in a ripped and damaged condition to the end of the ball. We did not apologize, because our presence of mind happened to be absent at the very moment that we had the greatest need of it. But we beg permission to do so now.

An excellent supper was served in the large dining room of the new What Cheer House on B street. We missed it there, somewhat. We were not accompanied by a lady, and consequently we were not eligible to a seat at the first table. We found out all about that at the Gold Hill ball, and we had intended to be all prepared for this one.

We engaged a good many young ladies last Tuesday to go with us, thinking that out of the lot we should certainly be able to secure one, at the appointed time, but they all seemed to have got a little angry about something—nobody knows what, for the ways of women are past finding out. They told us we had better go and invite a thousand girls to go to the ball. A thousand. Why, it was absurd. We had no use for a thousand girls. A thou—but those girls were as crazy as loons. In every instance, after they had uttered that pointless suggestion, they marched magnificently out of their parlors—and if you will believe us, not one of them ever recollected to come back again.

Why, it was the most unaccountable experience we ever heard of. We never enjoyed so much solitude in so many different places, in one evening before. But patience has its limits; we finally got tired of that arrangement—and at the risk of offending some of those girls, we stalked off to the Sanitary Ball alone without a virgin, out of that whole litter. We may have done wrong—we probably did do wrong to disappoint those fellows in that kind of style—but how could we help it? We couldn't stand the temperature of those parlors more than an hour at a time: it was cold enough to freeze out the heaviest stock-holder on the Gould & Curry's books.

However, as we remarked before, everybody spoke highly of the supper, and we believe they meant what they said. We are unable to say anything in the matter from personal knowledge, except that the tables were arranged with excellent taste, and more than abundantly supplied, and everything looked very beautiful, and very inviting, also; but then we had absorbed so much cold weather in those parlors, and had had so much trouble with those girls, that we had no appetite left. We only ate a boiled ham and some pies, and went back to the ball room. There were some very handsome cakes on the tables, manufactured by Mr. Slade, and decorated with patriotic mottoes, done in fancy icing. All those who were happy that evening agree that the supper was superb.

After supper the dancing was jolly. They kept it up till four in the morning, and the guests enjoyed themselves excessively. All the dances were performed, and the bill of fare wound up with a new style of plain quadrille called a medley, which involved the whole list. It involved us also. But we got out again—and we stayed out, with great sagacity.

But speaking of plain quadrilles reminds us of another new one—the Virginia reel. We found it a very easy matter to dance it, as long as we had thirty or forty lookers-on to prompt us. The dancers were formed in two long ranks, facing each other, and the battle opens with some light skirmishing between the pickets, which is gradually resolved into a general engagement along the whole line: after that, you have nothing to do but stand by and grab every lady that drifts within reach of you, and swing her. It is very entertaining, and elaborately scientific also; but we observed that with a partner who had danced it before, we were able to perform it rather better than the balance of the guests.

Altogether, the Sanitary Ball was a remarkably pleasant party, and we are glad that such was the case—for it is a very uncomfortable task to be obliged to say harsh things about entertainments of this kind. At the present writing we cannot say what the net proceeds of the ball will amount to, but they will doubtless reach quite a respectable figure—say $400.

DUE NOTICE—Moralists and philosophers have adjudged those who throw temptation in the way of the erring, equally guilty with those who are thereby led into evil; and we therefore hold the man who suffers that turkey to run at large just back of our office as culpable as ourselves, if some day that fowl is no longer perceptible to human vision. The Czar of Russia never cast his eye on the minarets of Byzantium half as longingly as we gaze on that old gobbler. Turkey stuffed with oysters is our weakness—our mouth waters at the recollection of sundry repasts of that character—and this bird aforementioned appears to us to have an astonishing capacity for oyster-stuffing. Wonder if those fresh oysters at Almack's are all gone? We grow ravenous—pangs of hunger gnaw our vitals—if tomorrow's setting sun gleams on the living form of that turkey, we yield our reputation for strategy.

THE NEW COURT HOUSE—Messrs. Unger & Denninger's new brick house, on B street, has been leased by the County Commissioners for court rooms and offices. The first floor, we believe, is to be used for a United States District Court room, and the second story will be partitioned into offices and a Probate Court room. It would probably have been better to have reversed this order of things, on account of the superior light and the freedom from dust and noise afforded by the upper story; yet it is possible that these advantages may be as necessary in one case as the other—we do not care about dictating much in the matter so long as no one will be likely to pay us for it.

But nevertheless, since the first story is to be used for the District Court, we wish to suggest that that box, that partition, be removed, and the whole of it set apart for that purpose. It would then be a large, handsome and well-lighted hall, whereas, in its present shape, it is not very greatly superior to the present court room on C street. A gentleman informed us yesterday that he thought the intention was to remove the partition, but he could not be positive about it.

THE MUSIC—Millington & McCluskey's band furnished the music for the Sanitary Ball on Thursday night, and also for the Odd Fellows' Ball the other evening in Gold Hill, and the excellence of the article was only equalled by the industry and perseverance of the performers. We consider that the man who can fiddle all through one of those Virginia Reels without losing his grip, may be depended upon in any kind of musical emergency.

Virginia City Territorial Enterprise
c. January 11, 1863

Local Column

HIGH PRICE OF PORK—In our record of probate proceedings today will be found the case of John Hill vs. John Doe Wentworth. As a matter of principle, it may be well enough to stand by your rights until the lake of fire and brimstone is no longer in a state of liquification, but whether it be good policy to do so at all times is a question which admits of argument. This case is an instance in point. The property involved is about twenty or thirty dollars' worth of pork in a crude state—we mean, two living hogs, probably worth but little more than ten dollars each; yet this suit to determine their ownership has already cost the parties to it some six or seven hundred dollars, and the defeated but plucky plaintiff has given notice that he will apply for a new trial! The new trial will double the bill of expenses, in all human probability.

We learn from gentlemen who were present at the trial today, that there were about thirty witnesses on the stand, and one of them a woman. The hog dispute afforded those concerned and the lookers-on a good deal of fun, but it was very costly. Those two distinguished pigs ought to be taken care of and exhibited at the first agricultural fair of Nevada Territory. At any rate, we shall officially spread the proceedings of this trial upon the records of the Washoe Agricultural, Mining and Mechanical Society, as evidence of the high value placed upon the hog in Nevada Territory.

Virginia City Territorial Enterprise
c. January 22, 1863

Territorial Sweets

The following, which will do to sweeten some bachelor's coffee with, was picked up in front of the International:

"DARLING: I have not had time to write you today—I have worked hard entertaining company. Do come and see your little pet. I yearn for the silvery cadence of your voice—I thirst for the bubbling stream of your affection.
"YOUR MADELINE."

We feel for that girl. The water privilege which she pines for so lovingly has probably dried up and departed, else her sweet note would not have been floating around the streets without a claimant. We feel for her deeply—and if it will afford her any relief, if it will conduce to her comfort, if it will satisfy her yearning even in the smallest degree, we will cheerfully call around and "bubble" awhile for her ourself, if she will send us her address.

Virginia City Territorial Enterprise
c. February 12, 1863

The Spanish

We slid down into the Spanish mine yesterday, to look after the rich strike which was made there lately.

[This in the time before elevators, when, as in the salt mines in Austria, one slides down a polished wooden bannister on a waxed leather apron to reduce the heat. It is a great ride down but a long hike back up. Ed.]

We found things going on at about their usual gait, and the general appearance of the mine in no respect differing from what it was before the recent flood. A few inches of water still remain in the lower gallery, but it interferes with nobody, and can be easily bailed out whenever it may be deemed necessary.

Every department of the Spanish mine is now in first class working order, owing to the able management of the general superintendent, Mr. J. P. Corrigan; the slight damage done by the inundation having been thoroughly repaired. In the matter of bracing and timbering the mine, an improvement upon the old plan has lately been added, which makes a large saving in the bill of expenses. This improvement consists in building the stations wider and higher, and filling up a wall of them here and there with refuse rock. Expenses are not only lightened thus, but such walls never rot, are never in danger of caving, need never be removed, and are altogether the strongest supports that a mine can have.

Intelligent people can understand, now, that about a hundred dollars a day may be saved in this way, without even taking into consideration the costly job of re-timbering every two or three years, which is rendered unnecessary by it—and by way of driving the proposition into heads like the Unreliable's, which is filled with oysters instead of brains, we will say that by building these walls, you are saved the time and labor of lowering heavy timbers 300 feet into the earth and hoisting up refuse rock the same distance; for you can leave the one in the woods, and pile the other into boxed-up stations as fast as you dig it out.

However, it is time to speak of the rich strike, now. This charming spot is two hundred and forty feet below the surface of the earth. It extends across the entire width of the ledge—from twenty-five to thirty feet—and has been excavated some twenty feet on the length of the lead, and to the depth of twenty-one feet. How much deeper it reaches, no man knoweth.

The face of the walls is of a dark blue color, sparkling with pyrites, or sulphurets, or something, and beautifully marbled with little crooked streaks of lightning as white as a loaf of sugar. This mass of richness pays from eight to twelve hundred dollars a ton just as it is taken from the ledge, without "sorting." Twenty thousand dollars' worth of it was hoisted out of the mine last Saturday; about two hundred and fifty tons have been taken out altogether.

The hoisting apparatus is about perfect: when put to its best speed, it can bail out somewhere in the neighborhood of a hundred and fifty tons of rock in daylight. The rich ore we have been talking about is sacked up as soon as it reaches the surface of the Territory, and shipped off to the Company's mill (the Silver State) at Empire City. The Silver State is a forty-stamp arrangement, with a thundering chimney to it, which anyone has noticed who has traveled from here to Carson. Mr. Dorsey is the superintendent, and Mr. Janin assayer.

Virginia City Territorial Enterprise
February 3, 1863

Letter from Carson

Carson, Tuesday Night

EDS. ENTERPRISE: I received the following atrocious document the morning I arrived here. It is from that abandoned profligate, the Unreliable, and I think it speaks for itself:

Carson City, Thursday Morning

TO THE UNRELIABLE—SIR: Observing the driver of the Virginia stage hunting after you this morning, in order to collect his fare, I infer you are in town.

In the paper which you represent, I noticed an article which I took to be an effusion of your muddled brain, stating that I had "cabbaged" a number of valuable articles from you the night I took you out of the streets in Washoe City and permitted you to occupy my bed.

I take this opportunity to inform you that I will compensate you at the rate of $20 per head for every one of those valuables that I received from you, providing you will relieve me of their presence. This offer can either be accepted or rejected on your part; but, providing you don't see proper to accept it, you had better procure enough lumber to make a box 4 x 8, and have it made as early as possible. Judge Dixson will arrange the preliminaries, if you don't accede. An early reply is expected by
  RELIABLE

Not satisfied with wounding my feelings by making the most extraordinary references and allusions in the above note, he even sent me a challenge to fight, in the same envelope with it, hoping to work upon my fears and drive me from the country by intimidation.

But I was not to be frightened; I shall remain in the Territory. I guessed his object at once, and determined to accept his challenge, choose weapons and things, and scare him, instead of being scared myself. I wrote a stern reply to him, and offered him mortal combat with bootjacks at a hundred yards.

The effect was more agreeable than I could have hoped for. His hair turned black in a single night, from excess of fear; then he went into a fit of melancholy, and while it lasted he did nothing but sigh, and sob, and snuffle, and slobber, and blow his nose on his coat-tail, and say "he wished he was in the quiet tomb"; finally, he said he would commit suicide—he would say farewell to the cold, cold world, with its cares and troubles, and go and sleep with his fathers, in perdition.

Then rose up this young man, and threw his demijohn out of the window, and took a glass of pure water, and drained it to the very, very dregs. And then he fell on the floor in spasms. Dr. Tjader was called in, and as soon as he found that the cuss was poisoned, he rushed down to the Magnolia Saloon and got the antidote, and poured it down him. As he was drawing his last breath, he scented the brandy and lingered yet a while upon the earth, to take a drink with the boys. But for this, he would have been no more and possibly a good deal less—in another moment.

So he survived; but he has been in a mighty precarious condition ever since. I have been up to see how he was getting along two or three times a day. He is very low; he lies there in silence, and hour after hour he appears to be absorbed in tracing out the figures in the wall paper. He is not changed in the least, though; his face looks just as natural as anything could be. There is no more expression in it than a turnip.

But he is a very sick man; I was up there a while ago, and I could see that his friends had begun to entertain hopes that he would not get over it. As soon as I saw that, all my enmity vanished; I even felt like doing the poor Unreliable a kindness, and showing him, too, how my feelings towards him had changed.

So I went and bought him a beautiful coffin, and carried it up and set it down on his bed, and told him to climb in when his time was up. Well, sir, you never saw a man so affected by a little act of kindness as he was by that. He let off a sort of war-whoop, and went to kicking things around like a crazy man, and he foamed at the mouth, and went out of one fit and into another faster than I could take them down in my note-book. I have got thirteen down, though, and I know he must have had two or three before I could find my pencil. I actually believe he would have had a thousand, if that old fool who nurses him hadn't thrown the coffin out of the window, and threatened to serve me in the same way if I didn't leave.

I left, of course, under the circumstances, and I learn that although the patient was getting better a moment before this circumstance, he got a good deal worse immediately afterward. They say he lies in a sort of a stupor now, and if they cannot rally him, he is gone in, as it were. They may take their own course now, though, and use their own judgment. I shall not go near them again, although I think I could rally him with another coffin.

I did not return to Virginia yesterday, on account of the wedding. The parties were Hon. James H. Sturtevant, one of the first Pi-Utes of Nevada, and Miss Emma Curry, daughter of Hon. A. Curry, who also claims that his is a Pi-Ute family of high antiquity. Curry conducted the wedding arrangements himself, and invited none but Pi-Utes. This interfered with me a good deal. However, as I had heard it reported that a marriage was threatened, I felt it my duty to go down there and find out the facts in the case. They said I might stay, as it was me; the permission was unnecessary, though—I calculated to do that anyhow. I promised not to say anything about the wedding, and I regard that promise as sacred—my word is as good as my bond.

At three o'clock in the afternoon, all the Pi-Utes went up stairs to the old Hall of Representatives in Curry's house, preceded by the bride and groom, and the bridesmaids and groomsmen (Miss Jo. Perkins and Miss Nettie Curry, and Hon. John H. Mills and Wm. M. Gillespie), and followed by myself and the fiddlers.

The fiddles were tuned up, three quadrille sets were formed on the floor. Father Bennett advanced and touched off the high contracting parties with the hymeneal torch (married them, you know), and at the word of command from Curry, the fiddle-bows were set in motion, and the plain quadrilles turned loose.

Thereupon, some of the most responsible dancing ensued that you ever saw in your life. The dance that Tam O'Shanter witnessed was slow in comparison to it. They kept it up for six hours, and then they carried out the exhausted musicians on a shutter, and went down to supper. I know they had a fine supper, and plenty of it, but I do not know much else. They drank so much champagne around me that I got confused, and lost the hang of things, as it were.

Mills, and Musser, and Sturtevant, and Curry, got to making speeches, and I got to looking at the bride and bridesmaids—they looked uncommonly handsome—and finally I fell into a sort of trance. When I recovered from it the brave musicians were all right again, and the dance was ready to commence. They went to slinging plain quadrilles around as lively as ever, and never rested again until nearly midnight, when the dancers all broke down and the party broke up. It was all mighty pleasant, and jolly, and sociable, and I wish to thunder I was married myself.

I took a large slab of the bridal cake home with me to dream on, and dreamt that I was still a single man, and likely to remain so, if I live and nothing happens—which has given me a greater confidence in dreams than I ever felt before. I cordially wish the newly married couple all kinds of happiness and posterity, though.

Richardson's case was continued to the next term of the District Court last Thursday, and the prisoner admitted to bail in the sum of $10,000—$7,000 on the charge of murder (the killing of Con Mason), and $3,000 on the charge of highway robbery.

Three new mining companies filed their certificates of incorporation in the County Clerk's and Territorial Secretary's offices last Saturday. Their ledges are located in the new Brown & Murphy District, in Lyon County. The names, etc., of the new companies are as follows: Jennie V. Thompson G. & S. M. Company, capital stock $220,000, in 2,200 shares of $100 each; Byron G. & S. M. Company, same number of shares, etc.; Lion G. & S. Company, capital stock $230,000, in 2,300 shares of $100 each. The following gentlemen are Trustees of all three companies: C. L. Newton, J. D. Thompson, J. Ball, G. C. Haswell and Wm. Millikin. The principal offices of the companies are in Carson City.

Virginia City Territorial Enterprise
February 8, 1863

Letter From Carson

Carson, Thursday Morning

EDS. ENTERPRISE: The community were taken by surprise last night, by the marriage of Dr. J. H. Wayman and Mrs. M. A. Ormsby. Strategy did it. John K. Trumbo lured the people to a party at his house, and corraled them, and in the meantime Acting Governor Clemens proceeded to the bride's dwelling and consolidated the happy couple under the name and style of Mr. and Mrs. Wayman, with a life charter, perpetual succession, unlimited marital privileges, principal place of business at ho—blast those gold and silver mining incorporations!

I have compiled a long list of them from the Territorial Secretary's books this morning, and their infernal technicalities keep slipping from my pen when I ought to be writing graceful poetical things. After the marriage, the high contracting parties and the witnesses there assembled adjourned to Mr. Trumbo's house.

The ways of the Unreliable are past finding out. His instincts always prompt him to go where he is not wanted, particularly if anything of an unusual nature is on foot. Therefore, he was present and saw those wedding ceremonies through the parlor windows. He climbed up behind Dr. Wayman's coach and rode up to Trumbo's—this shows that his faculties were not affected by his recent illness. When the bride and groom entered the parlor he went in with them, bowing and scraping and smiling in his imbecile way, and attempting to pass himself off for the principal groomsman.

I never saw such an awkward, ungainly lout in my life. He had on a pair of Jack Wilde's pantaloons, and a swallow-tail coat belonging to Lytle ("Schermerhorn's Boy"), and they fitted him as neatly as an elephant's hide would fit a poodle dog. I would be ashamed to appear in any parlor in such a costume. It never enters his head to be ashamed of anything, though. It would have killed me with mortification to parade around there as he did, and have people stepping on my coat tail every moment.

As soon as the guests found out who he was they kept out of his way as well as they could, but there were so many gentlemen and ladies present that he was never at a loss for somebody to pester with his disgusting familiarity. He worried them from the parlor to the sitting-room, and from thence to the dancing-hall, and then proceeded upstairs to see if he could find any more people to stampede. He found Fred. Turner, and stayed with him until he was informed that he could have nothing more to eat or drink in that part of the house. He went back to the dancing-hall then, but he carried away a codfish under one arm, and Mr. Curry's plug hat full of sour-krout under the other. He posted himself right where he could be most in the way, and fell to eating as comfortably as if he were boarding with Trumbo by the week. They bothered him some, though, because every time the order came to "all promenade," the dancers would sweep past him and knock his cod fish out of his hands and spill his sour-krout.

He was the most loathsome sight I ever saw; he turned everybody's stomach but his own. It makes no difference to him, either, what he eats when hungry. I believe he would have eaten a corpse last night, if he had one. Finally, Curry came and took his hat away from him and tore one of his coat tails off and threatened to thresh him with it, and that checked his appetite for a moment. Instead of sneaking out of the house, then, as anybody would have done who had any self respect, he shoved his codfish into the pocket of his solitary coat tail (leaving at least eight inches of it sticking out), and crowded himself into a double quadrille.

He had it all to himself pretty soon; because the order "gentlemen to the right" came, and he passed from one lady to another around the room, and wilted each and every one of them with the horrible fragrance of his breath. Even Trumbo, himself, fainted. Then the Unreliable, with a placid expression of satisfaction upon his countenance, marched forth and swept the parlors like a pestilence. When the guests had been persecuted as long as they could stand it, though, they got him to drink some kerosene oil, which neutralized the sour-krout and cod fish, and restored his breath to about its usual state, or even improved it, perhaps, for it generally smells like a hospital.

The Unreliable interfered with Col. Musser when he was singing the peanut song; he bothered William Patterson, Esq., when that baritone was singing, "Ever of thee I'm fondly dreaming"; he interrupted Epstein when he was playing on the piano; he followed the bride and bridegroom from place to place, like an evil spirit; and he managed to keep himself and his coat-tail eternally in the way.

I did hope that he would stay away from the supper-table, but I hoped against an impossibility. He was the first one there, and had choice of seats also, because he told Mr. Trumbo he was a groomsman; and not only that, but he made him believe, also, that Dr. Wayman was his uncle. Then he sailed into the ice cream and champagne, and cakes and things, at his usual starvation gait, and he would infallibly have created a famine, if Trumbo had not been particularly well fortified with provisions.

There is one circumstance connected with the Unreliable's career last night which it pains me to mention, but I feel that it is my duty to do it. I shall cut the melancholy fact as short as possible, however: seventeen silver spoons, a New Testament and a gridiron were missed after supper. They were found upon the Unreliable's person when he was in the act of going out at the back door.

Singing and dancing commenced at seven o'clock in the evening, and were kept up with unabated fury until half-past one in the morning, when the jolly company put on each other's hats and bonnets and wandered home, mighty well satisfied with Trumbo's "corn shucking," as he called it.

Well, you were particularly bitter about the "extra session" yesterday morning, and with very small cause, too, it seems to me. You rush in desperately and call out all the fire engines in the universe, and lo! there is nothing but a chunk of harmless fox-fire to squirt at after all. You slash away right and left at the lawyers, just as if they were not human like other people, subject to the same accidents of fortune and circumstances, moved by the same springs of action, and honest or dishonest according to the nature which God Almighty endowed them with. Stuff!

You talk like a wooden man. A man's profession has but little to do with his moral character. If we had as many preachers as lawyers, you would find it mixed as to which occupation could muster the most rascals. Then you pitch into the legislators, and say that, "with two or three exceptions, they are men who failed to complete their programmes of rascality," etc. Humbug! They never commenced any such programme. I reported their proceedings—I was behind the scenes, and I know. I talk sweepingly, perhaps—so do you, in that wild sentence. There might have been two or three first-class rascals in the Legislature—I have that number in my eye at the present moment—but the balance were fully as honest as you, and considerably more so than me.

I could prove this by simply reminding you of their names. Run over the list, and see if there are not some very respectable names on it. I have acknowledged that there were several scoundrels in the Legislature, but such a number, in as large a body as the last Assembly, could carry no measure, you know, and the men I am thinking of couldn't even influence one. The Lord originally intended them to do transportation duty in a jackass train, I think.

And then, how you talk about the pecuniary wants of our legislators: "Their hungry wallets yearn for a second assault on the greenbacks and franchises of the Territory." That is humbug, also. Take the House, for instance. I can name you fifteen members of that body whose pecuniary condition is very comfortable—who stand in no more pressing need of Territorial greenbacks than you do of another leg. And I can name you half a dozen others who are not suffering for food and raiment, and whom Providence will be able to take care of, I think, without bringing an extra session of the Nevada Legislature to pass.

You talk like a wooden man, I tell you. Why there are not enough "Territorial Greenbacks" in the Secretary's office and the Territorial Treasury put together to start a wholesale peanut stand with; and why should thirty-nine legislators want to neglect their business to go to Carson and gobble up and divide such a pittance? Bosh.

Somebody made a blunder; somebody did a piece of rascality. It was not the legislators, yet only they can set the matter right—and if they want to go back to the capital and do it, it is rather a credit to them than a dishonor. I cannot see anything very criminal in this conduct of theirs.

You are too brash, you know—that is what is the matter with you. You say you heard a report that the Acting Governor had decided to call an extra session. Well, what if you did? Don't you suppose that, being here, at the seat of government, I would naturally know a good deal more about it than anybody's reports? Reports lie—I do not. Why didn't you ask me for information? I always have an abundance of the article on hand.

  I will give you some now: the Acting Governor has not decided to call an extra session; he is not seriously thinking of such a thing at present; he is not expecting to think of it next week; he is not in favor of the measure, and does not wish to move in the matter unless a majority of the counties expressly desire it. Now, you have said a great many things in your article which you ought not to have said; you have done injustice to all the parties whom you have mentioned; you have hollered "Wolf!" when there was nothing present but the mildest sort of a lamb; and the properest course for you to pursue will be to screw down your throttle-valve and dry up.

  I have a strong inclination to continue this subject a while longer, but I promised to go down in town and get drunk with Curry and Trumbo, and Tom Bedford and Gillespie, before I leave for Virginia. My promises are sacred. I have also to receive a petition from citizens of Carson, with several thousand names on it, requesting me to extend my visit here a few years longer. It affords me great pleasure to state that several hundred sheets of this petition are covered with the autographs of intelligent and beautiful ladies.

Virginia City Territorial Enterprise
c. *February 17, 1863*

Local Column

  APOLOGETIC—We are always happy to apologize to a man when we do him an injury. We have wounded William Smiley's feelings, and we will heal them up again or bust. We said in yesterday's police record that Bill (excuse the familiarity, William) was drunk. We lied. It is our opinion that Sam Wetherill did, too, for he gave us the statement. We have gleaned the facts in the case, though, from William himself, and at his request we hasten to apologize. His offense was mildness itself. He only had a pitched battle with another man, and resisted an officer. That was all. Come up, William, and take a drink.

Virginia City Territorial Enterprise
c. February 17, 1863

Silver Bars—How Assayed

We propose to speak of some silver bars which we have been looking at, and to talk science a little, also, in this article, if we find that what we learned in the latter line yesterday has not escaped our memory. The bars we allude to were at the banking house of Paxton Thornburgh, and were five in number; they were the concentrated result of portions of two eight-day runs of the Hoosier State Mill, on Potosi rock.

The first of the bricks bore the following inscription, which is poetry stripped of flowers and flummery, and reduced to plain common sense: "No. 857; Potosi Gold and Silver Mining Company; Theall & Co., assayers; 688.48 ounces, gold, 020 fine, silver, 962 fine; gold $572.13, silver $1,229.47." Bars No. 836 and No. 858 bore about the same inscription, save that their values differed, of course, the one being worth $1,800, and the other a fraction under $1,300. The two largest bars were still in the workshop, and had not yet been assayed; one of them weighed nearly a hundred pounds and one was worth about $3,000, and the other, which contained over 900 ounces, was worth in the neighborhood of $2,000. The weight of the whole five bars may be set down in round numbers at 300 pounds, and their value at, say, $10,000. Those are about the correct figures.

We are very well pleased with the Hoosier State mill and the Potosi mine—we think of buying them. From the contemplation of this result of two weeks' mill and mining labor, we walked through the assaying rooms, in the rear of the banking house, with Mr. Theall, and examined the scientific operations there, with a critical eye. We absorbed much obtuse learning, and we propose to give to the ignorant the benefit of it.

After the amalgam has been retorted at the mill, it is brought here and broken up and put into a crucible (along with a little borax) of the capacity of an ordinary plug hat; this vessel is composed of some kind of pottery which stands heat like a salamander; the crucible is placed in a brick furnace; in the midst of a charcoal fire as hot as the one which the three Scriptural Hebrew children were assayed in; when the mass becomes melted, it is well stirred, in order to get the metals thoroughly mixed, after which it is poured into an iron brick mould; such of the base metals as were not burned up, remain in the crucible in the form of a "sing."

The next operation is the assaying of the brick. A small chip is cut from each end of it and weighed; each of these is enveloped in lead and placed in a little shallow cup made of bone ashes, called a cupel, and put in a small stone-ware oven, enclosed in a sort of parlor stove furnace, where it is cooked like a lost sinner; the lead becomes oxydized and is entirely absorbed by the pores of the cupel—any other base metals that may still linger in the precious stew, meet the same fate, or go up the chimney.

The gold and silver come from the cupel in the shape of a little button, and in a state of perfect purity; this is weighed once more, and what it has lost by the cooking process, determines the amount of base metal that was in it, and shows exactly what proportion of it the bar contains—the lost weight was base metal you understand, and was burned up or absorbed by the cupel.

The scales used in this service are of such extremely delicate construction that they have to be shut up in a glass case, since a breath of air is sufficient to throw them off their balance—so sensitive are they, indeed, that they are even affected by the particles of dust which find their way through the joinings of the case and settle on them. They will figure the weight of a piece of metal down to the thousandth part of a grain, with stunning accuracy. You might weigh a mosquito here, and then pull one of his legs off, and weigh him again, and the scales would detect the difference.

The smallest weight used—the one which represents the thousandth part of a grain—is composed of aluminum, which is the metallic base of common clay, and is the lightest metal known to science. It looks like an imperceptible atom clipped from the invisible corner of a piece of paper whittled down to an impossible degree of sharpness—as it were—and they handle it with pincers like a hair pin. But with an excuse for this interesting digression, we will return to the silver button again.

After the weighing, melting and re-weighing of it has shown the amount of base metal contained in the brick, the next thing to be done is to separate the silver and gold in it, in order to find out the exact proportions of these in the bar. The button is placed in a mattrass filled with nitric acid (an elongated glass bottle or tube, shaped something like a bell clapper) which is half buried in a box of hot sand—they called it a sand bath—on top of the little cupel furnace, where all the silver is boiled out of said button and held in solution (when in this condition it is chemically termed "nitrate of silver").

This process leaves a small pinch of gold dust in the bottom of the mattrass which is perfectly pure; its weight will show the proportion of pure gold in the bar, of course. The silver in solution is then precipitated with muriatic acid (or something of that kind—we are not able to swear that this was the drug mentioned to us, although we feel very certain that it was) and restored to metal again. Its weight, by the mosquito scales, will show the proportion of silver contained in the brick, you know.

Now just here, our memory is altogether at fault. We cannot recollect what in the world it is they do with the "dry cups." We asked a good many questions about them—asking questions is our regular business—but we have forgotten the answers. It is all owing to lager beer. We are inclined to think, though, that after the silver has been precipitated, they cook it a while in those little chalky-looking "dry cups," in order to turn it from fine silver dust to a solid button again for the sake of convenient handling—but we cannot begin to recollect anything about it.

We said they made a separate assay of the chips cut from each end of a bar; now if these chips do not agree—if they make different statements as to the proportions of the various metals contained in the bar, it is pretty good proof that the mixing was not thorough, and the brick has to be melted over again; this occurrence is rare, however. This is all the science we know. What we do not know is reserved for private conversation, and will be liberally inflicted upon anybody who will come here to the office and submit to it.

After the bar has been assayed, it is stamped as described in the beginning of this dissertation, and then it is ready for the mint. Science is a very pleasant subject to dilate upon, and we consider that we are as able to dilate upon it as any man that walks—but if we have been guilty of carelessness in any part of this article, so that our method of assaying as set forth herein may chance to differ from Mr. Theall's, we would advise that gentleman to stick to his own plan nevertheless, and not go to following ours—his is as good as any known to science. If we have struck anything new in our method, however, we shall be happy to hear of it, so that we can take steps to secure to ourselves the benefits accruing therefrom.

Virginia City Territorial Enterprise
February 19, 1863

Ye Sentimental Law Student

EDS. ENTERPRISE—I found the following letter, or Valentine, or whatever it is, lying on the summit, where it had been dropped unintentionally, I think. It was written on a sheet of legal cap, and each line was duly commenced within the red mark which traversed the sheet from top to bottom.

Solon appeared to have had some trouble getting his effusion started to suit him. He had begun it, "Know all men by these presents," and scratched it out again; he had substituted, "Now at this day comes the plaintiff, by his attorney," and scratched that out also; he had tried other sentences of like character, and gone on obliterating them, until, through much sorrow and tribulation, he achieved the dedication which stands at the head of his letter, and to his entire satisfaction, I do cheerfully hope.

But what a villain a man must be to blend together the beautiful language of love and the infernal phraseology of the law in one and the same sentence! I know but one of God's creatures who would be guilty of such depravity as this: I refer to the Unreliable. I believe the Unreliable to be the very lawyer's-cub who sat upon the solitary peak, all soaked in beer and sentiment, and concocted the insipid literary hash I am talking about. The handwriting closely resembles his semi-Chinese tarantula tracks.

Sugar Loaf Peak, February 14, 1863.

To the loveliness to whom these presents shall come, greeting:— This is a lovely day, my own Mary; its unencumbered sunshine reminds me of your happy face, and in the imagination the same doth now appear before me. Such sights and scenes as this ever remind me, the party of the second part, of you, my Mary, the peerless party of the first part.

The view from the lonely and segregated mountain peak, of this portion of what is called and known as Creation, with all and singular the hereditaments and appurtenances thereunto appertaining and belonging, is inexpressively grand and inspiring; and I gaze, and gaze, while my soul is filled with holy delight, and my heart expands to receive thy spirit-presence, as aforesaid. Above me is the glory of the sun; around him float the messenger clouds, ready alike to bless the earth with gentle rain, or visit it with lightning, and thunder, and destruction; far below the said sun and the messenger clouds aforesaid, lying prone upon the earth in the verge of the distant horizon, like the burnished shield of a giant, mine eyes behold a lake, which is described and set forth in maps as the Sink of Carson; nearer, in the great plain, I see the Desert, spread abroad like the mantle of a Colossus, glowing by turns, with the warm light of the sun, hereinbefore mentioned, or darkly shaded by the messenger clouds aforesaid; flowing at right angles with said Desert, and adjacent thereto, I see the silver and sinuous thread of the river, commonly called Carson, which winds its tortuous course through the softly tinted valley, and disappears amid the gorges of the bleak and snowy mountains—a simile of man!—leaving the pleasant valley of Peace and Virtue to wander among the dark defiles of Sin, beyond the jurisdiction of the kindly beaming sun aforesaid!

And about said sun, and the said clouds, and around the said mountains, and over the plain and the river aforesaid, there floats a purple glory—a yellow mist—as airy and beautiful as the bridal veil of a princess, about to be wedded according to the rites and ceremonies pertaining to, and established by, the laws or edicts of the kingdom or principality wherein she doth reside, and whereof she hath been and doth continue to be, a lawful sovereign or subject. Ah! my Mary, it is sublime! it is lovely! I have declared and made known, and by these presents do declare and make known unto you, that the view from Sugar Loaf Peak, as hereinbefore described and set forth, is the loveliest picture with which the hand of the Creator has adorned the earth, according to the best of my knowledge and belief, so help me God.

Given under my hand, and in the spirit-presence of the bright being whose love has restored the light of hope to a soul once groping in the darkness of despair, on the day and year first above written.

(Signed) SOLON LYCURGUS.

Law Student, and Notary Public in and for the said County of Storey, and Territory of Nevada.

To Miss Mary Links, Virginia (and may the laws have her in their holy keeping).

Virginia City Territorial Enterprise
February 25, 1863

Local Column

THE UNRELIABLE—This poor miserable outcast crowded himself into the Firemen's Ball, night before last, and glared upon the happy scene with his evil eye for a few minutes. He had his coat buttoned up to his chin, which is the way he always does when he has no shirt on. As soon as the managers found out he was there, they put him out, of course. They had better have allowed him to stay, though, for he walked straight across the street, with all his vicious soul aroused, and climbed in at the back window of the supper room and gobbled up the last crumb of the repast provided for the guests before he was discovered. This accounts for the scarcity of provisions at the Firemen's supper that night. Then he went home and wrote a particular description of our ball costume, with his usual meanness, as if such information could be of any consequence to the public. He never vouchsafed a single compliment to our dress, either, after all the care and taste we had bestowed upon it. We despise that man.

"MANY CITIZENS"—In another column of this paper will be found a card signed by "Many Citizens of Carson," stating that the County Commissioners of Ormsby county have removed the Sheriff from office and appointed someone else in his stead. They also ask whether the Commissioners really possess the power to remove the Sheriff, or the Governor of the Territory, or the President of the United States, at pleasure.

This is all well enough, except that in the face of our well known ability in the treatment of ponderous questions of unwritten law, these citizens have addressed their inquiries to the chief editor of this paper—a man who knows no more about legal questions than he does about religion—and so saturated with self-conceit is he, that he has even attempted, in his feeble way, to answer the propositions set forth in that note. We ignore his reply entirely, and notwithstanding the disrespect which has been shown us, we shall sink private pique for the good of our fellow men, and proceed to set their minds at rest on this question of power.

We declare that the County Commissioners do possess the power to remove the officers mentioned in that note, at pleasure. The Organic Act says so in so many words. We invite special attention to the first clause of section 2 of that document, where this language is used, if we recollect rightly: "The executive power and authority in and over said Territory of Nevada shall be vested in a Governor and other officers, who shall hold their offices for four years, and until their successors shall be appointed and qualified, unless sooner removed by the County Commissioners."

That is explicit enough, we take it. "Other officers" means any or all other officers, of course, else such dignitaries as it was intended to refer to would have been specifically mentioned; consequently, the President of the United States, and the Governor and Sheriff being "officers," come within the provisions of the law, and may be shoved out of the way by the Commissioners as quietly as they would abate a nuisance.

We might enlarge upon this subject until Solomon himself couldn't understand it—but we have settled the question, and we despise to go on scattering pearls before swine who have not asked us for them. In thus proving by the Organic Act, and beyond the shadow of a doubt, that the County Commissioners are invested with power to remove the Sheriff or the Governor or the President, whenever they see fit to do so, we have been actuated solely by a love of the godlike principles of right and justice, and a desire to show the public what an unmitigated ass the chief editor of this paper is.

Having succeeded to our entire satisfaction, we transfer our pen to matters of local interest, although we could prove, if we wanted to, that the County Commissioners not only possess the power to depose the officers above referred to but to hang them also, if they feel like it. When people want a legal opinion in detail, they must address their communications to us, individually, and not to irresponsible smatterers, like the chief editor.

THE FIREMEN'S BALL—About seventy couples assembled at Topliffe's Theatre night before last, upon the occasion of the annual ball of Virginia Engine Company No. 1. The hall was ablaze, from one end to the other, with flags, mirrors, pictures, etc.; and when the crowd of dancers had got into violent motion, and thoroughly fuddled with plain quadrilles, the looking-glasses multiplied them into a distracted and countless throng. Verily, the effect was charming to the last degree.

The decoration of the theatre occupied several days, and was done under the management of a committee composed of Messrs. Brokaw, Robinson, Champney, Claresy, Garvey and Sands, and they certainly acquitted themselves with marked ability. The floor was covered with heavy canvass, and we rather liked the arrangement—but the wind got under it and made it fill and sag like a circus tent, insomuch that it impeded the Varsovienne practice, and caused the ladies to complain occasionally.

Benham's "People's Band" made excellent music; however, they always do that. We have not one particle of fault to find with the ball; the managers kept perfect order and decorum, and did everything in their power to make it pass pleasantly to all the guests. They succeeded.

But of all the failures we have been called upon to chronicle, the supper was the grandest. It was bitterly denounced by nearly everybody who sat down to it—officers, firemen, men, women and children. Now, the supposition is that somebody will come out in a card and deny this, and attribute base motives to us: but we are not to be caught asleep, or even napping, this time—we have got all our proofs at hand, and shall explode at anybody who tries to show that we cannot tell the truth without being actuated by unworthy motives.

Chief Engineer Peasley and officer Birdsall said that the supper contract was for a table supplied with everything the market could afford, and in such profusion that the last who came might fare as well as the first (the contractor to receive a stipulated sum for each supper furnished)—and they also say that no part or portion of that contract was entirely fulfilled. The entertainment broke up about four o'clock in the morning, and the guests returned to their homes well satisfied with the ball itself, but not with the supper.

SMALL POX—From Carson we learn, officially, that Dr. Munckton has been sent down to Pine Nut Springs to look after some cases of smallpox, reported as existing among the Washoe Indians there. It is said that three men and a mahala are afflicted with it; the doctor intends vaccinating their attendants and warning the other Indians to keep away. Capt. Jo says one of the Indians caught the disease from a shirt given him by a white man. We do not believe any man would do such a thing as that maliciously, but at the same time, any man is censurable who is so careless as to leave infected clothing lying about where these poor devils can get hold of it. The commonest prudence ought to suggest the destruction of such dangerous articles.

SCHOOL-HOUSE—An addition is being built to the public school house, and will be completed and put in order for occupation as soon as possible. Mr. Mellvile's school has increased to such an extent that the old premises were found insufficient to accommodate all the pupils. As soon as the new building is completed, the school will be divided into three departments—advanced, intermediate and infant—and one of these will occupy it.

TRIAL TODAY—Sam Ingalls, who attempted the life of Pease the other day with a bowie knife, will be up before Judge Atwill today on a charge of drawing a deadly weapon. A case of this kind should never be allowed to pass without a severe rebuke, and if the evidence finds the prisoner guilty, he will probably catch it today; if it does not, why, no one wants him rebuked, of course.

DISTRICT COURT—The testimony for both sides in the case of the Burning Moscow vs. Madison Company was completed yesterday, and the lawyers will begin to throw hot shot at each other this morning—which is our military way of saying that the arguments of counsel herein will be commenced today. A great deal of interest is manifested in this suit, and the lobbies will be crowded during its trial.

SUICIDE—We learn by a note received last night per Langton's Express, that a German named John Meyer, a wood dealer in Downieville, committed suicide there on the night of the 19th inst., by blowing his brains out with a pistol. The cause is supposed to have been insanity.

TELEGRAPHIC—A message for S. S. Harman remains uncalled for at the Telegraph office.

Virginia City Territorial Enterprise
February 26, 1863

Reportorial

He became a newspaper reporter, and crushed Truth to earth and kept her there; he bought and sold his own notes, and never paid his board; he pretended great friendship for Gillespie, in order to get to sleep with him; then he took advantage of his bed fellow and robbed him of his glass eye and his false teeth; of course he sold the articles, and Gillespie was obliged to issue more county scrip than the law allowed, in order to get them back again; the Unreliable broke into my trunk at Washoe City, and took jewelry and fine clothes and things, worth thousands and thousands of dollars; he was present, without invitation, at every party and ball and wedding which transpired in Carson during thirteen years.

But the last act of his life was the crowning meanness of it: I refer to the abuse of me in the Virginia Union of last Saturday, and also to a list of Langton's stage passengers sent to the same paper by him, wherein my name appears between those of "Sam Chung" and "Sam Lee." This is his treatment of me, his benefactor. That malicious joke was his dying atrocity. During thirteen years he played himself for a white man: he fitly closed his vile career by trying to play me for a Chinaman. He is dead and buried now, though: let him rest, let him rot. Let his vices be forgotten, but let his virtues be remembered: it will not infringe much upon any man's time.

P. S.—By private letters from Carson, since the above was in type, I am pained to learn that the Unreliable, true to his unnatural instincts, came to life again in the midst of his funeral sermon, and remains so to this moment. He was always unreliable in life—he could not even be depended upon in death. The shrouded corpse shoved the coffin lid to one side, rose to a sitting posture, cocked his eye at the minister and smilingly said, "O let up, Dominie, this is played out, you know—loan me two bits!" The frightened congregation rushed from the house, and the Unreliable followed them, with his coffin on his shoulder. He sold it for two dollars and a half, and got drunk at a "bit house" on the proceeds. He is still drunk.

Virginia City Territorial Enterprise
c. March 1, 1863

Local Column

CALICO SKIRMISH—Five Spanish women, of unquestionable character, were arraigned before Judge Atwill yesterday, some as principals and some as accessories to a feminine fight of a bloodthirsty description in A street. It was proved that one of them drew a navy revolver and a bowie-knife and attempted to use them upon another of the party, but being prevented, she fired three shots through the floor, for the purpose of easing her mind, no doubt. She was bound over to keep the peace, and the whole party dismissed.

Virginia City Territorial Enterprise
c. March 3, 1863

A Sunday in Carson

I arrived in this noisy and bustling town of Carson at noon today, per Langton's express. We made pretty good time from Virginia, and might have made much better, but for Horace Smith, Esq., who rode on the box seat and kept the stage so much by the head she wouldn't steer. I went to church, of course—I always go to church when I—when I go to church—as it were. I got there just in time to hear the closing hymn, and also to hear the Rev. Mr. White give out a long metre doxology, which the choir tried to sing to a short-metre tune. But there wasn't music enough to go around: consequently, the effect was rather singular than otherwise. They sang the most interesting parts of each line, though, and charged the balance to "profit and loss;" this rendered the general intent and meaning of the doxology considerably mixed, as far as the congregation were concerned, but inasmuch as it was not addressed to them, anyhow, I thought it made no particular difference.

By an easy and pleasant transition, I went from church to jail. It was only just down stairs—for they save men eternally in the second story of the new court house, and damn them for life in the first. Sheriff Gasherie has a handsome double office fronting on the street, and its walls are gorgeously decorated with iron convict-jewelry. In the rear are two rows of cells, built of bomb-proof masonry and furnished with strong iron doors and resistless locks and bolts. There was but one prisoner—Swayze, the murderer of Derickson—and he was writing; I do not know what his subject was, but he appeared to be handling it in a way which gave him great satisfaction . . .

Virginia City Territorial Enterprise
March 4, 1863

City Marshall Perry

John Van Buren Perry, recently re-elected City Marshal of Virginia City, was born a long time ago, in County Kerry, Ireland, of poor but honest parents, who were descendants, beyond question, of a house of high antiquity. The founder of it was distinguished for his eloquence; he was the property of one Baalam, and received honorable mention in the Bible.

John Van Buren Perry removed to the United States in 1792—after having achieved a high gastronomical reputation by creating the first famine in his native land—and established himself at Kinderhook, New Jersey, as a teacher of vocal and instrumental music. His eldest son, Martin Van Buren, was educated there, and was afterwards elected President of the United States; his grandson, of the same name, is now a prominent New York politician, and is known in the East as 'Prince John'; he keeps up a constant and affectionate correspondence with his worthy grandfather, who sells him feet in some of his richest wildcat claims from time to time.

While residing at Kinderhook, Jack Perry was appointed Commodore of the United States Navy, and he forthwith proceeded to Lake Erie and fought the mighty marine conflict, which blazes upon the pages of history as "Perry's Victory." In consequence of this exploit, he narrowly escaped the Presidency.

Several years ago Commodore Perry was appointed Commissioner Extraordinary to the Imperial Court of Japan, with unlimited power to treat. It is hardly worthwhile to mention that he never exercised that power; he never treated anybody in that country, although he patiently submitted to a vast amount of that sort of thing when the opportunity was afforded him at the expense of the Japanese officials. He returned from his mission full of honors and foreign whisky, and was welcomed home again by the plaudits of a grateful nation.

After the war was ended, Mr. Perry removed to Providence, Rhode Island, where he produced a complete revolution in medical science by inventing the celebrated "Pain Killer" which bears his name. He manufactured this liniment by the shipload, and spread it far and wide over the suffering world; not a bottle left his establishment without his beneficent portrait upon the label, whereby, in time, his features became as well known unto burned and mutilated children as Jack the Giant Killer's.

When pain had ceased throughout the universe Mr. Perry fell to writing for a livelihood, and for years and years he poured out his soul in pleasing and effeminate poetry.

His very first effort, commencing:

"How doth the little busy bee
Improve each shining hour," etc.

gained him a splendid literary reputation, and from that time forward no Sunday-school library was complete without a full edition of his plaintive and sentimental "Perry-Gorics." After great research and profound study of his subject, he produced that wonderful gem which is known in every land as "The Young Mother's Apostrophe to Her Infant," beginning:

"Fie! fie! oo itty bitty pooty sing!
To poke oo footsy-tootsys into momma's eye!"

This inspired poem had a tremendous run, and carried Perry's fame into every nursery in the civilized world. But he was not destined to wear his laurels undisturbed: England, with monstrous perfidy, at once claimed the "Apostrophe" for her favorite son, Martin Farquhar Tupper, and sent up a howl of vindictive abuse from her polluted press against our beloved Perry. With one accord, the American people rose up in his defense, and a devastating war was only averted by a public denial of the paternity of the poem by the great Proverbial over his own signature. This noble act of Mr. Tupper gained him a high place in the affection of this people, and his sweet platitudes have been read here with an ever augmented spirit of tolerance since that day.

The conduct of England toward Mr. Perry told upon his constitution to such an extent that at one time it was feared the gentle bard would fade and flicker out altogether; wherefore, the solicitude of influential officials was aroused in his behalf, and through their generosity he was provided with an asylum in Sing Sing prison, a quiet retreat in the state of New York. Here he wrote his last great poem, beginning:

> "Let dogs delight to bark and bite,
> For God hath made them so—
> Your little hands were never made
> To tear out each other's eyes with—"

and then proceeded to learn the shoemaker's trade in his new home, under the distinguished masters employed by the commonwealth.

Ever since Mr. Perry arrived at man's estate his prodigious feet have been a subject of complaint and annoyance to those communities which have known the honor of his presence. In 1835, during a great leather famine, many people were obliged to wear wooden shoes, and Mr. Perry, for the sake of economy, transferred his boot-making patronage from the tan-yard which had before enjoyed his custom, to an undertaker's establishment—that is to say, he wore coffins.

At that time he was a member of Congress from New Jersey, and occupied a seat in front of the Speaker's throne. He had the uncouth habit of propping his feet upon his desk during prayer by the chaplain, and thus completely hiding that officer from every eye save that of Omnipotence alone. So long as the Hon. Mr. Perry wore orthodox leather boots the clergyman submitted to this infliction and prayed behind them in singular solitude, under mild protest; but when he arose one morning to offer up his regular petition, and beheld the cheerful apparition of Jack Perry's coffins confronting him, "The jolly old bum went under the table like a sick porpus" (as Mr. P. feelingly remarks), "and never shot off his mouth in that shanty again."

Mr. Perry's first appearance on the Pacific Coast was upon the boards of the San Francisco theaters in the character of "Old Pete" in Dion Boucicault's "Octoroon." So excellent was his delineation of that celebrated character that "Perry's Pete" was for a long time regarded as the climax of histrionic perfection.

Since John Van Buren Perry has resided in Nevada Territory, he has employed his talents in acting as City Marshal of Virginia, and in abusing me because I am an orphan and a long way from home, and can therefore be persecuted with impunity. He was re-elected day before yesterday, and his first official act was an attempt to get me drunk on champagne furnished to the Board of Aldermen by other successful candidates, so that he might achieve the honor and glory of getting me in the station-house for once in his life. Although he failed in his object, he followed me down C street and handcuffed me in front of Tom Peasley's, but officers Birdsall and Larkin and Brokaw rebelled against this unwarranted assumption of authority, and released me—whereupon I was about to punish Jack Perry severely, when he offered me six bits to hand him down to posterity through the medium of this biography, and I closed the contract. But after all, I never expect to get the money.

Virginia City Territorial Enterprise
March 7, 1863

Champagne With the Board of Brokers

By a sort of instinct we happened in at Almack's just at the moment that the corks were about to pop, and discovering that we had intruded we were retreating when Daggett, the soulless, insisted upon our getting with the Board of Brokers, and we very naturally did so. The President had already been toasted, the Vice-President had likewise been complimented in the same manner. Mr. Mitchell had delivered an address through his unsolicited mouth-piece, Mr. Daggett, whom he likened unto Baalam's ass—and very aptly too—and the press had been toasted, and he had attempted to respond and got overcome by something—feelings perhaps—when that ever lasting, omnipresent, irrepressible, "Unreliable" crowded himself into the festive apartment, where he shed a gloom upon the Board of Brokers, and emptied their glasses while they made speeches. The imperturbable impudence of that iceberg surpasses anything we ever saw.

By a concerted movement the young man was partially put down at length, however, and the Board launched out into speech-making again, but finally somebody put up five feet of "Texas," which changed hands at eight dollars a foot, and from that they branched off into a wholesale bartering of "wildcat"—for their natures were aroused by the first smell of blood, of course—and we adjourned to make this report. The Board will begin its regular meetings Monday next.

Virginia City Territorial Enterprise
c. April 1, 1863

Examination of Teachers

A grand examination of candidates for positions as teachers in our public schools was had yesterday in one of the rooms of the Public School in this city. Some twenty-eight candidates were present—twenty-three of whom were ladies and five gentlemen. We do the candidates but simple justice when we say that we have never seen more intelligent faces in a crowd of the size.

The following gentlemen constituted the Board of Examiners: Dr. Geiger, Mr. J. W. Whicher and John A. Collins. We observed that Messrs. Feusier, Adkison and Robinson of the Board of Trustees were also present yesterday. Printed questions are given to each of the candidates, the answers to which are written out and handed in with the signature of the applicant appended. These are all examined in private by the Board, and those who have best acquitted themselves are selected as teachers. In all, we believe, about twelve teachers are to be chosen.

Upon each of the following subjects a great number of questions are to be answered: general questions, methods of teaching, object teaching; spelling, reading, writing, defining, arithmetic, grammar, geography, natural philosophy, history of the United States, physiology and hygiene, chemistry, algebra, geometry, natural history, astronomy—in all, eighteen subjects, with about as many questions upon each. Yesterday they had got as far as the ninth subject, grammar, at the time of our visit, and we presume have got but little further. Today the examination will be resumed.

If there is anything that terrifies us it is an examination. We don't even like an examination in a Police Court. In vain we looked from face to face yesterday through the whole list of candidates for signs of fright or trepidation. All appeared perfectly at ease, though quite in earnest. We took a look at some of the questions and were made very miserable by barely glancing them over. We became much afraid that some member of the Board would suddenly turn upon us and require us on pain of death or a long imprisonment to answer some of the questions.

Under the head of "Object Teaching," we found some ten questions—some of them, like a wheel within a wheel, containing ten questions in one. We barely glanced at the list, reading here and there a question, when we felt great beads of perspiration starting out upon our brow—our massive intellect oozing out. Happening to read a question like this, "Name four of the faculties of children that are earliest developed," we at once became anxious to get out of the room. We expected each moment that one of the Board would seize us by the collar and ask, "Why is it?" or something of the kind, and we wanted to leave—thought we would feel better in the open air.

When the answers of all the candidates are opened and read we will try to be on hand; we are anxious for information on those "four faculties." We think the above a good deal like the conundrum about the young man who "went to the Sandwich Islands; learned the language of the Kanakas, came home, got married, got drunk, went crazy, was sent to Stockton—Why is it?"

Then under the same head we noticed ten questions about mining for silver ores and ten more about the reduction of silver ores. Why these twenty-three "school marms" are expected to be posted on amalgamating processes is more than we can guess. As this is a mining country, we presume it is necessary for a lady to give satisfactory answers to such questions as the following, before being entrusted with the education of our little Washoeites: "What is your opinion of the one-ledge theory? Have you seen the Ophir horse? Have you conscientious scruples as to black dyke? Are you committed to the sage-brush process? Give your opinion on vein matter, and state your reasons for thinking so; and tell wherein you differ with those who do not agree with you."

Virginia City Territorial Enterprise
April 3, 1863

Local Column

A DISTINGUISHED VISITOR—Madame Clara Kopka arrived in Virginia a few days since, and is still sojourning in the city. To many of our citizens the name will be unfamiliar, yet such is by no means the case in the hospitals and upon the battle-fields of the East, where she has devoted nearly twelve months to arduous labor in tending the sick and wounded soldiers. In this service she has endured all the hardships and privations of camp life, without hope or desire of reward, and to the serious detriment of her health.

She comes among us partly to satisfy a taste for travel, and partly to gather renewed vigor by a change of climate. She asked Mayor Arick for a homestead, supposing, in the simplicity of her heart, that the barren but beautiful landscape which surrounds Virginia was free to any who thought they could make use of it. Unfortunately, this is not the case; but the Silver Terrace Company could give Madame the homestead she covets without inconveniencing themselves in the least, and we have an idea that they will consider it a pleasure to do so.

Madame Kopka brings with her a bundle of letters from military officers, from brigade and subordinate surgeons in the army, from Secretary Stanton, and letters of recommendation to General Halleck, all of which speak of her in the highest terms of praise. We cannot spare room for these letters, but we publish two newspaper extracts which will answer every purpose, perhaps. The first is from a long article, written by an army surgeon, in the N. Y. Home Journal of September 13th, and the other from the N. Y Tribune of July 5th . . .

THE LOIS ANN—This claim is situated in a ravine which runs up in a northwesterly direction out of American Flat, and is on the Ophir Grade, about two miles and a half from Gold Hill. The ledge did not crop out, but was uncovered by a small slide in the hillside, and found by Mr. Lightford, the present Superintendent, and located some four or five weeks ago. A well timbered incline has since been sunk upon it to the depth of twenty-five feet, and work in it is still going on day and night, although a stream of water from the vein materially interferes with the operations of the men.

In the bottom of the incline the ledge is about ten feet wide, has a casing of blue clay, and is well defined; a great quantity of quartz has been taken from it, which looks exactly like third or fourth-class Ophir, but it won't pay to crush yet awhile, although choice specimens of it have assayed as high as ninety-two dollars to the ton.

We visited the mine in company with Mr. H. C. Brown and Mr. Lightford, the Superintendent, and we share their opinion, that there is big pay rock in it somewhere, and it is only necessary to sink a reasonable depth to find it. Such promising indications as have been found in this claim are not often discovered so near the surface. Three north extensions have been located on the Lois Ann, and shafts sunk, and the lead struck on the first and third, the character and appearance of the rock in both instances proving identical with that of the original—coarse crystallized quartz, of a porous nature, and of a dark blue color like Comstock rock.

There are fourteen hundred feet in the discovery claim, and the property is owned principally by mill men of Gold Hill. One of the best indications about the Lois Ann is at present much the most troublesome—we refer to the stream of water which pours from the ledge; work in the incline will have to be suspended on account of it and a tunnel commenced from the ravine—this will be about a hundred and fifty feet long, and will tap the lead at a depth of seventy-five feet.

A mill-site has been taken up in the vicinity with the intention of turning the water to useful account in case the ledge proves as excellent as it is expected it will. Another good-looking ledge lies back of the Lois Ann, and parallel with it, which belongs to the same company. There is a claim of a thousand feet in the vicinity of these leads which is called the Zanesville, and the rock from it pays in gold from the very surface; every pound of it is saved, and mill men who have tested it say it will yield about a hundred dollars to the ton; there is only a mere trace of silver in it. The ledge is only about two feet wide, in the bottom of a shaft twelve feet deep, but is increasing in width slowly; possibly the Zanesville may peter out and go to thunder, but there is no prospect of such a result at present. It is rich, but as it is only a gold ledge, and is so small, we have less confidence in it than in the Lois Ann.

ISLAND MILL—The Island Mill, built on Carson river by Mr. Hite, of Gold Hill, is about completed now, and the machinery was set in motion yesterday to see if there was anything wrong about it. The result was satisfactory, and the Island Mill will go to work formally and forever next Tuesday.

GOULD & CURRY—They struck it marvelously rich in a new shaft in the Gould & Curry mine last Saturday night. We saw half a ton of native silver at the mouth of the tunnel, on Tuesday, with a particle of quartz in it here and there, which could be readily distinguished without the aid of a glass. That particular half ton will yield somewhere in the neighborhood of ten thousand dollars. We have long waited patiently for the Gould & Curry to flicker out, but we cannot discover much encouragement about this last flicker. However, it is of no consequence—it was a mere matter of curiosity anyhow; we only wanted to see if she would, you know.

THE MINSTRELS—We were present at La Plata Hall about two minutes last night, and heard Sam. Pride's banjo make a very excellent speech in English to the audience. The house was crowded to suffocation.

Virginia City Territorial Enterprise
April 12, 1863

Advice to the Unreliable on Church-Going

In the first place, I must impress upon you that when you are dressing for church, as a general thing, you mix your perfumes too much; your fragrance is sometimes oppressive; you saturate yourself with cologne and bergamot, until you make a sort of Hamlet's Ghost of yourself, and no man can decide, with the first whiff, whether you bring with you air from heaven or from hell. Now, rectify this matter as soon as possible; last Sunday you smelled like a secretary to a consolidated drug store and barber shop. And you came and sat in the same pew with me; now don't do that again.

In the next place when you design coming to church, don't lie in bed until half past ten o'clock and then come in looking all swelled and torpid, like a doughnut. Do reflect upon it, and show some respect for your personal appearance hereafter.

There is another matter, also, which I wish to remonstrate with you about. Generally, when the contribution box of the missionary department is passing around, you begin to look anxious, and fumble in your vest pockets, as if you felt a mighty desire to put all your worldly wealth into it—yet when it reaches your pew, you are sure to be absorbed in your prayer-book, or gazing pensively out of the window at far-off mountains, or buried in meditation, with your sinful head supported by the back of the pew before you. And after the box is gone again, you usually start suddenly and gaze after it with a yearning look, mingled with an expression of bitter disappointment (fumbling your cash again meantime), as if you felt you had missed the one grand opportunity for which you had been longing all your life.

Now, to do this when you have money in your pockets is mean. But I have seen you do a meaner thing. I refer to your conduct last Sunday, when the contribution box arrived at our pew—and the angry blood rises to my cheek when I remember with what gravity and sweet serenity of countenance you put in fifty cents and took out two dollars and a half ...

Virginia City Territorial Enterprise
c. *April 16, 1863*

Horrible Affair

For a day or two a rumor has been floating around that five Indians had been smothered to death in a tunnel back of Gold Hill, but no one seemed to regard it in any other light than as a sensation hoax gotten up for the edification of strangers sojourning within our gates. However, we asked a Gold Hill man about it yesterday, and he said there was no shadow of a jest in it—that it was a dark and terrible reality. He gave us the following story as being the version generally accepted in Gold Hill.

That town was electrified on Sunday morning with the intelligence that a noted desperado had just murdered two Virginia policemen, and had fled in the general direction of Gold Hill. Shortly afterward, some one arrived with the exciting news that a man had been seen to run and hide in a tunnel a mile or a mile and a half west of Gold Hill. Of course it was Campbell—who else would do such a thing, on that particular morning, of all others?

So a party of citizens repaired to this spot, but each felt a natural delicacy about approaching an armed and desperate man in the dark, and especially in such confined quarters; wherefore they stopped up the mouth of the tunnel, calculating to hold on to their prisoner until some one could be found whose duty would oblige him to undertake the disagreeable task of bringing forth the captive.

The next day a strong posse went up, rolled away the stones from the mouth of the sepulchre, went in and found five dead Indians!—three men, one squaw and one child, who had gone in there to sleep, perhaps, and been smothered by the foul atmosphere after the tunnel had been closed up. We still hope the story may prove a fabrication, notwithstanding the positive assurances we have received that it is entirely true.

The intention of the citizens was good, but the result was most unfortunate. To shut up a murderer in a tunnel was well enough, but to leave him there all night was calculated to impair his chances for a fair trial—the principle was good, but the application was unnecessarily "hefty." We have given the above story for truth—we shall continue to regard it as such until it is disproven.

Virginia City Territorial Enterprise
c. April 19, 1863

Local Column

ELECTRICAL MILL MACHINERY—Mr. Wm. L. Card, of Silver City, has invented a sort of infernal machine, which is to turn quartz mills by electricity. It consists of wheels and things, and—however, we could not describe it without getting tangled. Mr. Card assures us that he can apply his invention to all the mills in Silver City, and work the whole lot with one powerful Grove battery. We believe—and if we had galvanic sense enough to explain the arrangement properly, others would also. A patent has already been applied for.

Virginia City Territorial Enterprise
c. May 19, 1863

Letter from Mark Twain

San Francisco, May 16, 1863

EDS. ENTERPRISE: The Unreliable, since he has been here, has conducted himself in such a reckless and unprincipled manner that he has brought the whole Territory into disrepute and made its name a reproach, and its visiting citizens objects of suspicion. He has been a perfect nightmare to the officers of the Occidental Hotel. They give him an excellent room, but if, in prowling about the house, he finds another that suits him better, he "locates" it (that is his slang way of expressing it).

Judging by his appearance what manner of man he was, the hotel clerk at first gave him a room immediately under the shingles—but it was found impossible to keep him there. He said he could not stand it, because spinning round and round, up that spiral staircase, caused his beer to ferment, and made him foam at the mouth like a soda fountain; wherefore, he descended at the dead of night and "jumped" a room on the second floor (the very language he used in boasting of the exploit). He said they served an injunction on him there, "and," says he, "if Bill Stewart had been down here, Mark, I'd have sued to quiet title, and I'd have held that ground, don't you know it?" And he sighed; and after ruminating a moment, he added, in a tone of withering contempt: "But these lawyers won't touch a case unless a man has some rights; humph! they haven't any more strategy into 'em than a clam. But Bill Stewart—thunder! Now, you just take that Ophir suit that's coming off in Virginia, for instance—why, God bless you, Bill Stewart'll worry the witnesses, and bullyrag the Judge, and buy up the jury and pay for 'em; and he'll prove things that never existed—hell! What won't he prove! That's the idea—what won't he prove, you know? Why, Mark, I'll tell you what he done when—"

The Unreliable was interrupted here by a messenger from the hotel office, who handed him several sheets of legal cap, very neatly folded. He took them and motioned the young man to retire. "Now," said he, confidentially, "do you know what that is, Sweetness?" I said I thought it was a wash bill, or a hotel bill, or some thing of that kind. His countenance beamed with admiration: "You've struck it, by the Lord; yes, sir, that's just what it is—it's another of them d—d assessments; they levied one on me last week, and I meant to go and see a lawyer about it, but"—The Unreliable simmered down into a profound reverie, and I waited in silence to see what species of villainy his fertile brain would bring forth.

At last he started up exultingly, with a devilish light in his eye: "I've got them in the door, Mark! They've been trying all they knew how to freeze me out, but they can't win. This hotel ain't incorporated under the laws of the Territory, and they can't collect—they are only a lot of blasted tenants in common! O, certainly" (with bitter scorn), "they'll get rich playing me for a Chinaman, you know." I forbear to describe how he reveled in the prospect of swindling the Occidental out of his hotel bill—it is too much humiliation even to think of it.

This young man insisted upon taking me to a concert last night, and I refused to go at first, because I am naturally suspicious of him, but he assured me that the Bella Union Melodeon was such a chaste and high-toned establishment that he would not hesitate to take any lady there who would go with him. This remark banished my fears, of course, and we proceeded to the house of amusement.

We were the first arrivals there. He purchased two pit-tickets for twenty-five cents apiece; I demurred at this kind of hospitality, and reminded him that orchestra seats were only fifty cents, and private boxes two dollars and a half. He bent on me a look of compassion, and muttered to himself that some people have no more sense than a boiled carrot—that some people's intellects were as dark as the inside of a cow.

He walked into the pit, and then climbed over into the orchestra seats as coolly as if he had chartered the theatre. I followed, of course. Then he said, "Now, Mark, keep your eye skinned on that doorkeeper, and do as I do." I did as he did, and I am ashamed to say that he climbed a stanchion and took possession of a private box. In due course several gentlemen performers came on the stage, and with them half a dozen lovely and blooming damsels, with the largest ankles you ever saw. In fact, they were dressed like so many parasols—as it were. Their songs, and jokes, and conundrums were received with rapturous applause. The Unreliable said these things were all copyrighted; it is probably true—I never heard them anywhere else. He was well pleased with the performance, and every time one of the ladies sang, he testified his approbation by knocking some of her teeth out with a bouquet.

The Bella Union, I am told, is supported entirely by Washoe patronage. There are forty-two single gentlemen here from Washoe, and twenty-six married ones; they were all at the concert last night except two—both unmarried. But if the Unreliable had not told me it was a moral, high-toned establishment, I would not have observed it.

Hon. Wm. H. Davenport, of Virginia, and Miss Mollie Spangler, of Cincinnati, Ohio, were married here on the 10th instant, at the residence of Colonel John A. Collins. Among the invited guests were Judge Noyes and lady, Messrs. Beecher and Franz, of Virginia, and Mr. Mark Twain; among the uninvited I noticed only the Unreliable. It will probably never be known what became of the spoons.

The bridal party left yesterday for Sacramento, and may be expected in Virginia shortly. Old fat, jolly B. C. Howard, a Lyon County Commissioner, is here, at the Russ House, where he will linger a while and then depart for his old home in Vermont, to return again in the Fall. Col. Raymond, of the Zephyr-Flat mill, is in the city, also, and taking up a good deal of room in Montgomery Street and the Bank Exchange; he has invested in some fast horses, and I shall probably take them over to Washoe shortly. There are multitudes of people from the Territory here at the three principal hotels—consequently provisions are scarce. If you will send a few more citizens down we can carry this election, and fill all these city offices with Carson and Virginia men.

There is not much doing in stocks just now, especially in the Boards. But I suspect it is the case here as it is in Virginia, that the Boards do precious little of the business. Many private sales of Union (Gold Hill) and Yellow Jacket have transpired here during the past week at much higher prices than you quote those stocks at. Three hundred feet of Golden Gate changed hands at $100 per foot, and fifty feet at $110; but a telegram from Virginia yesterday, announcing that they had "struck it"—and moderately rich—in the San Francisco, raised both stocks several figures, as also the Golden Eagle (first south extension of the Golden Gate), which had been offered the day before at $30 a foot. Two hundred feet of Oriental were sold at private sale today at $7 a foot. Now, you hear no talk in Virginia but the extraordinary dullness of the San Francisco market. Humbug! It may be dull in the Boards, but it is lively enough on the street. If you doubt it, say so, and I will move around a little and furnish you with all the statistics you want.

I meant to say something glowing and poetical about the weather, but the Unreliable has come in and driven away refined emotion from my breast. He says: "Say it's bully, you tallow brained idiot! that's enough; anybody can understand that; don't write any of those infernal, sick platitudes about sweet flowers, and joyous butterflies, and worms and things, for people to read before breakfast. You make a fool of yourself that way; everybody gets disgusted with you; stuff! be a man or a mouse, can't you?"

I must go out now with this conceited ass—there is no other way to get rid of him.

Virginia City Territorial Enterprise
c. June 21, 1863

Letter from Mark Twain
All About Fashions

San Francisco, June 19

EDS. ENTERPRISE:—I have just received, per Wells-Fargo, the following sweet scented little note, written in a microscopic hand in the center of a delicate sheet of paper—like a wedding invitation or a funeral notice—and I feel it my duty to answer it:

VIRGINIA, June 16.

"MR. MARK TWAIN—Do tell us something about the fashions. I am dying to know what the ladies of San Francisco are wearing. Do, now, tell us all you know about it, won't you? Pray excuse brevity, for I am in such a hurry. BETTIE.

"P. S.—Please burn this as soon as you have read it."

"Do tell us"—and she is in "such a hurry." Well, I never knew a girl in my life who could write three consecutive sentences without italicizing a word. They can't do it, you know. Now, if I had a wife, and she—however, I don't think I shall have one this week, and it is hardly worthwhile to borrow trouble.

Bettie, my love, you do me proud. In thus requesting me to fix up the fashions for you in an intelligent manner, you pay a compliment to my critical and observant eye and my varied and extensive information, which a mind less perfectly balanced than mine could scarcely contemplate without excess of vanity. Will I tell you something about the fashions? I will, Bettie—you better bet you bet, Betsey, my darling. I learned those expressions from the Unreliable; like all the phrases which fall from his lips, they are frightfully vulgar—but then they sound rather musical than otherwise.

A happy circumstance has put it in my power to furnish you the fashions from headquarters—as it were, Bettie: I refer to the assemblage of fashion, elegance and loveliness called together in the parlor of the Lick House last night—[a party given by the proprietors on the occasion of my paying up that little balance due on my board bill]. I will give a brief and lucid description of the dresses worn by several of the ladies of my acquaintance who were present. Mrs. B. was arrayed in a superb speckled foulard, with the stripes running fore and aft, and with collets and camails to match; also, a rotonde of Chantilly lace, embroidered with blue and yellow dogs, and birds and things, done in cruel, and edged with a Solferino fringe four inches deep—lovely. Mrs. B. is tall, and graceful and beautiful, and the general effect of her costume was to render her appearance extremely lively.

Miss J. W. wore a charming robe polonais of scarlet *ruche a la vieille,* with yellow fluted flounces of rich bombazine, fourteen inches wide; low neck and short sleeves; also a Figaro vest of bleached domestic—selvedge edge turned down with a back-stitch, and trimmed with festoons of blue chicoree taffetas—gay?—I reckon not. Her head-dress was the sweetest thing you ever saw: a bunch of stately ostrich plumes—red and white—springing like fountains above each ear, with a crown between, consisting of a single fleur de soliel, fresh from the garden—Ah, me! Miss W. looked enchantingly pretty; however, there was nothing unusual about that—I have seen her look so, even in a milder costume.

Mrs. J. B. W. wore a heavy rat-colored brocade silk, studded with large silver stars, and trimmed with organdy; balloon sleeves of nankeen pique, gathered at the wrist, cut bias and hollowed out some at the elbow; also, a bournous of black Honiton lace, scolloped, and embroidered in violent colors with a battle piece representing the taking of Holland by the Dutch; low neck and high-heeled shoes; gloves; palm leaf fan; hoops; her head-dress consisted of a simple maroon colored Sontag, with festoons of blue illusion depending from it; upon her bosom reposed a gorgeous bouquet of real sage brush, imported from Washoe. Mrs. W. looked regally handsome. If every article of dress worn by her on this occasion had been multiplied seven times, I do not believe it would have improved her appearance any.

Miss C. wore an elegant Cheveux de la Reine (with ruffles and furbelows trimmed with bands of guipre round the bottom), and a mohair Garibaldi shirt; her unique head-dress was crowned with a graceful pomme de terre (Limerick French), and she had her hair done up in papers—greenbacks. The effect was very rich, partly owing to the market value of the material, and partly to the general loveliness of the lady herself.

Miss A. H. wore a splendid Lucia de Lammermoor, trimmed with green baize: also, a cream-colored mantilla shaped pardessus, with a deep gore in the neck, and embellished with a wide greque of taffetas ribbon, and otherwise garnished with ruches, and radishes and things. Her coiffure was a simple wreath of sardines on a string. She was lovely to a fault.

Now, what do you think of that effort, Bettie (I wish I knew your other name) for an unsanctified newspaper reporter, devoid of a milliner's education? Doesn't it strike you that there are more brains and fewer oysters in my head than a casual acquaintance with me would lead one to suppose? Ah, well—what I don't know, Bet, is hardly worth the finding out, I can tell you.

I could have described the dresses of all the ladies in that party, but I was afraid to meddle with those of strangers, because I might unwittingly get something wrong, and give offense. You see strangers never exercise any charity in matters of this kind—they always get mad at the least inaccuracies of description concerning their apparel, and make themselves disagreeable. But if you will just rig yourself up according to the models I have furnished you, Bets, you'll do, you know—you can weather the circus.

You will naturally wish to be informed as to the most fashionable style of male attire, and I may as well give you an idea of my own personal appearance at the party. I wore one of Mr. Lawlor's shirts, and Mr. Ridgway's vest, and Dr. Wayman's coat, and Mr. Camp's hat, and Mr. Paxton's boots, and Jerry Long's white kids, and Judge Gilchrist's cravat, and the Unreliable's brass seal-ring, and Mr. Tollroad McDonald's pantaloons—and if you have an idea that they are anyways short in the legs, do you just climb into them once, sweetness. The balance of my outfit I gathered up indiscriminately from various individuals whose names I have forgotten and have now no means of ascertaining, as I thoughtlessly erased the marks from the different garments this morning. But I looked salubrious, B., if ever a man did.

San Francisco Daily Morning Call
July 9, 1863

Mark Twain's Letter
Home Again

Virginia City, Nevada Territory, July 5, 1863

EDITORS CALL—After an absence of two months, I stand in the midst of my native sagebrush once more; and in the midst of bustle and activity, and turmoil and confusion, to which lunchtime in the Tower of Babel was foolishness. B and C streets swarm with men, and horses, and wagons, and pack-trains, and dry-goods, and quartz, and bricks, and stone, and lumber, to such a degree that it is almost impossible to navigate them. And then the infernal racket—O, for the solitude of Montgomery Street again! Everybody is building, apparently. The boundaries of the city of Virginia have not been extended during the past two months, but the number of houses has been fearfully increased—doubled, I may say. Some portions of the town have grown clear out of my recollection since I have been away. Maguire has erected a spacious and beautiful theatre on D street, exactly after the pattern of the Opera House in San Francisco, and it is nightly crowded with admirers of Mr. Mayo, Mrs. Hayne, and other "theatricides," whose names are familiar to Californians.

The Henness Pass

I came by the Henness Pass route. I don't like it. I brought my other shirt along, and they charged me extra baggage. Besides, Uncle John Atchison, Mr. Harris and Mr. Chapelle were in the party, and they created a famine at every station we stopped at. They fell upon the Barnum Restaurant in Sacramento, and ate the proprietor out of house and home; then they attacked the first station this side of Lincoln, and brought ruin and desolation upon it. I am a mighty responsible artist at a dinner-table myself, when I get a chance—but I never got one until we arrived at Lake City, on Wednesday evening. We met the down stage there, with five or six men in it who were considerably battered and bruised by a recent upset. They were unable to eat. But the landlord lost nothing by it—I disposed of those extra rations. The only man among the wounded who was seriously hurt was a Mr. Tomlinson, from Humboldt Bay—shoulder dislocated. We seventeen passengers, however, traveled without fear of accident on this part of the route—from Nevada to Tracy's—as our driver was the best in the world except Woodruff (they call him Wood), who drives on the Placerville route from Genoa or Carson to Strawberry. They gave us a fish breakfast at Hunter's, on the Truckee—trout, Uncle John said, but it was hardly tender enough for that—I expect it was whale. We dashed by the Ophir on Thursday morning at half-past eleven o'clock, twenty-nine hours out from Sacramento—which reminds me of an anecdote, one of Mr. Merritt's, President of Imperial Gold and Silver Mining Company.

What Our Future Prosperity Depends Upon

Thus. Mr. Nathaniel Page, of San Francisco, was coming to Virginia one morning, in one of the Pioneer coaches, and enjoying the conversation of a sociable old sot, who decorated the middle seat. The sociable man pointed to the hillside, and remarked:

"When I first come here, two years ago, that Savage, there, 'n the Hale, 'n the Norcrus, 'n the Potosi, could be had for the askin' - any of 'em. Now look at 'em! (hic) Bilin', ain't they? H__ll! thousands couldn't touch 'em this very minute!"

Mr. Page said, "Well, those claims have increased in value rapidly—but do you think they will continue to do so?"

To which the sociable man replied, "Blessed if I know—'n no other man don't know, either. It's all owin' (hic) to how many more d__d fools comes here f'm Sanfercisco!"

The Fourth in Virginia

Yesterday was the greatest day Virginia ever saw. From morning till night her streets were crowded to suffocation with citizens, and soldiers, and fire companies, and the air was filled with the music of brass bands and the booming of cannon. I traversed the city in company with Billy Welch, of the California mine, in his "Washoe carriage" (being favored with the vacant seat aft the middle gangway, on that gentleman's little mule) and had a notable opportunity of wondering where such multitudes of people could have come from, and of never arriving at any satisfactory conclusion about it. The reading of the poem, and the Farewell Address, and the President's Message and accompanying documents, and so forth, came off in the afternoon, at the theatre. Of course, the house could only contain a very small fraction of the public, but that fraction was well satisfied with the exercises.

Mr. Frank Mayo read the poem (written by Joseph T. Goodman, Esq.,) which was a masterly production, as was amply attested by the tremendous applause with which it was received. Had I dreamed of such an enthusiastic reception as that, I would have dashed off a dusty old poem myself for the occasion. Thomas Fitch, Esq., delivered the oration. I don't know Mr. Fitch personally, but by reputation I don't like him. He is a "born" orator, though. If he always swings the English language as grandly as he did yesterday, I shall always be happy to hear him. He is a regular masked battery. He lulls you into a treacherous repose, with a few mild and graceful sentences, and then suddenly explodes in your midst with a bombshell of eloquence which shakes you to your very foundations.

Yesterday evening, a grand display of fireworks on Virginia Hill finished the Fourth of July festivities in this metropolis. Our wonderfully clear atmosphere vouchsafed to the pyrotechnics a splendor and brilliancy never attained at lower altitudes. Various figures and mottoes were represented, and the beauty of the designs and the excellence of the execution did infinite credit to Virginia.

Man Shot

The good order and freedom from disturbance which prevailed yesterday were the subject of general remark. I hardly think old citizens were fooled by it though. If they did not speak of it openly, many of them must have been speculating inwardly as to what man we were likely to have for breakfast. The fearful question was solved—or almost solved—just before midnight. Two Irishmen got to fighting in the San Francisco Saloon, and the proprietor of the establishment, Mike Millenovich, attempted to separate them. Two policemen—McGee and Scott—came in, attracted by the noise, and a general row ensued, in the course of which nine pistol shots were fired, one of which broke Millenovich's arm, and another entered his side, inflicting an ugly and probably fatal wound. I get this meagre and unsatisfactory statement from an eyewitness, who says "they made it so warm for him in there that he don't rightly know much about it." I entertain a similar opinion myself. Another witness tells me several outsiders were wounded by chance shots, but I have been unable to stumble upon any such.

The Mines

I cannot say anything about the mines this time, because I have not had time to visit them since I got home. That villainous trip over the mountains has relaxed my tremendous energies to some extent, also. From the increasing richness of the developments being made in the Hale & Norcross mine, however, I think you may count on a great advance in the price of that stock within the next few days.

False Report

There was a report about town last night, that Charles Strong, Esq., Superintendent of the Gould & Curry, had been shot and very effectually killed. I asked him about it at church this morning. He said there was no truth in the rumor. And speaking of the church, I am at this moment suffering with an itching to do up the fashions there, but I expect it might not be an altogether safe speculation.

San Francisco Daily Morning Call
July 15, 1863

Mark Twain's Letter

Virginia City, Nevada Territory, July 12, 1863

Editors *Morning Call*—Last week the weather was passably cool here, but it has moderated a good deal since then. The thermometer stands at a thousand, in the shade, today. It will probably go to a million before night. But the evenings are as cool and balmy as a shroud—wherefore, we refrain from grumbling. The weather took a curious freak yesterday: it actually clouded up and rained for five minutes—the first time such a thing has occurred here within my recollection. Several of the drops were assayed at once, of course, and found to be genuine; but they contained neither gold nor silver. Had the storm lasted an hour, it would have been incorporated under the Territorial law.

The races over the Winters course at Washoe City have commanded a good deal of interest during the past week. Marcus D. Boruck, editor of the San Francisco *Spirit of the Times*, attended them, for the purpose of reporting the proceedings for his paper. So far, Joe Winters' Miami is the winning horse. The race yesterday was two-mile heats, best three in five, and the competitors Miami, Strideaway and Kate Mitchell. Miami won, in three straight heats. Time: 1:53, 1:54, 1:55. Tomorrow finishes the season.

A mass meeting was held at Maguire's Opera House this afternoon for the purpose of raising a Sanitary Fund for the relief of soldiers wounded in the recent great battles in Pennsylvania and at Vicksburg. The enterprise was so insufficiently advertised that the theatre was not more than half full, and I was a little disappointed in the sum collected. They could have done about half as well in any other town of the same population, and I dislike to see Virginia fail to go ahead of all similar cities. Not more than a dozen or so of our wealthy men were present, and none of our great men were represented by authority. However, the meeting was very enthusiastic. Mr. R. M. Daggett was elected President, and Wm. M. Stewart, Esq., set the ball in motion with a short, stirring speech, and a check for $500; Col. John A. Collins followed with a speech and another for $500; and in a few minutes about $6,000 was subscribed altogether. This is fourteen thousand dollars short of what ought to have been collected. However, we shall come out all right before the week is out. Committees will canvass the county for the next three days, and on Thursday evening the Sanitary Fund will take a benefit at Maguire's Opera House; the free-list will be suspended, and the price of tickets placed at two or three dollars to all parts of the house. It will be a matter of small consequence what the play is—the theatre will be packed to its utmost capacity. Between the acts the audience will be permitted to subscribe to the fund, whether they want to or not. Mr. Paul proposed, today, that inasmuch as our former donations had gone to the New York and Cincinnati commissions, we now raise $20,000, cast into a huge silver block, inscribe "Vicksburg" upon it, and send it to St. Louis. The idea is sound.

Three of the Pioneer coaches met with accidents day before yesterday, this side of Placerville. One of them rolled down a slight precipice, and was smashed to pieces. Mr. Teschemacher, of San Francisco, was in it, but escaped uninjured. Mr. F. T. Moss had three ribs broken, and Mr. G. T. Sewall, of Humboldt District, received a small bruise or so. Mr. Sewall is the profound Justice of the Peace who held an inquest last Fall at Gravelly Ford, on the Humboldt River, on a petrified man who had been sitting there, cemented to the bed-rock, for the last three or four hundred years. The citizens wished to blast him out and bury him, but Judge S. refused to allow the sacrilege to be committed.

I have been around among mines this week. The Savage Company are keeping five mills going, and shipping bullion every day. I descended the main shaft of the Hale & Norcross, three hundred feet, and found they had not yet struck the ledge in the lower level, and will not for the next five or six days. The Chollar Company are putting up the finest and most extensive pumping and hoisting machinery in the Territory. They are shipping bullion regularly, and will increase the quantity vastly as soon as their new works are completed, say eight weeks hence. The Potosi Company are also erecting hoisting machinery at the C Street shaft. The Virginia Rogers Company are at work again, they tell me. I went all through the Ophir, too, through the extensive excavations in the "north mine," and thence under the Spanish, by way of the "fifth gallery," to the "south mine." In this portion of the mine the Company are drifting south on the ledge to find the rich streak of ore lately struck in the Central - they have about fifty feet to drift yet.

The yield of the Ophir—in the Company's own mills—was nearly $200,000 last month. The Gould & Curry mine doubled this yield, perhaps, but the rock was worked in many mills other than their own. The Silver City mines are coming out handsomely, and are growing in favor every day. Those of Gold Hill are being worked with increased energy and profit, and new machinery of an expensive character has been added to several of them lately. The Echo Company are making preparations to sink a new shaft in the vicinity of the Succor Mill, as it is dangerous to work the old incline, on account of its caving propensities. The last batch of rock from the Echo—thirty tons, third-class—yielded seventy-one dollars to the ton in the Pioneer Mill. The first-class ore goes clear out of sight into the thousands. The Echo is probably the richest mine in Gold Hill District. Work on the Yellow Jacket and Belcher is progressing as usual, and the stock continues to advance in price. Two months hence will see these mines pretty thoroughly opened, and prove them, doubtless, to be among the best in Washoe.

The Humboldt Register man has taken umbrage at something I said in my last letter—about the day of excitements in Humboldt being over—the people having gone soberly to work, and left that sort of thing to newer districts. He says Humboldt never dealt in excitements. Now, in my opinion—however, on second thought I will not discuss this matter with that editor. I can "lam" him.

I will conclude by hashing up a little general news for you:

Dispatches from Salt Lake say that Judge Mott, of this District, is there, on his way to Virginia.

The Hoosier State Mill, between here and Gold Hill, was sold by Messrs. Blasdell & Pray, a day or two since, to Messrs. George Hurst and Jake Clark, for forty thousand dollars, cash. It is an excellent little eight-stamp mill, and worth the money.

A billiard tournament came off here during the week, between two of your most distinguished players, A. W. Jamieson and J. W. Little. The game (five hundred points) was played on a carom table, and Jamieson won it, beating his competitor one hundred and seven. Mr. Jamieson has not his superior on the Pacific coast.

In the theatrical line, we are to have a complimentary benefit to Mr. and Mrs. Chas. Pope next Wednesday evening at the Court House, and about Tuesday evening that sickest of all sentimental dramas, "East Lynne," will be turned loose upon us at the Opera House. It used to afford me much solid comfort to see those San Franciscans whine and snuffle and slobber all over themselves at Maguire's Theatre, when the consumptive "William" was in the act of "handing in his checks," as it were, according to the regular programme of East Lynne—and now I am to enjoy a season of happiness again, I suppose. If the tears flow as freely here as I count upon, water privileges will be cheap in Virginia next week. However, Mrs. Julia Dean Hayne don't "take on" in the piece like Miss Sophie Edwin; wherefore, she fails to pump an audience dry, like the latter.

Now, from the sentimental to the practical: The big chimney at the Gould & Curry mill is finished at last. It is one hundred and fifteen feet high, and handsomely based and capped with cut stone.

I forgot to say that Maguire's new opera house here is a little larger and rather handsomer than its counterpart in San Francisco, and is crowded seven nights in the week.

San Francisco Daily Morning Call
July 18, 1863

Mark Twain's Letter

Virginia City, Nevada Territory, July 16, 1863

Editors *Morning Call*—I have been all through the Ophir mine this morning, and down to the sixth gallery, three hundred and thirteen feet below the surface.

Looking into the Spanish from the fifth gallery, I could see nothing but a chaos of huge crushed and splintered timbers, and masses of earth and stone, with no aperture large enough for us to crawl into. The crumbling down of handfuls of dirt and stones showed that the caving and settling was still going on. The new shaft to be sunk in front of the ledge will put the mine all right again; the Company could sink on the north end of the claim and go to taking out ore at once, if necessary.

Ophir Damages

Fifty feet or more of the north ends of the second, third and fourth galleries in the Ophir have caved in—the two latter at seven o'clock, last evening. No caving of any consequence occurred this morning, though where we stood, in the fifth gallery, near the Spanish line, two piles of rubbish had come through from above, and some of the timbers, eighteen inches square and six feet long, were split like brooms from top to bottom, by the tremendous weight bearing upon them, and a small portion of that extremity of the gallery may be crushed in today, although Mr. Wilder, the Superintendent, has hopes of saving it. If it lasts until tomorrow, it will be safe, and it is being rapidly double-timbered.

As Good As Ever

Thus, so far, the fifth and sixth galleries are intact, and the Company are only working in those. The caving of the upper galleries has been an advantage rather than an injury, as the Company would have had to go to the expense of filling them up if Nature had not come forward and done it herself.

The Mine Not Really Injured

In the sixth gallery we found a few inches of water, which is owing to the fact that the pump had to be stopped two hours to allow the workmen to timber a part of the incline which had caved in. The pump is working again, and the incline will soon be entirely repaired. We might have avoided the water and seen more of the sixth gallery, by descending a deep shaft from the fifth gallery, but there was no one to man the windlass. Ophir is better stock today than it was a week ago. As I said before, the mine was being worked only in the fifth and sixth galleries, and these are uninjured. There is ore enough at Ophir City to run the Ophir Mill three months, and there is a two months' supply at the Woodworth Mill. Six days hence they will be hoisting ore again, and going on as usual, as if nothing had happened.

San Francisco Daily Morning Call
July 23, 1863

Mark Twain's Letter

Virginia City, Nevada Territory, July 19

Judicial Broil

We have had a pleasant little judicial broil here, during the past week, the seeds of which were planted at the last session of the Legislature. Judge Jones, who dealt retail justice in the Third District, hankered after the wholesale trade of the First and the dignity of sitting in judgment upon the great mining cases of Virginia; and inasmuch as Judge Mott, the incumbent of the post, had been elected to represent the Territory in Congress, the Legislature passed a law appointing Judge Jones to this District, and altering the terms of the Court. On its way to the Governor's office to be ratified by his signature, the bill was accidentally torn up and the fragments shoved into a mud-hole, in a fit of absence of mind by somebody.

Here was the devil to pay. Judge Jones went to bed that night as Judge of the First Judicial District, and got up in the morning as Judge of the Third, as usual; for the Legislature had adjourned sine die, and in doing so, had also adjourned the Governor's law-making functions for a year, inasmuch as these divisions of authority, like two fond lovers, cannot exist apart. However, a new bill, as much like the original as the enrolling clerks could make it, was hatched out, and Gov. Nye and the officers of the Legislature "took the chances" and signed it, thus creating Jones Judge of the First District once more. But the said Judge Jones was a baldheaded Samson from that moment; for he was a great man in Israel, but utterly shorn of his power. Simply because the "Act" wherein his strength should have lain, was born out of wedlock—was born in Legislative vacation—the bastard offspring of an emasculated Governor and four impotent Legislative officers! as it were. Well, here was trouble again; some folks said Jones was Judge, and others said he wasn't, and the vexed question was submitted by the bar of Virginia to Judge Norton, of California, who ruled that the new law was of no more binding effect than if it had been created by a Board of Aldermen, although he did not express his opinion in just that language.

Judge Mott went East on business, and as the time drew near for the holding of the May term of this court (according to the old law) the Virginia bar requested acting Governor Clemens to appoint Jones Judge for that term, which was done. Jones accepted, and opened the Court, thus tacitly acknowledging the new law a dead letter and the old one still in force, since the new law called for a term to being in March (which was never held) but provided for none to commence on the first Monday in May. The term concluded, everybody supposed Judge Jones would return to Dayton and open his own court - but he didn't. He allowed the Third District people to worry along without a Court.

The other day a telegram was received from Salt Lake announcing that Judge Mott was there on his way to Virginia, whereupon Judge Jones took possession of the District Clerk's office here ("jumped it," as we phrase it), turned out D. M. Hanson's deputy, and appointed a Clerk of his own choosing. Hanson carried off the keys and the seal of the office, and Jones immediately had a new seal manufactured. Moreover, he put some spunky roughs on guard in the office, with orders to hold it to the bitter end against all comers. The Sheriff don't know whose authority to obey, so he declines to respect the new seal, and refused to serve any papers at all. I have not heard that Judge Jones has appointed a new Sheriff yet. Judge Mott arrived last Friday, and has gone to Carson, avowing his intention to return and resume the functions of Judge of the District, in spite of thunder. If he succeeds in ousting Jones, what in the mischief are we to do with that official? For the indignant lawyers of Dayton have requested him not to come back there any more.

Theatricals

Theatricals flourish in Virginia just now. "East Lynne" has been played to tearful crowds every night during the past week, at Maguire's new opera house. On Thursday evening the citizens gave a complimentary benefit to Mr. and Mrs. Charles Pope, at the Court House, which was largely attended. Tomorrow evening, Mrs. Leighton's troupe will commence, in a new hall, on the corner of C and Taylor streets.

General Benevolence

The Sanitary Fund took a benefit at Maguire's last Wednesday evening, where collections amounting to over three thousand dollars were taken up. The sum now in the hands of the treasurer foots up about thirteen thousand dollars, which will soon be augmented to twenty thousand, and shipped East. Rev. Mr. Rising has also gathered together about two thousand dollars for the United States Christian Commission, and started it for New York, in the form of a silver bar, last Thursday.

The Caved Mines

I traveled through the Ophir mine a few days ago, and the next day about a million tons of it caved in. If I am to blame, I will pay for it. I waited a while for it to do its heaviest caving, and then went through the mine again. I found that the damage did not amount to much. The three galleries destroyed had been worked out, and were no longer any use to the company. It would have been necessary to fill them up, anyhow, and the "cave" only saved them that trouble. The mine is all the better off for it. The fifth and sixth galleries were the only ones being worked, and they were left uninjured. The Superintendent is nearly ready to commence hoisting ore again. The Spanish Company are sinking a new shaft in front of their mine, now. Had they done this in the first place, the cave would not have seriously interfered with them.

About Other Mines

They "struck it rich" in the Leon (Gold Hill) yesterday, and that stock is going up rapidly, just now.

Mr. Castle, of San Francisco, is here, probably on business for the Echo Company. This claim is now divided into three companies of five hundred feet each, and is very valuable stock. The old incline is under repair, now, and the ore taken from it will pay all the expenses of working the different divisions of the mine, and in the meantime an eight foot shaft is being sunk two hundred and fifty feet north, and steam hoisting and pumping apparatus ordered for it.

The Golden Gate and San Francisco Companies are still sinking. The shaft on the first is down two hundred and ninety feet, and that on the other two hundred and forty-five; neither will drift until water is reached.

The "North Ophir" is coming into favor again. As nuggets of pure silver as large as pieces of chalk were found in liberal quantities in the ledge, the mine was pronounced "salted," and the stock fell form $60 to $13 a foot. However, during the last day or two a hundred experienced miners have examined the claim, and laughed at the idea of its having been salted. Among them were Mr. Hillyer, Mr. Deidesheimer, formerly superintendent, and Mr. Dickey, formerly foreman of the great original Ophir, and these gentlemen state that they frequently found such pieces of pure silver in the latter mine near the surface two or three years ago. Their testimony has removed the stain from the North Ophir's character, and the stock has already begun to recover.

Immigration

The tide of immigration is flowing in freely, now from the plains, but the graybacks go on to California, where they will get rid of their green-backs and then come back to Washoe.

Billiard Match

Mr. A. W. Jamieson has accepted a challenge to play a match game of billiards here within the next sixty days, against some man to be produced by Ralph Benjamin. The game will consist of 1,500 points, on a carom table; stakes $1,000. Mr. Jamieson has deposited $500 forfeit.

San Francisco Daily Morning Call
July 30, 1863

Mark Twain's Letter

Virginia City, Nevada Territory, July 26, 1863

The Judicial War Ended

THE WAR between Judges Jones and Mott, about the Judgeship of this District, has come to an end, it grieves me to say, without bloodshed. Not that I cared a straw, either way, but then the people expected blood, and the sovereign people should never be baulked in their desires. Yes, Judge Mott returned from the East, and marched up and reinstalled D. M. Hanson in the District Clerk's office, without a show of resistance from anybody. This manner of ending a war which promised so much destruction and desolation, is what the late William Shakspeare would have called a "lame and impotent conclusion," and I concur.

Tribute to California

I have every reason to believe that at this moment California contains the most moral, honest, virtuous, upright, high-toned, Christian population that exists upon the earth. God be praised for his mercy! O, happy, happy Commonwealth, within whose boundaries thieves and assassins abide not! Because all those fellows are over here, you know. Numerous? Why, about two-thirds of us are professional thieves, according to my estimate. Nothing that can be stolen is neglected. Watches that never would go in California, generally go fast enough before they have been in the Territory twenty-four hours; horses that—[but this house being on fire at the present moment, and it being no time to be choice in the matter of language, I expect I had better "get up and dust," as it were.]

Apology for a Letter

I just send this to show that I had commenced my regular letter, though I was never permitted to finish it, because of that fire at the White House, yesterday. I discovered that the room under mine was on fire, gave the alarm, and went down to see how extensive it was likely to be. I thought I had plenty of time, then, and went back and changed my boots. The correctness of my judgment is apparent in this instance; for, so far from having a week to fool around in, I came near not escaping from the house at all. I started to the door with my trunk, but I couldn't stand the smoke, wherefore I abandoned that valuable piece of furniture in the hall, and returned and jumped out at the window. But I gathered up my San Francisco letter and shoved it into my pocket. Now do you know that trunk was utterly consumed, together with its contents, consisting of a pair of socks, a package of love-letters, and $300,000 worth of "wildcat" stocks? Yes, Sir, it was; and I am a bankrupt community. Plug hat, numerous sets of complete harness—all broadcloth—lost—eternally lost.

However, the articles were borrowed, as a general thing. I don't mind losing them. But I had notes burned up there, from which I meant to elaborate a letter which all San Francisco would have read and been the better for it—been redeemed by it—so to speak. I had gossip in abundance, concerning San Francisco people sojourning among us. What I lost by the fire don't amount to a great deal, but what they have lost in the non-completion of that letter, it is impossible to estimate. I started out with an apology—if I have done so, well; if I have not, I'm d__d if I read this note again to find it out.

San Francisco Daily Morning Call
August 2, 1863

Dispatches by the State Line
(Specially to the Daily Morning Call)
Tom Fitch in a Duel--Officer Interposes

VIRGINIA, August 1.—Thomas Fitch, editor of the *Union*, challenged J. T. Goodman, editor of the *Enterprise*. They went out to fight this morning, with navy revolvers, at fifteen paces. The police interfered and prevented the duel.

Virginia City Territorial Enterprise
August 2, 1863

A Duel Prevented

WHEREAS, Thomas Fitch, editor of the *Union*, having taken umbrage at an article headed "The Virginia Union—not the Federal," written by Joseph T. Goodman, our chief editor, and published in these columns; and whereas said Fitch having challenged said Goodman to mortal combat, naming John Church as his "friend;" and whereas the said Goodman having accepted said challenge, and chosen Thos. Peasley to appoint the means of death—

Therefore, on Friday afternoon it was agreed between the two seconds that the battle should transpire at nine o'clock yesterday morning (which would have been late in the day for most duelists, but it was fearfully early for newspaper men to have to get up)—place, the foot of the canyon below the Gould & Curry mill; weapons, navy six-shooters; distance, fifteen paces; conditions, the first fire to be delivered at the word, the others to follow at the pleasure of the targets, as long as a chamber in their pistols remained loaded.

To say that we felt a little proud to think that in our official capacity we were about to rise above the recording of ordinary street broils and the monotonous transactions of the Police Court to delineate the ghastly details of a real duel would be to use the mildest of language. Much as we deplored the state of things which was about to invest us with a new dignity, we could not help taking much comfort in the reflection that it was out of our power, and also antagonistic to the principles of our class, to prevent the state of things above mentioned. All conscientious scruples, all generous feelings must give way to our inexorable duty—which is to keep the public mind in a healthy state of excitement, and experience has taught us that blood alone can do this.

At midnight, in company with young Wilson, we took a room at the International, to the end that through the vigilance of the watchman we might not be suffered to sleep until past nine o'clock. The policy was good—our strategy was faultless. At six o'clock in the morning we were on the street, feeling as uncomfortable in the gray dawn as many another early bird that founded its faith upon the inevitable worm and beheld too late that that worm had failed to come in time, for the friends of the proposed deceased were interfering to stop the duel, and the officers of the law were seconding their efforts. But the two desperadoes finally gave these meddlers the slip, and drove off with their seconds to the dark and bloody ground. Whereupon young Wilson and ourself at once mounted a couple of Olin's fast horses and followed in their wake at the rate of a mile a minute.

Since then we enjoy more real comfort in standing up than sitting down, being neither iron-clad nor even half-soled. But we lost our bloody item at last—for Marshal Perry arrived early with a detachment of constables, and also Deputy Sheriff Blodgett came with a lot of blasted Sheriffs, and the battleground lying in Storey County, these miserable, meddling whelps arrested the whole party and marched them back to town. And at the very moment that we were suffering for a duel. The whole force went off down there and left the city at the mercy of thieves and incendiaries. Now, that is about all the strategy those fellows know.

We have only to add that Goodman and Fitch were obliged to give bonds in the sum of $5,000 each to keep the peace, and if anything were lacking to make this robbery of the reporters complete, that last circumstance furnished the necessary material. In interfering with our legitimate business, Mr. Perry and Mr. Blodgett probably think they are almighty smart, but we calculate to get even with them.

Virginia City Territorial Enterprise
August 4, 1863

An Apology Repudiated

We are to blame for giving "the Unreliable" an opportunity to misrepresent us, and therefore refrain from repining to any great extent at the result. We simply claim the right to deny the truth of every statement made by him in yesterday's paper, to annul all apologies he coined as coming from us, and to hold him up to public commiseration as a reptile endowed with no more intellect, no more cultivation, no more Christian principle than animates and adorns the sportive jackass rabbit of the Sierras. We have done.

San Francisco Daily Morning Call
August 6, 1863

Mark Twain's Letter
Fire Matters

After the destructive fire of last Sabbath, the insurance agents declared that they would take no more risks on Virginia property until the city should consent to invest it with a greater degree of safety. The Fire Department also held a meeting, and petitioned the Board of Aldermen to furnish the different Fire Companies with more hose, and to order that the old cisterns be thoroughly repaired, and new ones of greater capacity constructed. The Board concluded to answer the prayer of the petition, and ran the risk of the next Legislature indorsing their action—from which you are to understand that the law only allows the city to contract debts to the amount of $15,000, and she did that months ago. We have two excellent engines and hose companies, and a hook and ladder company; the organization of a third engine company is nearly completed.

Agricultural Fair

The Washoe Agricultural, Mining and Mechanical Association (you see, the daily habit of naming mining claims in this country has enabled our people to acquire a flow of language in that particular which they are justly proud of, and are ready upon all occasions to display) will open its first annual fair on the race grounds at Carson, on the second Monday in October, and continue the same during five days. Perhaps it will increase the public confidence in this infant experiment to know that by Legislative enactment I am Recording Secretary of it, at an exorbitant salary, payable quarterly in Territorial scrip, subject to the mild discount of seventy-five percent.

A Duel Ruined

The *Virginia Union* and the *Territorial Enterprise* have been sparring at each other for some time, and I watched the contest with great satisfaction, because I felt within me a presentiment that somebody was going to get into trouble. On the 30th of July, the thing culminated in an article in the *Enterprise*, headed "The Virginia Union—not the Federal," which was extremely personal towards Thomas Fitch, Esq., editor of the Union. Mr. Fitch immediately challenged Mr. Goodman, the author of it, naming John Church, Esq., as his "friend." Mr. Goodman accepted, and appointed Thomas Peasley, Esq., to act with Mr. Church in arranging the preliminaries and bossing the funerals. Yesterday morning, I followed the parties to the foot of the canyon below the Gould & Curry mill, to see them destroy each other with navy revolvers at fifteen paces, but the officers of the law arrived in time to spoil the sport. They arrested the principals, and brought them back to town, where they were placed under bonds in the sum of five thousand dollars each, to keep the peace.

Theatricals

The dramatic company at Maguire's new opera house continues to draw good houses. Having finished his engagement, Mr. Frank Mayo, who has won many friends and admirers during his sojourn among us, left yesterday for Esmeralda, partly on business, but principally for recreation. Mrs. Julia Dean Rayne will depart for San Francisco shortly; previously, however, as I am informed by Mr. Buchanan, she is to receive a benefit and a silver brick at the hands of our citizens. Mrs. W. H. Leighton will begin an engagement at the opera house on Tuesday. Mrs. R. A. Perry takes a benefit tomorrow evening. Several theatrical stars will arrive from the Bay during the present week. Harry Brown is here, but whether on theatrical business or not, I am not informed.

Territorial Politics

Governor Nye arrived in the Territory last week, and has visited Virginia twice since. And in this connection I will just mention that financiering for official honors in the gift of the future State of Washoe has already begun. The Governor is spoken of for the position of United States Senator, and while the chances are very much against him, it would puzzle a wiser man than thy servant to say who they are in favor of. As nearly as I can come at it, there are a thousand candidates for Washoe congressmen. The election of delegates to the State Convention will come off in September, and the Convention itself will meet at Carson early in November. I have mentioned Governor Nye, but I came near forgetting to give you the names of the other aspirants for Senatorial distinction—as I learn them from street gossips, I mean. These are Chief Justice Turner, Governor J. Neely Johnson, William M. Steward, John K. Lovejoy, and several others whom I do not recollect. Of these, Mr. Stewart could poll much the largest vote, perhaps. Judge Mott has not yet resigned the post of Territorial delegate to Congress, but it is thought he will, eventually. In case he does, the friends of Hon. John B. Winters propose to run him for delegate, if he will consent. The people here know him, respect him, and have confidence in him, and he could be elected very easily.

Military Arrest

Lieutenant Mathewson came up from the fort and arrested Hal. Clayton a few days ago, for persisting in the utterance of disloyal sentiments, notwithstanding the repeated warnings which he had previously received. He is now at the fort.

Washoe Cavalry

Captain Baldwin's and Captain Zabriske's Companies of Territorial Cavalry are now full, armed, equipped, and under marching orders for Salt Lake City.

Phelan Coming

The great tournament to come off here on the 14th of September, between A. W. Jamison and Wm. Goldthwaite, has begun to excite some attention in the East. Several distinguished old sports residing in that part of the world have already signified their intention of being present at it, and among the rest, Mr. Phelan, the ancient champion, has written his old friend, Mr. Benjamin, of this place, that he will arrive here about that time.

Steam-Printing in Washoe

The Virginia *Daily Enterprise* was enlarged to the size of the *San Francisco Evening Bulletin* on the 1st. of August. It was the first newspaper started on the Eastern Slope, and is succeeding better than pioneers of any description usually do. It is now printed on a large double-cylinder steam press—the first one ever brought into the territory, and the only one in it now. It did its first work here on the 31st of July, thus inaugurating steam-printing among us on the anniversary of the discovery of the great Comstock lead, which event had occurred on that day four years previously.

Judge Jones Resigned

Judge Horatio M. Jones, who "jumped" Judge Mott's Court here two weeks ago, and afterwards yielded its possession to the latter officer, has forwarded to Washington his resignation of the position of Associate Justice of the Supreme Court of Nevada Territory.

Carson Races

The racing season on the Carson Course will begin tomorrow, and promises to prove one of unusual interest. Mr. Boruck, of the San Francisco *Spirit of the Times*, says that at no time in California for years have such crowds assembled upon like occasions as were present at the recent races over the Winters Course at Washoe City.

Mines, Etc.

The astonishingly rich vein of ore struck on the surface the other day, a yard or two back of the Ophir incline, continues to hold out well, and shows no inclination to suspend payment. It has been traced some distance, and is being very thoroughly prospected. Joseph Woodworth, who was present at the time of the discovery, I believe, says that a portion of this vein, further south, was worked for a while by the Ophir Company three years ago and $600,000 taken from the shaft. Mr. Earle is here, and many other San Franciscans, but want of time has kept me from prying into their affairs, wherefore I am unable to tell you what they are up to. I shall be better posted, next time.

An engine of one hundred and fifty horse power is being built for the Gould & Curry mill, and the extra forty stamps for that establishment are on hand and will be added to it shortly. The Savage is now turning out ore equal to the richest produced by the Gould & Curry, perhaps; and that taken from the Hale & Norcross at present, is of a better quality, even, than the yield of last week. Both of these companies continue to make large shipments of bullion to the Bay.

Building

If the stock fever here seems less rampant than usual, attribute it to the fact that everybody is engaged in building just now and cannot spare time to gamble. During the past three months, the long lines of frame shanties in B and C streets have been transformed into imposing two and three-story bricks, and the work still goes on with undiminished ardor. If I had a thousand brick yards I suppose I could use them all in Virginia just now. I haven't got a thousand brick-yards though, and if my luck continues to run along about as usual, I don't suppose I ever will have.

Foot Race

A foot race was run this afternoon on the "divide" between Virginia and Gold Hill. Forbes and Adams (the "emigrant") were the competitors; distance one hundred yards, stakes one thousand dollars a side. Forbes won easily, coming out three or four feet ahead.

San Francisco Daily Morning Call
August 13, 1863

Mark Twain's Letter

Virginia City, August 8, 1863

I hope it will afford you some gratification to know that I have a cough, and a cold in my head, and a sore throat, and a voice like a trombone; for, verily, it affords me none. I feel as cheerful as a funeral. However, Lake Bigler will restore me to the full enjoyment of a life of virtue and usefulness tomorrow.

The City of Virginia

From an article written by Mr. Barack, of the *Spirit of the Times*, I gather the following facts concerning Virginia. They will be interesting to such of our citizens as are sojourning in San Francisco, and also instructive to your own: "In all those attributes which go to make up a great commercial and business emporium, Virginia is the second city on the Pacific coast. Her population is nearly double that of Sacramento; is double that of Portland, Oregon, and is four times as great as that of Stockton or Marysville. Taking in the population of Gold Hill, which stands in the same relation to Virginia that the Mission Dolores does to San Francisco, we have at least twenty thousand inhabitants.

"This is well for a city only three years old. Did San Francisco surpass these figures in her infancy? The city contains upwards of twenty-eight hundred wooden houses; five of stone; eighty-seven of brick; already completed; twenty-eight in an unfinished state; and contracts out for thirty- seven more. The brick edifices are of all sorts and sizes, ranging from modest one story-and-a-half affairs to imposing four-story buildings worthy of Montgomery Street. Last year, the taxable property of Virginia amounted to six millions of dollars. This year it is eleven millions."

Permit one more extract: "The amount of business done in Virginia is positively immense and astonishing. It never ceases, and seems to grow by what it feeds on. In extent, value, and constancy, it is more like a city of ten times its age and population. It is remarkable in all the phases it presents, and is another high and enduring monument to the energy and enterprise of the American people. The completion of the Central Railroad will make Virginia a gigantic inland metropolis, and, independent of that, what I have already seen assures me that, five years from the present writing, by means of its own natural growth, it will have attained a population of forty or fifty thousand inhabitants." That prophecy is certainly within bounds, and will infallibly be fulfilled.

More Fire Companies

Within the past two weeks, two new Engine Companies have been organized here. We now have four.

Visiting Brethren

Hon. T. G. Phelps is in the city, and addressed a large union meeting on B Street last evening. Hon. John B. Winters arrived yesterday, from San Francisco, to look after some mining interests. Judge Cannon and Judge Gilchrist are resting here; they are on their way to Reese River, with a new fifteen-stamp mill, made to order in your city. Mr. E. H. Leonard, largely interested in the Mission Woolen Factory, will reach Virginia tomorrow or next day. This being his first journey in this direction, he is traveling leisurely by private conveyance, and taking a good look at the country as he passes along. Mr. Orrick Johnson, the livery stage pioneer of San Francisco, arrived in Virginia a few days since, with a large supply of horses and carriages for his new stable, recently built here.

Theatricals

Mr. Frank Mayo and Mrs. Julia Dean Rayne left this morning for San Francisco. The citizens tendered Mrs. Rayne a benefit on last Friday evening, at which she was presented with a small silver brick by a few of her friends. It is said that "Mr. Trench, the well-known first architect of the old Metropolitan Theatre, in San Francisco, is about to build a superb theatre in Virginia." Now, my information is to the effect that Jo. Trench, the well-known millman of Silver City, is to build it; yet Jo. Trench and Trench the Metropolitan architect may abide in the same corpulent, good-natured carcass, for all I know. Charles Pope will be lessee and manager at the new establishment. Mr. Sutliff, of San Francisco, is about to erect a fine music hall in Virginia, to be fifty feet wide by one hundred feet long. He hopes to have it completed within the next two months.

Legal Battle

William M. Stewart, Esq., a lawyer, well known in California and Washoe, had a fight in the District Court, a day or two since, with G. D. Keeney, Esq., another member of the profession. Kenney fought with his fists and fingernails, and Stewart fought with a cork inkstand. The result was that the latter became dyed in blood and the former in ink. Judge Mott separated the warriors before any serious damage was done. No duel anticipated.

Railroad Meeting

Governor Nye, and Messrs. Floyd, John H. Atchinson, John H. Kinkead and H. F. Rice, visited Virginia yesterday, to attend a meeting of the Virginia and Truckee Railroad Company. I am informed by them that the business transacted will be furnished me next Wednesday. This road will have a branch to Carson, and when completed will pay heavier dividends on the money invested than any other railroad in the world. With the notes and estimates in my possession, I could easily demonstrate this proposition, if the limited space afforded in a newspaper letter would admit of it.

No Democratic Convention

The call for a Territorial Democratic Convention has been withdrawn by those having authority to do so.

Mining Affairs

The Chollar Company have almost completed their new works, the finest and costliest in the Territory, The pump is twelve inches in diameter, the hoisting apparatus is as perfect as San Francisco could furnish, and the engine is of one hundred horse power. The new shaft has reached its depth of nearly three hundred feet. The Chollar Company's weighty assessments are about at an end. The Hale & Norcross continues to supply a number of mills with choice rock; the stock has advanced to $2,600 in this market. The Echo Company, Gold Hill, are sacking and shipping large quantities of rich ore to San Francisco; the second and third class rock is worked in the mills of the Territory.

Since the discovery of the rich vein back of the Ophir incline, two weeks ago, from five to seven tons of ore, ranging in value from $1,500 to $8,000 a ton, have been taken from it daily, and shipped to the Bay, with occasionally a few hundred pounds of $10,000 rock. The yield now is in the neighborhood of ten tons a day, as I am informed by the Superintendent. The Mississippi Silver Mining Company, Silver Hill, have sent their Superintendent to your city after steam hoisting and pumping machinery. The rock taken from the principal shaft will pay handsomely. In the case of the Belcher vs. Koh-i-noor Company, Judge Mott granted an injunction against the latter yesterday. The Belcher gave bonds in the sum of $80,000.

Virginia City Territorial Enterprise
August 19, 1863

Letter from Mark Twain

EDS. ENTERPRISE: Never mind the date—I haven't known what day of the month it was since the fourth of July. In reality, I am not well enough to write, but am angry now, and like our old Methodist parson at home in Missouri, who started in to produce rain by a season of fervent prayer, "I'll do it or bust."

I notice in this morning's ENTERPRISE a lame, impotent abortion of a biography of Marshal Perry, and I cannot understand what you mean by it. You either want to impose upon the public with an incorrect account of that monster's career (compiled from items furnished by himself, I'll warrant), or else you wish to bring into disrepute my own biography of him, which is the only correct and impartial one ever published. Which is it? If you really desired that the people should know the man they were expected to vote for, why did you not republish that history?

By referring to it you will see that your own has not a word of truth in it. Jack Perry has made you believe he was born in New York, when in reality he was born in New Jersey; he has told you he was a pressman—on the contrary, he is by occupation a shoemaker—by nature a poet, and by instinct a great moral humbug. If I chose, I could enumerate a dozen more instances to prove that, in his own vulgar phraseology, Jack Perry has successfully played you for a Chinaman. I suppose if he had told you the size of his boots was No. 5, you wouldn't have known enough to refrain from publishing the absurdity. Now the next time you want any facts about Jack Perry, perhaps you had better refer to the standard biography compiled by myself, or else let me hash them up for you.

You have rushed into these biographies like a crazy man, and I suppose you have found out by this time that you are no more fitted for that sort of thing than I am for a circus rider (which painfully reminds me that my last horseback trip at Lake Bigler, on that razor-bladed beast of Tom Nye's, has lengthened my legs and shortened my body some). If I could devote more time to composition and less to coughing, I would write all those candidates' biographies over again, just to show you how little you know about it.

I must have led a gay life at Lake Bigler, for it seems a month since I flew up there on the Pioneer coach, alongside of Hank Monk, the king of stage drivers. But I couldn't cure my cold. I was too careless. I went to the lake (Lake Bigler I must beg leave to call it still, notwithstanding, if I recollect rightly, it is known among sentimental people as either Tahoe Lake or Yahoo Lake—however, one of the last will do as well as the other, since there is neither sense nor music in either of them), with a voice like a bull frog, and by indulging industriously in reckless imprudence, I succeeded in toning it down to an impalpable whisper in the course of seven days.

I left there in the Pioneer coach at half-past one on Monday morning, in company with Mayor Arick, Mr. Boruck and young Wilson (a nice party for a Christian to travel with, I admit), and arrived in Carson at five o'clock—three hours and a half out. As nearly as I can estimate it, we came down the grade at the rate of a hundred miles an hour; and if you do not know how frightfully deep those mountain gorges look, let me recommend that you go, also, and skim along their edges at the dead of night.

I left Carson at two o'clock with Dyer—Dyer, the polite Dyer, the accommodating—Dyer, of the Carson and Steamboat stage line, and reached the Steamboat Springs Hotel at dusk, where all others who are weary and hungry are invited to come, and be handsomely provided for by Messrs. Holmes & Stowe. At Washoe we ate a supper of unimpeachable squareness at the Washoe Exchange, where I found Hon. J. K. Lovejoy, Dr. Bowman, and Captain Rawlings—there may have been other old acquaintances present, but the champagne that Lovejoy drank confused my vision so much that I cannot recollect whether there were or not.

I learned here that the people who own ranches along Steamboat Creek are very indignant at Judge Mott for granting an injunction to the Pleasant Valley Mill Company, whereby they are prohibited from using the water in the stream upon their lands. They say the mill company purchased the old Smith ranch and that portion of the creek which passes through it, and now they assume the right to deprive ranchmen owning property two or three miles above their lines from irrigating their lands with water which the mill company never before pretended to claim.

They further state that the mill men gave bonds in the trivial sum of $1,000, whereas the damage already done the crops by the withdrawal of the water amounts to more than $20,000. Again, the idea is that the mill men need the water to wet a new ditch which they have been digging, and after that is accomplished they will pay the amount of the bond and withdraw the injunction. Moreover—so the story runs—Judge Mott promised a decision in the case three weeks ago, and has not kept his word. The citizens of Galena, in mass meeting assembled, have drawn up a petition praying that the Judge will redress their grievances today, without further delay. If the prayer is unheeded, they will turn the water on their ranches tomorrow in defiance of the order of the court.

I believe I have recounted all these facts just as I got them; but if I haven't, I can't help it, because I have lost my note-book again. I think I could lose a thousand notebooks a week if I had them. And, moreover, if you can ferret out the justice of the above proceedings, you are a better lawyer than I am—and here comes Orrick Johnson's Virginia stage again, and I shall have to fling in my benediction before I sing the doxology, as usual. Somehow or other, I can never get through with what I have to say.

Virginia City Territorial Enterprise
August 25, 1863

Letter from Mark Twain
Steamboat Springs Hotel

August 23, 1863.

The Springs

EDS. ENTERPRISE: I have overstepped my furlough a full week—but then this is a pleasant place to pass one's time. These springs are ten miles from Virginia, six or seven from Washoe City and twenty from Carson. They are natural—the devil boils the water, and the white steam puffs up out of crevices in the earth, along the summits of a series of low mounds extending in an irregular semi-circle for more than a mile. The water is impregnated with a dozen different minerals, each one of which smells viler than its fellow, and the sides of the springs are embellished with very pretty parti-colored incrustations deposited by the water. From one spring the boiling water is ejected a foot or more by the infernal force at work below, and in the vicinity of all of them one can hear a constant rumbling and surging, somewhat resembling the noises peculiar to a steamboat in motion—hence the name.

The Hotel

The Steamboat Springs Hotel is very pleasantly situated on a grassy flat, a stone's throw from the hospital and the bath houses. It is capable of accommodating a great many guests. The rooms are large, "hard-finished" and handsomely furnished; there is an abundant supply of pure water, which can be carried to every part of the house, in case of fire, by means of hose; the table is furnished with fresh vegetables and meats from the numerous fine ranches in the valley, and lastly, Mr. Stowe is a pleasant and accommodating landlord, and is ably seconded by Messrs. Haines, Ellsworth and Bingham.

These gentlemen will never allow you to get ill-humored for want of polite attention—as I gratefully remember, now, when I recall the stormy hours of Friday, when that accursed "Wake-up Jake" was in me. But I haven't got to that, yet. God bless us! it is a world of trouble, and we are born to sorrow and tribulation—yet, am I chiefest among sinners, that I should be prematurely damned with "Wake-up Jake," while others not of the elect go free? I am trying to go on with my letter, but this thing bothers me; verily, from having "Wake-up Jake" on the stomach for three days, I have finally got it on the brain. I am grateful for the change. But I digress.

The Hospital

Dr. Ellis, the proprietor of the Springs, has erected a large, tastefully designed, and comfortable and well ventilated hospital, close to the bath-houses, and it is constantly filled with patients afflicted with all manner of diseases. It would be a very profitable institution, but a great many who come to it half dead, and leave it again restored to robust health, forget to pay for the benefits they have received. Others, when they arrive, confess at once that they are penniless, yet few men could look upon the sunken cheeks of these, and upon their attenuated forms and their pleading, faded eyes, and refuse them the shelter and assistance we all may need some day. Without expectation of reward, Dr. Ellis gives back life, hope and health to many a despairing, poverty-stricken devil; and when I think of this, it seems so strange that he could have had the meanness to give me that "Wake-up Jake."

However, I am wandering away from the subject again. All diseases (except confirmed consumption) are treated successfully here. A multitude of invalids have attended these baths during the past three years, yet only an insignificant number of deaths have occurred among them.

I want to impress one thing upon you: it is a mistaken notion that these Springs were created solely for the salvation of persons suffering venereal diseases. True, the fame of the baths rests chiefly upon the miracles performed upon such patients, and upon others afflicted with rheumatism, erysipelas, etc., but then all ordinary ailments can be quickly and pleasantly cured here without a resort to deadly physic.

More than two-thirds of the people who come here are afflicted with venereal diseases—fellows who know that if "Steamboat" fails with them they may as well go to trading feet with the undertaker for a box—yet all here agree that these baths are none the less potent where other diseases are concerned. I know lots of poor, feeble wretches in Virginia who could get a new lease of life by soaking their shadows in Steamboat Springs for a week or two. However, I must pass on to

The Baths

My friend Jim Miller has charge of these. Within a few days the new bath-house will be finished, and then twelve persons may bathe at once, or if they be sociable and choose to go on the double-bed principle, four times as many can enjoy the luxury at the same time. Persons afflicted with loathsome diseases use bath-rooms which are never entered by the other patients.

You get up here about six o'clock in the morning and walk over to the bath-house; you undress in an anteroom and take a cold shower-bath—or let it alone, if you choose; then you step into a sort of little dark closet floored with a wooden grating, up through which come puffs and volumes of the hottest steam you ever performed to (because the awkwardest of us feel a hankering to waltz a little under such circumstances, you know), and then if you are alone, you resolve to have company thenceforward, since to swap comments upon your sensations with a friend must render the dire heatless binding upon the human constitution.

I had company always, and it was the pleasantest thing in the world to see a thin-skinned invalid cavorting around in the vapory obscurity, marveling at the rivers of sweat that coursed down his body, cursing the villainous smell of the steam and its bitter, salty taste—groping around meanwhile, for a cold corner, and backing finally, into the hottest one, and darting out again in a second, only remarking "Outch!"—and repeating it when he sits down, and springs up the same moment off the hot bench.

This was fun of the most comfortable character; but nothing could be more agreeable than to put your eye to the little square hole in the door, and see your boiled and smoking comrade writhing under the cold shower-bath, to see him shrink till his shoulders are level with the top of his head, and then shut his eyes and gasp and catch his breath, while the cruel rain pattered down on his back and sent a ghastly shiver through every fibre of his body. It will always be a comfort to me to recall these little incidents.

After the shower-bath, you return to the anteroom and scrub yourself all over with coarse towels until your hide glows like a parlor carpet—after which you feel as elastic and vigorous as an acrobat. Then if you are sensible, you take no exercise, but just eat your breakfast and go to bed—you will find that an hour's nap will not hurt you any.

The Wake-Up Jake

A few days ago I fell a victim to my natural curiosity and my solicitude for the public weal. Everybody had something to say about "Wake-up Jake." If a man was low-spirited; if his appetite failed him; if he did not sleep well at night; if he were costive; if he were bilious; or in love; or in any other kind of trouble; or if he doubted the fidelity of his friends or the efficacy of his religion, there was always some one at his elbow to whisper, "Take a 'wake-up,' my boy."

I sought to fathom the mystery, but all I could make out of it was that the "Wake-up Jake" was a medicine as powerful as "the servants of the lamp," the secret of whose decoction was hidden away in Dr. Ellis' breast. I was not aware that I had any use for the wonderful "wake-up," but then I felt it to be my duty to try it, in order that a suffering public might profit by my experience—and I would cheerfully see that public suffer perdition before I would try it again.

I called upon Dr. Ellis with the air of a man who would create the impression that he is not so much of an ass as he looks, and demanded a "Wake up-Jake" as unostentatiously as if that species of refreshment were not at all new to me. The Doctor hesitated a moment, and then fixed up as repulsive a mixture as ever was stirred together in a tablespoon. I swallowed the nauseous mess, and that one meal sufficed me for the space of forty-eight hours. And during all that time, I could not have enjoyed a viler taste in my mouth if I had swallowed a slaughter-house.

I lay down with all my clothes on, and with an utter indifference to my fate here or hereafter, and slept like a statue from six o'clock until noon. I got up, then, the sickest man that ever yearned to vomit and couldn't. All the dead and decaying matter in nature seemed buried in my stomach, and I "heaved, and retched, and heaved again," but I could not compass a resurrection—my dead would not come forth. Finally, after rumbling, and growling, and producing agony and chaos within me for many hours, the dreadful dose began its work, and for the space of twelve hours it vomited me, and purged me, and likewise caused me to bleed at the nose.

I came out of that siege as weak as an infant, and went to the bath with Palmer, of Wells, Fargo & Co., and it was well I had company, for it was about all he could do to keep me from boiling the remnant of my life out in the hot steam. I had reached that stage wherein a man experiences a solemn indifference as to whether school keeps or not.

Since then, I have gradually regained my strength and my appetite, and am now animated by a higher degree of vigor than I have felt for many a day. 'Tis well. This result seduces many a man into taking a second, and even a third "Wake-up Jake," but I think I can worry along without any more of them. I am about as thoroughly waked up now as I care to be. My stomach never had such a scouring out since I was born. I feel like a jug. If I could get young Wilson or the Unreliable to take a "Wake-up Jake," I would do it, of course, but I shall never swallow another myself—I would sooner have a locomotive travel through me. And besides, I never intend to experiment in physic any more, just out of idle curiosity.

A "Wake-up Jake" will furbish a man's machinery up and give him a fresh start in the world—but I feel I shall never need anything of that sort any more. It would put robust health, and life and vim into young Wilson and the Unreliable—but then they always look with suspicion upon any suggestion that I make.

Good-Bye

Well, I am going home to Virginia today, though I dislike to part from the jolly boys (not to mention iced milk for breakfast, with eggs laid to order, and spiced oysters after midnight with the Reverend Jack Holmes and Bingham) at the Steamboat Springs Hotel. In conclusion, let me recommend to such of my fellow citizens as are in feeble health, or are wearied out with the cares of business, to come down and try the hotel, and the steam baths, and the facetious "Wake-up Jake." These will give them rest, and moving recreation—as it were.

Virginia City Territorial Enterprise
August 27, 1863

Local Column

YE BULLETIN CYPHERETH—The *Bulletin* folks have gone and swallowed an arithmetic; that arithmetic has worked them like a "Wake-up Jake," and they have spewed up a multitude of figures. We cypher up the importance of the Territory sometimes so recklessly that our self-respect lies torpid within us for weeks afterwards—but we see now that our most preposterous calculations have been as mild as boardinghouse milk; we perceive that we haven't the nerve to do up this sort of thing with the *Bulletin.*

It estimates the annual yield of the precious metals at $730,000,000! Bully! They say figures don't lie—but we doubt it. We are distanced—that must be confessed; yet, appalled as we are, we will venture upon the *Bulletin*'s "boundless waste" of figures, and take the chances. A Gould & Curry bar with $2,000 in it weighs nearly 100 pounds; $100,000 worth of their bullion would weigh between two and two and a half tons; it would take two of Wells Fargo's stages to carry that $100,000 without discommoding the passengers; it would take 100 stages to carry $5,000,000, 2,000 stages to carry $100,000,000, and 14,600 stages to carry the *Bulletin*'s annual yield of $730,000,000!

Wells, Fargo & Co. transport all the bullion out of the Territory in their coaches, and to attend to this little job, they would have to send forty stages over the mountains daily throughout the year, Sundays not excepted, and make each of the forty carry considerably more than a ton of bullion!—yet they generally send only two stages, and the greatest number in one day, during the heaviest rush, was six coaches; they didn't each carry a ton of bullion, though, old smarty from Hong Kong.

The *Bulletin* also estimates the average yield of ore from our mines at $1,000 a ton! Bless your visionary soul, sixty dollars—where they get it "regular like"—is considered good enough in Gold Hill, and it is a matter of some trouble to pick out many tons that will pay $400. From sixty to two hundred is good rock in the Ophir, and when that company, or the Gould & Curry, or the Spanish, or any other of our big companies get into a chamber that pays over $500, they ship it to the Bay, my boy. But they don't ship thousands of tons at a time, you know.

In Esmeralda and Humboldt, ordinary "rich rock" yields $100 to $200, and when better is found, it is shipped also. Reese River appears to be very rich, but you can't make an "average" there yet awhile; let her mines be developed first. We place the average yield of the ore of our Territory at $100 a ton—that is high enough; we couldn't starve, easily, on forty-dollar rock.

Lastly, the *Bulletin* puts the number of our mills at 150. That is another mistake; the number will not go over a hundred, and we would not be greatly amazed if it even fell one or two under that. While we are on the subject, though, we might as well estimate the "annual yield" of the precious metals, also; we did not intend to do it at first.

Mr. Valentine, Wells Fargo's handsome and accomplished agent, has handled all the bullion shipped through the Virginia office for many a month. To his memory—which is excellent—we are indebted for the following exhibit of the company's business in the Virginia office since the first of January, 1862: From January 1st to April 1st, about $270,000 worth of bullion passed through that office; during the next quarter, $570,000; next quarter, $800,000; next quarter, $956,000; next quarter, $1,275,000; and for the quarter ending on the 30th of last June, about $1,600,000. Thus in a year and a half, the Virginia office only shipped $5,330,000 in bullion. During the year 1862 they shipped $2,615,000, so we perceive the average shipments have more than doubled in the last six months. This gives us room to promise for the Virginia office $500,000 a month for the year 1863, and now, perhaps, judging by the steady increase in the business, we too, like the *Bulletin*, are "underestimating," somewhat. This gives us $6,000,000 for the year. Gold Hill and Silver City together can beat us—we will give them eight, no, to be liberal, $10,000,000. To Dayton, Empire City, Ophir and Carson City, we will allow an aggregate of $8,000,000, which is not over the mark, perhaps, and may possibly be a little under it. To Esmeralda we give $4,000,000. To Reese River and Humboldt $2,000,000, which is liberal now, but may not be before the year is out.

So we prognosticate that the yield of bullion this year will be about $30,000,000. Placing the number of mills in the Territory at 100, this gives to each the labor of $300,000 in bullion during the twelve months. Allowing them to run 300 days in the year (which none of them more than do) this makes their work average $1,000 a day—one ton of the *Bulletin*'s rock, or ten of ours. Say the mills average 20 tons of rock a day and this rock worth $50 as a general thing, and you have got the actual work of our 100 mills figured down just about to a spot—$1,000 a day each, and $30,000,000 a year in the aggregate.

Oh no!—we have never been to school—we don't know how to cypher. Certainly not—we are probably a natural fool, but we don't know it. Anyhow, we have mashed the *Bulletin*'s estimate all out of shape and cut the first left-hand figure off its $730,000,000 as neatly as a regular banker's clerk could have done it.

San Francisco Daily Morning Call
August 29, 1863

Dispatches by the State Line
(Specially to the Daily Morning Call)

Disastrous Fire at Virginia City—Seventy Buildings Burned

VIRGINIA CITY, August 28—1:40 P.M.—Fire broke out in a wood-pile at the back of Pat Lynch's building, between Union and Sutton Avenue, at half-past eleven o'clock today. The fire extended from Lynch's, at the south of Taylor street, to the new Court House; thence up the hill, to Summit Street; southerly to Taylor and South, burning some seventy residences and frame buildings. The fire is still raging, but will probably be kept from the business portion of the city. It is impossible to give particulars before night.

The Virginia City Fire - Firemen's Riot
One Man Shot Dead - Incendiaries Arrested.

VIRGINIA CITY, August 28—10 P. M. Four blocks, frame buildings, burned to-day, between B and Howard streets and Taylor and Sutton Avenue—loss, three hundred thousand dollars.

A riot afterwards occurred between No. 1 and No. 2 engine companies; probably fifteen men slightly hurt, and half a dozen badly. John Cullen, of No. 2, shot Edward Richardson, a miner, through the lungs, killing him instantly. Cullen is under arrest. A. and L. A. Vorbe, arrested as incendiaries, were let out on five thousand dollars bail. All stores and liquor shops have been closed by order of the City Marshal. A dozen special Deputy Sheriffs have been appointed for tonight. All quiet at present.

San Francisco Daily Morning Call
August 30, 1863

Mark Twain's Letter
"Mark" Gets Invalided and Goes to Tahoe

EDITORS MORNING CALL—Some things are inevitable. If you tell a girl she is pretty, she will "let on" that she is offended; if seventeen men travel by stagecoach, they will grumble because they cannot all have outside seats; if you leave your room vacant all the forenoon to give the chambermaid a chance to put it in order, you will find that urbane but inflexible officer ready to begin her labors there at the exact moment of your return. These are patent—but I am able to add another to the list of inevitable things: if you get a week's leave of absence for a visit to Lake Bigler, or to Steamboat Springs, you will transcend the limits of your furlough. I speak from personal knowledge. I carried over to the lake a heavy cold, and acted so imprudently during a week, that it constantly grew heavier and heavier—until at last it came near outweighing me. Lake Bigler is a paradise to a healthy person, but there is too much sailing, and fishing, and other dissipation of a similar nature going on there to allow a man with a cold time to nurse it properly.

From Thence to Steamboat Springs

I was exceedingly sorry to leave the place, but I knew if I stayed there, and nothing interfered with my luck, I should die before my time—wherefore I journeyed back over the mountains last Monday, and have since been an interesting invalid at Steamboat Springs. These are boiling hot, and emit steam enough to run all the mills in the Territory. Learned men say the water is heated by a combination of combustible chemicals—the unlearned say it is done by a combination of combustible devils. However, like Governor Roop, I consider that it is no business of mine to inquire into the means which the Creator has seen fit to make use of in the consummation of his will regarding this or any other portion of his handiwork.

A Rich Decision

And possibly it may be interesting to you to know how Governor Roop came to deliver himself of that burst of inspiration. Two years ago, during the season of avalanches, Tom Rust's ranch slid down from the mountain side and pretty nearly covered up a ranch belonging to Dick Sides. Some of the boys in Carson thought the circumstance offered a fair opportunity for playing a hoax on our former simple-minded Attorney-General, old Mr. Bunker, and they got Sides to employ him to bring suit in a Referee's Court for the recovery of his ranch; which Mr. S. did, alleging that Rust now claimed the surface of the ground as his own, although he freely admitted that the ranch underneath it belonged to Sides, who, it grieved him to reflect, would probably never see his property again. Mr. Bunker was naturally stunned at so preposterous a proposition, and bade his client be of good cheer, and count without fear upon the restoration of his rights.

The Courtroom was crowded; Roop, as Judge Referee, presided with a grave dignity in keeping with his lofty position; the Sheriff guarded the sacred precincts of the Court from disturbance and indecorum with exaggerated vigilance. The witnesses were examined, and all the evidence of any value went in favor of General Bunker's client. The General appeared, with eleven solemn law-books under his arm, and with the light of triumph beaming in his eye, and made a ponderous speech of two hours in length. The opposing counsel replied feebly, by design, and the case went to the judge. All who heard Judge Roop's inspired decision, and noted the holy serenity of his countenance when he gave it, will cherish the memory of it while they continue to live in a world where meteors of joy flash only at intervals athwart a sky darkened with clouds of sorrow always.

He said: "Gentlemen, I have listened with profound interest to the arguments of counsel in this important case, and while I admit that the reasoning of the distinguished gentleman who appeared for the plaintiff was almost resistless, and that all the law and evidence adduced are in favor of his client, yet considerations of a far more sacred and exalted nature than these compel me to decide for the defendant, and to decree that the property remain in his possession. The Almighty created the earth and all that is in it, and who shall presume to dictate to Him the disposition of His handiwork? If He saw that defendant's ranch was too high up the hill, and chose, in His infinite wisdom, to move it down to a more eligible location, albeit to the detriment of the plaintiff and his ranch, it is meet that we bow in humble submission to His will, without inquiring into His motives or questioning His authority. My verdict, therefore, is, gentlemen, that the plaintiff, Sides, has lost his ranch by the dispensation of God!"

The monstrous verdict paralyzed Mr. Bunker where he stood. The crowd of spectators, defying the Sheriffs, shook the house with laughter. But after the Court adjourned, poor Bunker, oblivious of the joke, hunted up Governor Roop, and asked to appeal the case. The great judge frowned upon him, with severe dignity, for a moment, and then replied solemnly, that there was no appeal from the decision of the Lord! Cursing Roop's imbecility, the General told me afterwards that the only recourse ever offered his client was the privilege, if the defendant would give his consent, of either removing Rust's ranch, or digging his own out from under it! That hoax finally drove Mr. Bunker back to New Hampshire, and lost to us the densest intellect the President ever conferred upon the Territory.

The Hotel and Its Occupants

But I digress. Being in the vicinity of Dick Sides' ranch overcame me with the memories of other days. As I was saying, these Springs are situated in Steamboat Valley, something over twenty miles from Carson, and about half that distance from Gold Hill and Virginia, and are visited daily by stagecoaches from those places. There is a hospital, kept by Dr. Ellis, the proprietor of the Springs, which is neat, roomy and well-ventilated. The Steamboat Springs Hotel, kept by Mr. Stowe and Mr. Holmes, formerly of Sacramento, is capable of accommodating a great many guests, and has constantly a large number within its walls; the table is not as good as that at the Occidental, but the sleeping apartments are unexceptionable. In the bath houses near the hospital, twelve persons may bathe at once, or four times that number if they be individuals who like company.

There are about thirty-five patients, suffering under all kinds and degrees of affliction, in the hospital at present; there are also several at the hotel. Some walk with canes, some with crutches, some limp about without artificial assistance, and some do not pretend to walk at all, and look dejected and baggy; they mope about languidly and slowly; there is no eagerness in their eyes, and in their faces only sad indifference; the features of some are marred by old sores, and—but if it is all the same to you, I will speak of pleasanter things.

The steam baths here restore to health, or at least afford relief, to all classes of patients but consumptives. These must seek assistance elsewhere. Erysipelas, rheumatism, and most other human distempers have been successfully treated here for three years. Scarcely a case has been lost; the majority are sent home entirely cured, and none go away without having derived some benefit.

The Effect of a Bath

The boiling, steaming Springs send their jets of white vapor up out of fissures in the earth, extending in an irregular semi-circle for more than a mile; the water has a sulphurous smell, and a crust, composed of sulphur and other villainous drugs, is deposited by it in the beds of the little streams that flow from the Springs. The Indians (who don't mind an offensive smell, you know) boil their meat, when they have any, poor devils! in this sickening water. When you are shut up in the little dark bath rooms, with a dense cloud of scalding rising up around you and compelling you to schottisch whether you want to or not, you are obliged to keep your mouth open or smother, and this enables you to taste copper, and sulphur, and ipecac, and turpentine, and blood, hair and corruption—not to mention the multitude of other ghastly tastes in the steam which you cannot recollect the names of. And when you come out, and before you get to the cold shower-bath, you notice that you smell like a buzzard's breath, and are disgusted with your own company; but after your clothes are on again, you feel as brisk and vigorous as an acrobat and your disrespect for the fragrant bath lingers with you no longer.

Has a Quarrel with "John Halifax"

Hark! methinks that sound—ah, no, it cannot be—and yet, it is! it is! Now, all those exclamations are original with me, but they were superinduced by reading that high-flown batch of contradictions and inconsistencies, "John Halifax, Gentleman." The "sound" referred to was simply a call to our regular "hash," and I only wanted to see how such silly language would fit so sensible a subject, under the circumstances; though I cannot stop now to discuss it.

San Francisco Daily Morning Call
September 3, 1863

Dispatches by the State Line
(Specially to the Daily Morning Call)

Important from Nevada Territory

The Election in Virginia City, Gold Hill, Carson and Dayton, N.T., Yesterday.

Splendid Union Triumph – Suicide of a Pioneer – Jack McNabb Shooting Policeman – Talk of a Vigilance Committee, etc., etc.

VIRGINIA, SEPTEMBER 2— Virginia polled 2,737 votes; Gold Hill, 1,086. The straight Union ticket is elected by an overwhelming majority. Same in Dayton and Silver City.

James A. Rogers, one of the earliest pioneers, blew his brains out this evening. Cause, "discouraged." He had been very low with the mountain fever for some time.

We had fifty extra policemen on duty all day. They were kept busy.

This afternoon, Jack McNabb, a notorious desperado, shot at a negro. He was not arrested. Afterwards, he created a disturbance, and Officers Watson and Birdsall tried to arrest him, when he shot Birdsall in the breast, and a special officer, named Burns, in the arm. Birdsall is not expected to live till morning. The people wanted to hang McNabb, but were prevented by the officers. Gen. Van Bokkelen, Territorial Provost-Marshal, asserted his authority, guarded the jail, and closed the saloons and stores. The city is infested with thieves, assassins and incendiaries. There is some little talk of a Vigilance Committee.

San Francisco Daily Morning Call
September 3, 1863

Mark Twain's Letter

August 30, 1863

We shipped ten thousand dollars in silver bars to the Sanitary Fund yesterday. But I cannot write today; I have no more animation than a sick puppy. However, I suppose I ought to inform the public about a circumstance which happened in the Court House this morning, and which was a most

Unfortunate Blunder

The Union League holds its meetings in the District Court Room on certain nights during the week; on Sundays the services of the First Presbyterian Church are held in the same apartment. This morning an Irish member of the League, who had been drinking a good deal, came reeling down the street, and as he passed the Court House, he chanced to look in; he saw the Rev. Mr. White (who had just sat down after the first prayer) occupying the pulpit—the place of the President of his society; he also saw familiar faces among the congregation, and he concluded at once that the Union League was in session.

With drunken promptness, he marched in at once, as soon as his mind was made up. He reached the centre of the room in safety, and supported himself in an unstable manner by resting one hand upon the railing; with the other he removed from his mouth a cigar, one-half of which was chewed to mush; he spat—partly on the floor, and principally on his chin—then hiccoughed, with such startling emphasis as to jerk his hat to the back part of his head; after which he gave the sign of salutation, and said: "Misrer Pres'zent: They been imposing on me at the mine, but d__n my thiev'n soul but I'll get even wid 'em, you know! [Sensation.] The fo'man o' Th' Pride o' the West has dis-dis-ch-(hic!)-airged me, bekase I'm a bloody d__d Blaick Republikin! " Seeing a familiar face in the congregation, he addressed his remarks to the owner of it, pointing there with his dilapidated cigar: "D'ye know me, Kuhrnel, an' " - [Voice: "But my good friend" --] "Be d__d to yer good friend! an' can't ye see it's meself that has the flewr? Ah! now, there's ould John A. Collins, an' h-(hic!) -e's wan o' the principal brethetin. I'll tell ye the whole of the dhirty thievin' saircumstance, ye see."

By this time, men, women, children and parson were smothering with suppressed laughter, as the dancing eyes that looked out over white handkerchiefs plainly testified. Col. Collins rose to his feet, blushing like a lobster, and succeeded in making the persecuted Irishman understand that he was not telling his troubles to the Union League, but to the First Presbyterian Church. The information stunned him. He stood a moment gathering again the ideas which had been scattered by this bombshell, and then backed himself out of the house, bowing repeatedly, and ejaculating: "Ladies and gentlemen, I beg yer pairdon. I thought 'twas the Union Laig. I did, upon my sowl; but I beg yer pairdon, ladies and gintlemen—I beg yer pairdon!" They used to go to Goldsmith's church to laugh, and remain to pray; but the Presbyterians here reversed the thing this morning.

Virginia City Territorial Enterprise
c. September 4, 1863

Bigler vs. Tahoe

I hope some bird will catch this Grub the next time he calls Lake Bigler by so disgustingly sick and silly a name as "Lake Tahoe." I have removed the offensive word from his letter and substituted the old one, which at least has a Christian English twang about it whether it is pretty or not.

Of course Indian names are more fitting than any others for our beautiful lakes and rivers, which knew their race ages ago, perhaps, in the morning of creation, but let us have none so repulsive to the ear as "Tahoe" for the beautiful relic of fairy-land forgotten and left asleep in the snowy Sierras when the little elves fled from their ancient haunts and quitted the earth. They say it means "Fallen Leaf"—well suppose it meant fallen devil or fallen angel, would that render its hideous, discordant syllables more endurable? Not if I know myself.

I yearn for the scalp of the soft-shell crab—be he injun or white man—who conceived of that spoony, slobbering, summer-complaint of a name. Why, if I had a grudge against a half-price nigger, I wouldn't be mean enough to call him by such an epithet as that; then, how am I to hear it applied to the enchanted mirror that the viewless spirits of the air make their toilets by, and hold my peace? "Tahoe"—it sounds as weak as soup for a sick infant. "Tahoe" be—forgotten! I just saved my reputation that time. In conclusion, "Grub," I mean to start to Lake Bigler myself, Monday morning, or somebody shall come to grief.

Virginia City Territorial Enterprise
September 17, 1863

Letter From Mark Twain

San Francisco, September 13, 1863

Over the Mountains

EDITORS ENTERPRISE: The trip from Virginia to Carson by Messrs. Carpenter & Hoog's stage is a pleasant one, and from thence over the mountains by the Pioneer would be another, if there were less of it. But you naturally want an outside seat in the day time, and you feel a good deal like riding inside when the cold night winds begin to blow; yet if you commence your journey on the outside, you will find that you will be allowed to enjoy the desire I speak of unmolested from twilight to sunrise. An outside seat is preferable, though, day or night.

All you want to do is to prepare for it thoroughly. You should sleep forty-eight hours in succession before starting so that you may not have to do anything of that kind on the box. You should also take a heavy overcoat with you. I did neither. I left Carson feeling very miserable for want of sleep, and the voyage from there to Sacramento did not refresh me perceptibly. I took no overcoat and I almost shivered the shirt off myself during that long night ride from Strawberry Valley to Folsom.

Our driver was a very companionable man, though, and this was a happy circumstance for me, because, being drowsy and worn out, I would have gone to sleep and fallen overboard if he had not enlivened the dreary hours with his conversation. Whenever I stopped coughing, and went to nodding, he always watched me out of the corner of his eye until I got to pitching in his direction, and then he would stir me up and inquire if I were asleep. If I said "No" (and I was apt to do that), he always said "it was a bully good thing for me that I warn't, you know," and then went on to relate cheerful anecdotes of people who had got to nodding by his side when he wasn't noticing, and had fallen off and broken their necks. He said he could see those fellows before him now, all jammed and bloody and quivering in death's agony—"G'lang! d—n that horse, he knows there's a parson and an old maid inside, and that's what makes him cut up so; I've saw him act jes' so more'n a thousand times!"

The driver always lent an additional charm to his conversation by mixing his horrors and his general information together in this way. "Now," said he, after urging his team at a furious speed down the grade for a while, plunging into deep bends in the road brimming with a thick darkness almost palpable to the touch, and darting out again and again on the verge of what instinct told me was a precipice, "Now, I seen a poor cuss—but you're asleep again, you know, and you've rammed your head agin' my side-pocket and busted a bottle of nasty rotten medicine that I'm taking to the folks at the Thirty-five Mile House; do you notice that flavor? ain't it a ghastly old stench? The man that takes it down there don't live on anything else, it's vittles and drink to him; anybody that ain't used to him can't go a-near him; he'd stun 'em—he'd suffocate 'em; his breath smells like a graveyard after an earthquake—you Bob! I allow to skelp that ornery horse, yet, if he keeps on this way; you see he's been on the overland till about two weeks ago, and every stump he sees he cal'lates it's an Injun."

I was awake by this time, holding on with both hands and bouncing up and down just as I do when I ride a horse back. The driver took up the thread of his discourse and proceeded to soothe me again: "As I was a saying, I see a poor cuss tumble off along here one night—he was monstrous drowsy, and went to sleep when I'd took my eye off of him for a moment—and he fetched up agin a boulder, and in a second there wasn't anything left of him but a promiscus pile of hash! It was moonlight, and when I got down and looked at him he was quivering like jelly, and sorter moaning to himself, like, and the bones of his legs was sticking out through his pantaloons every which way, like that." (Here the driver mixed his fingers up after the manner of a stack of muskets, and illuminated them with the ghostly light of his cigar.) "He warn't in misery long though. In a minute and a half he was deader'n a smelt—Bob! I say I'll cut that horse's throat if he stays on this route another week."

In this way the genial driver caused the long hours to pass sleeplessly away, and if he drew upon his imagination for his fearful histories, I shall be the last to blame him for it, because if they had taken a milder form I might have yielded to the dullness that oppressed me, and got my own bones smashed out of my hide in such a way as to render me useless forever after—unless, perhaps, someone chose to turn me to account as an uncommon sort of hat-rack.

Mr. Billet is Complimented by a Stranger

Not a face in either stage was washed from the time we left Carson until we arrived in Sacramento; this will give you an idea of how deep the dust lay on those faces when we entered the latter town at eight o'clock on Monday morning. Mr. Billet, of Virginia, came in our coach, and brought his family with him—Mr. R. W. Billet of the great Washoe Stock and Exchange Board of Highwaymen—and instead of turning his complexion to a dirty cream color, as it generally serves white folks, the dust changed it to the meanest possible shade of black: however, Billet isn't particularly white, anyhow, even under the most favorable circumstances.

He stepped into an office near the railroad depot, to write a note, and while he was at it, several lank, gawky, indolent immigrants, fresh from the plains, gathered around him. Missourians—Pikes—I can tell my brethren as far as I can see them. They seemed to admire Billet very much, and the faster he wrote the higher their admiration rose in their faces, until it finally boiled over in words, and one of my countrymen ejaculated in his neighbor's ear, "Dang it, but he writes mighty well for a nigger!"

The Menken—Written Expecially for Gentlemen

When I arrived in San Francisco, I found there was no one in town—at least there was nobody in town but "the Menken"—or rather, that no one was being talked about except that manly young female. I went to see her play "Mazeppa," of course. They said she was dressed from head to foot in flesh-colored "tights," but I had no opera-glass, and I couldn't see it, to use the language of the inelegant rabble. She appeared to me to have but one garment on—a thin tight white linen one, of unimportant dimensions; I forget the name of the article, but it is indispensable to infants of tender age—I suppose any young mother can tell you what it is, if you have the moral courage to ask the question.

With the exception of this superfluous rag, the Menken dresses like the Greek Slave; but some of her postures are not so modest as the suggestive attitude of the latter. She is a finely formed woman down to her knees; if she could be herself that far, and Mrs. H. A. Perry the rest of the way, she would pass for an unexceptionable Venus. Here every tongue sings the praises of her matchless grace, her supple gestures, her charming attitudes. Well, possibly, these tongues are right. In the first act, she rushes on the stage, and goes cavorting around after "Olinska"; she bends herself back like a bow; she pitches headforemost at the atmosphere like a battering ram; she works her arms, and her legs, and her whole body like a dancing-jack: her every movement is as quick as thought; in a word, without any apparent reason for it, she carries on like a lunatic from the beginning of the act to the end of it. At other times she "whallops" herself down on the stage, and rolls over as does the sportive pack-mule after his burden is removed. If this be grace then the Menken is eminently graceful.

After a while they proceed to strip her, and the high chief Pole calls for the "fiery untamed steed"; a subordinate Pole brings in the fierce brute, stirring him up occasionally to make him run away, and then hanging to him like death to keep him from doing it; the monster looks round pensively upon the brilliant audience in the theatre, and seems very willing to stand still—but a lot of those Poles grab him and hold on to him, so as to be prepared for him in case he changes his mind. They are posted as to his fiery untamed nature, you know, and they give him no chance to get loose and eat up the orchestra.

They strap Mazeppa on his back, fore and aft, and face upper most, and the horse goes cantering up-stairs over the painted mountains, through tinted clouds of theatrical mist, in a brisk exciting way, with the wretched victim he bears unconsciously digging her heels into his hams, in the agony of her sufferings, to make him go faster. Then a tempest of applause bursts forth, and the curtain falls. The fierce old circus horse carries his prisoner around through the back part of the theatre, behind the scenery, and although assailed at every step by the savage wolves of the desert, he makes his way at last to his dear old home in Tartary down by the footlights, and beholds once more, O, gods! the familiar faces of the fiddlers in the orchestra. The noble old steed is happy, then, but poor Mazeppa is insensible—"ginned out" by his trip, as it were.

Before the act closes, however, he is restored to consciousness by his doting old father, the king of Tartary; and the next day, without taking time to dress—without even borrowing a shirt, or stealing a fresh horse—he starts off on the fiery untamed, at the head of the Tartar nation, to exterminate the Poles, and carry off his own sweet Olinska from the Polish court. He succeeds, and the curtain falls upon a bloody combat, in which the Tartars are victorious.

"Mazeppa" proved a great card for Maguire here; he put it on the boards in first-class style, and crowded houses went crazy over it every night it was played. But Virginians will soon have an opportunity of seeing it themselves, as "the Menken" will go direct from our town there without stopping on the way.

The '"French Spy" was played last night and the night before, and as this spy is a frisky Frenchman, and as dumb as an oyster, Miss Menken's extravagant gesticulations do not seem so overdone in it as they do in "Mazeppa." She don't talk well, and as she goes on her shape and her acting, the character of a fidgety "dummy" is peculiarly suited to her line of business. She plays the Spy, without words, with more feeling than she does Mazeppa with them.

I am tired writing, now, so you will get no news in this letter. I have got a notebook full of interesting hieroglyphics, but I am afraid that by the time I am ready to write them out, I shall have forgotten what they mean. The lady who asked me to furnish her with the Lick House fashions shall have them shortly—or if I ever get time, I will dish up those displayed at the great Pioneer ball, at Union Hall, last Wednesday night.

The Golden Era
September 20, 1863

How to Cure a Cold

It is a good thing, perhaps, to write for the amusement of the public, but it is a far higher and nobler thing to write for their instruction—their profit—their actual and tangible benefit. The latter is the sole object of this article.

If it prove the means of restoring to health one solitary sufferer among my race—of lighting up once more the fire of hope and joy in his faded eyes—of bringing back to his dead heart again the quick, generous impulses of other days—I shall be amply rewarded for my labor; my soul will be permeated with the sacred delight a Christian feels when he has done a good, unselfish deed.

Having led a pure and blameless life, I am justified in believing that no man who knows me will reject the suggestions I am about to make, out of fear that I am trying to deceive him.

Let the public do itself the honor to read my experience in doctoring a cold, as herein set forth, and then follow in my footsteps.

When the White House was burned in Virginia, I lost my home, my happiness, my constitution and my trunk.

The loss of the two first named articles was a matter of no great consequence, since a home without a mother or a sister, or a distant young female relative in it, to remind you by putting your soiled linen out of sight and taking your boots down off the mantle-piece, that there are those who think about you and care for you, is easily obtained.

And I cared nothing for the loss of my happiness, because, not being a poet, it could not be possible that melancholy would abide with me long.

But to lose a good constitution and a better trunk were serious misfortunes. I had my Gould and Curry in the latter, you recollect; I may get it back again, though—I came down here this time partly to bully-rag the Company into restoring my stock to me.

On the day of the fire, my constitution succumbed to a severe cold caused by undue exertion in getting ready to do something.

I suffered to no purpose, too, because the plan I was figuring at for the extinguishing of the fire was so elaborate that I never got it completed until the middle of the following week.

The first time I began to sneeze, a friend told me to go and bathe my feet in hot water and go to bed.

I did so.

Shortly afterward, another friend advised me to get up and take a cold shower-bath. I did that also.

Within the hour, another friend assured me that it was policy to "feed a cold and starve a fever."

I did both.

I thought it best to fill myself up for the cold, and then keep dark and let the fever starve a while.

In a case of this kind, I seldom do things by halves; I ate pretty heartily; I conferred my custom upon a stranger who had just opened his restaurant that morning; he waited near me in respectful silence until I had finished feeding my cold, when he inquired if the people about Virginia were much afflicted with colds?

I told him I thought they were.

He then went out and took in his sign.

I started down toward the office, and on the way encountered another bosom friend, who told me that a quart of salt water, taken warm, would come as near curing a cold as anything in the world.

I hardly thought I had room for it, but I tried it anyhow.

The result was surprising; I must have vomited three-quarters of an hour; I believe I threw up my immortal soul.

Now, as I am giving my experience only for the benefit of those who are troubled with the distemper I am writing about, I feel that they will see the propriety of my cautioning them against following such portions of it as proved inefficient with me—and acting upon this conviction, I warn them against warm salt water.

It may be a good enough remedy, but I think it is too severe. If I had another cold in the head, and there was no course left me but to take either an earthquake or a quart of warm salt water, I would cheerfully take my chances on the earthquake.

After the storm which had been raging in my stomach had subsided, and no more good Samaritans happening along, I went on borrowing handkerchiefs again and blowing them to atoms, as had been my custom in the early stages of my cold, until I came across a lady who had just arrived from over the plains, and who said she had lived in a part of the country where doctors were scarce, and had from necessity acquired considerable skill in the treatment of simple "family complaints."

I knew she must have had much experience, for she appeared to be a hundred and fifty years old.

She mixed a decoction composed of molasses, aquafortis, turpentine, and various other drugs, and instructed me to take a wine-glass full of it every fifteen minutes.

I never took but one dose; that was enough; it robbed me of all moral principle, and awoke every unworthy impulse of my nature.

Under its malign influence, my brain conceived miracles of meanness, but my hands were too feeble to execute them; at that time had it not been that my strength had surrendered to a succession of assaults from infallible remedies for my cold, I am satisfied that I would have tried to rob the graveyard.

Like most other people, I often feel mean, and act accordingly, but until I took that medicine I had never reveled in such supernatural depravity and felt proud of it.

At the end of two days, I was ready to go to doctoring again. I took a few more unfailing remedies, and finally drove my cold from my head to my lungs.

I got to coughing incessantly, and my voice fell below Zero; I conversed in a thundering bass two octaves below my natural tone; I could only compass my regular nightly repose by coughing myself down to a state of utter exhaustion, and then the moment I began to talk in my sleep, my discordant voice woke me up again.

My case grew more and more serious every day.

Plain gin was recommended; I took it.

Then gin and molasses; I took that also.

Then gin and onions; I added the onions and took all three.

I detected no particular result, however, except that I had acquired a breath like a buzzard's.

I found I had to travel for my health. I went to Lake Bigler with my reportorial comrade, Adair Wilson. It is gratifying to me to reflect that we traveled in considerable style; we went in the Pioneer coach, and my friend took all his baggage with him, consisting of two excellent silk handkerchiefs and a daguerrotype of his grandmother.

I had my regular gin and onions along.

Virginia, San Francisco and Sacramento were well represented at the Lake House, and we had a very healthy time of it for a while. We sailed and hunted and fished and danced all day, and I doctored my cough all night.

By managing in this way, I made out to improve every hour in the twenty-four.

But my disease continued to grow worse. A sheet-bath was recommended. I had never refused a remedy yet, and it seemed poor policy to commence then; therefore I determined to take a sheet-bath, notwithstanding I had no idea what sort of arrangement it was.

It was administered at midnight, and the weather was very frosty. My breast and back were bared, and a sheet (there appeared to be a thousand yards of it) soaked in ice-water, was wound around me until I resembled a swab for a Columbiad.

It is a cruel expedient. When the chilly rag touches one's warm flesh, it makes him start with sudden violence and gasp for breath just as men do in the death agony. It froze the marrow in my bones and stopped the beating of my heart. I thought my time had come. Young Wilson said the circumstance reminded him of an anecdote about a negro who was being baptised, and who slipped from the Parson's grasp and came near being drowned; he floundered around, though, and finally rose up out of the water considerably strangled and furiously angry, and started ashore at once, spouting water like a whale, and remarking with great asperity that "One o' dese days, some gen'lman's nigger gwyne to git killed wid jes' sich dam foolishness as dis!"

Then young Wilson laughed at his silly, pointless anecdote, as if he had thought he had done something very smart. I suppose I am not to be affronted every day, though, without resenting it—I coughed my bedfellow clear out of the house before morning.

Never take a sheet-bath—never. Next to meeting a lady acquaintance, who, for reasons best known to herself, don't see you when she looks at you and don't know you when she does see you, it is the most uncomfortable thing in the world.

It is singular that such a simile as that, happened to occur to me; I haven't thought of that circumstance a dozen times today. I used to think she was so pretty, and gentle, and graceful, and considerate, and all that sort of thing.

But I suspect it was all a mistake.

In reality, she is as ugly as a crab; and there is no expression in her countenance, either; she reminds me of one of those dummies in the milliner shops. I know she has got false teeth, and I think one of her eyes is glass. She can never fool me with that French she talks, either; that's Cherokee—I have been among that tribe myself. She has already driven two or three Frenchmen to the verge of suicide with that unchristian gibberish. And that complexion of her's is the dingiest that ever a white woman bore - it is pretty nearly Cherokee itself. It shows out strongest when it is contrasted with her monstrous white sugar-shoveled bonnet; when she gets that on, she looks like a sorrel calf under a new shed. I despise that woman, and I'll never speak to her again. Not unless she speaks to me, anyhow.

But as I was saying, when the sheet-bath failed to cure my cough, a lady friend recommended the application of a mustard plaster to my breast.

I believe that would have cured me effectually, if it had not been for young Wilson.

When I went to bed I put my mustard plaster—which was a very gorgeous one, eighteen inches square—where I could reach it when I was ready for it.

But young Wilson got hungry in the night, and ate it up.

I never saw anybody have such an appetite; I am confident that lunatic would have eaten me if I had been healthy.

After sojourning a week at Lake Bigler, I went to Steamboat Springs, and besides the steam baths, I took a lot of the vilest medicines that were ever concocted. They would have cured me, but I had to go back to Virginia, where, notwithstanding the variety of new remedies I absorbed every day, I managed to aggravate my disease by carelessness and undue exposure.

I finally concluded to visit San Francisco, and the first day I got here a lady at the Lick House told me to drink a quart of whisky every twenty-four hours, and a friend at the Occidental recommended precisely the same course.

Each advised me to take a quart—that makes half a gallon. I calculate to do it or perish in the attempt.

Now, with the kindest motives in the world, I offer for the consideration of consumptive patients the variegated course of treatment I have lately gone through. Let them try it—if it don't cure them, it can't more than kill them.

Virginia City Territorial Enterprise
c. October 20, 1863

First Annual Fair of the Washoe Agricultural, Mining and Mechanical Society

Carson City, October 19, 1863

The Triumphal Parade

Late on Saturday afternoon, after the announcement of the awards in class A had been made, all the stock that had received premiums formed in a sort of triumphal procession, with the band at the head, and the stock following in the order of precedence to which they were entitled by the decision of the Judges, and marched down to the city, through the principal streets of which they paraded two or three times back and forth before final dismissal. The parade of so many fine animals in the streets was really a very fine sight, and was witnessed by everybody with much pleasure, being the first grand parade of the kind ever seen in the Territory.

Great Pantomine Speech

While waiting at the race course on Saturday for the arrival of some of the officers from the Pavilion, some of the boys belonging to the brass band in attendance concluded to do what they could for the amusement of those present, and so took possession of the platform from which the awards were to be made. One of the party was introduced to the audience as a very eloquent gentleman, who had volunteered to favor those present with a speech on the success of the Fair. The speaker took his position and made a polite bow to his audience, another of the musicians prepared to take down the speech and the third acted in the capacity of bottle holder.

The speaker soon launched forth, and in a few moments had worked himself up into a tremendous state of excitement. His lips worked convulsively, though no sound escaped them. He pointed toward the rocky peaks of the Sierras, then at the surrounding brown hills, finishing with a complacent wave of his hand toward the broad valley in which he stood. He was leaning far over the railing of the platform in the middle of a most eloquent appeal to the crowd, occasionally pointing heavenward, when his bottle-holder was suddenly overtaken by a violent fit of admiration, which he felt constrained to manifest by a most vigorous stamping upon the boards of the platform—so vigorous that he burst through one of the boards and hung suspended by the arms.

A keg of nails was kicked over in the row, and the great oratorical effort came to an end amid the prolonged shouts and cheers of the crowd. I was favored with a look at the speech as taken down by the reporter, and give the following extract: "____! ____! ____? ____! (?)____; ____, ____, ____!!! ____." There were some ten pages in the same style, but as your readers will perhaps be better pleased with the extract I have given than with the whole speech, as taken down by the reporter, I will omit the balance.

Races Saturday Afternoon

The challenge of "Deuces" against the field on Friday, for $300, catch-weights, barring "Breckinridge," was accepted by "Kate Mitchell," but today she was lame and forfeited. After the failure of these horses to run, a race was gotten up between three Spanish nags, for a purse of $27.50, single dash of a mile. In starting "Grey Dick" and the black nag, "Sheep," got off at the tap of the drum, but the sorrel horse "Split-ear," was held by his owner. "Sheep" and "Grey Dick" dashed forward, when the cry of "Come back!" was raised by several, also by a voice or two on the Judges' stand.

"Grey Dick" 's rider came back, but the rider of "Sheep" (Johnny Craddock), after riding back a short distance and ascertaining that the drum had tapped, turned about and rode leisurely around the track, winning the race and purse, according to the decision of the Judges and the rules of the Carson Racing Club. The decision was that once the drum was tapped, it was a go—the riders not being required to pay any attention to the calls to come back from anybody.

Outside bets were declared drawn. A new race was now made up between the same nags. Theo. Winters paid the entrance fees for the three horses, amounting to $15; purse, $20; single dash of a mile. The horses got a very fair start; on the first quarter "Sheep" got the lead, "Grey Dick" came next, and "Split-ear" brought up the rear. "Sheep" still held his own on nearing the home-stretch, but "Grey Dick" soon began to gain on him, and they were soon head and head.

Both riders used the whip freely on the home-stretch and the race was more stubbornly contested than any one that has taken place on the track this week. The betting had been very free on "Sheep" and "Grey Dick," "Sheep" seeming to be the favorite, and the excitement was intense. "Sheep" passed the score 6 inches ahead of "Grey Dick," winning the purse; time, 1:58.

A purse of $16.25 was now made up, the same horses to run, single dash of one mile. "Grey Dick" had the track, "Split-ear" second, "Sheep" third. The horses got a very good start. "Grey Dick" led for the first half mile, "Sheep" following closely and "Split-ear" far behind. "Grey Dick" kept the lead down the home stretch, the others following in about the same order in which they passed the half mile post, and came in three lengths ahead of "Sheep," "Split-ear" being three or four hundred yards behind. "Grey Dick" won the purse; time, 2:08.

A purse of $25 was now made up for a slow race—the slowest horse of the three to win—riders to change horses. "Split-ear" had the track, "Sheep" second, "Grey Dick" third. "Sheep's" owners had given him all the water he could drink on the sly, and from the start he was behind and kept at least three hundred yards behind all the way round the track, "Grey Dick" came in first, "Split-ear" second and "Sheep" rolled along far behind. "Sheep" won the race and purse; time 2:17.

A Hint to Carson

There are some things that kept running through my mind while looking through the city of Carson, and considering the peculiarities of its site, that I cannot refrain from jotting down here, though not coming strictly under the head of the Fair. However, they were suggested by improvements made on the Plaza in preparing for the holding of the Fair, and may, therefore, be considered as one of its legitimate fruits.

I think that every person who attended the Fair must have been most forcibly struck with the great improvement made in the appearance of the Plaza by the planting of evergreens on it in front of and about the Pavilion; this first led me to consider the site of the town and the many advantages its location afforded for making it one of the prettiest and pleasantest cities on the Eastern Slope.

Situated on a wide, and almost level, plain, at but a short distance from the eastern base of the Sierras, with numerous fine mountain streams tumbling down the hills behind it, Carson might have every street as well supplied with ditches of water as are those of Salt Lake City. The water from these ditches might be made to cause a thousand gardens in the city to "bloom as the rose." At no very great expense, the water of one of the mountain streams nearby might be brought upon the Plaza in pipes, and used to supply fountains in various parts of the grounds; about these fountains willows and plats of flowers might be planted, which, with a liberal sprinkling of cottonwood and other trees in various parts, would make it a far prettier place than the "Willows," near San Francisco.

With some such improvements Carson would be apt to attract nearly all the wealthy men owning mines and mills, or doing business in this part of the Territory—they would all wish to reside in or near so pretty and pleasant a place. If the Plaza was turned into a park as pleasant and beautiful as it might be made, it would soon become a general place of resort on Saturdays and Sundays for all the young people, and pleasure seekers in general, of all the neighboring towns and cities.

If the present Pavilion is allowed to stand where it is, it should be raised at least six to eight feet higher than it is by putting under it some kind of basement; then, with a broad flight of steps at the entrance of each wing, it would be a really imposing edifice, and one that would at once elicit the admiration of every stranger passing through the town.

Mr. Curry, one of the most public-spirited men in Carson, has already put a beautiful and substantial fence around the Plaza, and has offered to build a fountain that will throw a stream some twenty-five feet high, provided the Water Company, now about supplying water to the city, would furnish the amount of water needed. The people of Carson have, as I remarked above, the foundations for the handsomest city on the Eastern Slope, and the fault will lie with themselves if they don't make it such.

The Fair a Success and a Valuable Lesson

I have not yet been able to obtain the exact amount of all the receipts of the Fair, and will therefore defer all mention of sums. The receipts in full will shortly be obtained and published; I may, however, say that I heard it stated that the receipts would be much more than adequate to the liquidation of all outstanding liabilities of the Society, and that the $2,000 appropriated by the Legislature could be allowed to stand over untouched for the Fair of next year.

A number of the members of the Society have acted most generously, and done much toward contributing to the financial success of the institution. Theodore Winters in the start donated the Society $200; afterwards he presented to the Society all his winnings, amounting to $225, and has in various other ways aided the institution to near the amount of $1,000.

The owners of the Carson Race Course, as I took occasion to mention in a former letter, acted in the most liberal and handsome manner by the Society, in giving them the free use of all their grounds and buildings, to say nothing of the fact of their having worked all the week like Trojans for the success of the Fair. Mr. Gillespie, the Secretary, and many other officers of the Society labored day and night during the progress of the exhibition, that nothing might be left undone that could further the plans or aid the triumphant result of an institution which too many had predicted would die in an inglorious fizzle.

But we have no "fizzle" to chronicle. We have not, it is very true, made the grandest display of the kind ever seen on the Pacific Coast, but there have been much worse. We came to the exhibition, many of us, with a feeling of dubiousness in our hearts—half ashamed to tell where we were going, even when on the way. When we came away, we felt quite proud, held up our heads, and said we'd "been to the Fair!"

We have most of us been dwellers in the mountains and delvers in the mines, and knew little of the agricultural capacity of our valleys; we had rather supposed that we should be obliged always to look to California for our supplies of such articles of farm produce as we might need; but we have now had a faint glimpse of what may be done upon our soil, and feel no hesitancy in calling upon all who wish to till the earth in a land where the soil yields a bountiful return, and the best market in the world is open at the door of the cultivator, to come and occupy the land lying ready and free for all settlers. All who are now engaged in the cultivation of the soil of Washoe, and were present at the exhibition—and even those who only hear of it from the reports going forth—will now go to work in greater earnestness and with more confidence. Especially will this be the case with those contemplating fruit culture; and we shall expect soon to see orchards in all our valleys and vineyards gracing the slopes of all our hills.

Virginia City Territorial Enterprise
October 28, 1863

A Bloody Massacre Near Carson

From Abram Curry, who arrived here yesterday afternoon from Carson, we have learned the following particulars concerning a bloody massacre which was committed in Ormsby County night before last. It seems that during the past six months a man named P. Hopkins, or Philip Hopkins, has been residing with his family in the old log house just at the edge of the great pine forest which lies between Empire City and Dutch Nick's. The family consisted of nine children—five girls and four boys—the oldest of the group, Mary, being nineteen years old, and the youngest, Tommy, about a year and a half.

Twice in the past two months Mrs. Hopkins, while visiting in Carson, expressed fears concerning the sanity of her husband, remarking that of late he had been subject to fits of violence, and that during the prevalence of one of these he had threatened to take her life. It was Mrs. Hopkins' misfortune to be given to exaggeration, however, and but little attention was paid to what she said.

About ten o'clock on Monday evening Hopkins dashed into Carson on horseback, with his throat cut from ear to ear, and bearing in his hand a reeking scalp from which the warm, smoking blood was still dripping, and fell in a dying condition in front of the Magnolia saloon. Hopkins expired in the course of five minutes, without speaking. The long red hair of the scalp he bore marked it as that of Mrs. Hopkins. A number of citizens, headed by Sheriff Gasherie, mounted at once and rode down to Hopkins' house, where a ghastly scene met their gaze. The scalpless corpse of Mrs. Hopkins lay across the threshold, with her head split open and her right hand almost severed from the wrist. Near her lay the ax with which the murderous deed had been committed.

In one of the bedrooms six of the children were found, one in bed and the others scattered about the floor. They were all dead. Their brains had evidently been dashed out with a club, and every mark about them seemed to have been made with a blunt instrument. The children must have struggled hard for their lives, as articles of clothing and broken furniture were strewn about the room in the utmost confusion. Julia and Emma, aged respectively fourteen and seventeen, were found in the kitchen, bruised and insensible, but it is thought their recovery is possible. The eldest girl, Mary, must have taken refuge, in her terror, in the garret, as her body was found there, frightfully mutilated, and the knife with which her wounds had been inflicted still sticking in her side. The two girls, Julia and Emma, who had recovered sufficiently to be able to talk yesterday morning, state that their father knocked them down with a billet of wood and stamped on them. They think they were the first attacked.

They further state that Hopkins had shown evidence of derangement all day, but had exhibited no violence. He flew into a passion and attempted to murder them because they advised him to go to bed and compose his mind. Curry says Hopkins was about forty-two years of age, and a native of western Pennsylvania; he was always affable and polite, and until very recently we had never heard of his ill treating his family. He had been a heavy owner in the best mines of Virginia and Gold Hill, but when the San Francisco papers exposed the game of cooking dividends in order to bolster up our stocks he grew afraid and sold out, and invested to an immense amount in the Spring Valley Water Company of San Francisco. He was advised to do this by a relative of his, one of the editors of the *San Francisco Bulletin*, who had suffered pecuniarily by the dividend-cooking system as applied to the Daney Mining Company recently.

Hopkins had not long ceased to own in the various claims on the Comstock lead, however, when several dividends were cooked on his newly acquired property, their water totally dried up, and Spring Valley stock went down to nothing. It is presumed that this misfortune drove him mad and resulted in his killing himself and the greater portion of his family. The newspapers of San Francisco permitted this water company to go on borrowing money and cooking dividends, under cover of which cunning financiers crept out of the tottering concern, leaving the crash to come upon poor and unsuspecting stockholders, without offering to expose the villainy at work. We hope the fearful massacre detailed above may prove the saddest result of their silence.

Virginia City Territorial Enterprise
October 29, 1863

I Take It All Back

The story published in the *Enterprise* reciting the slaughter of a family near Empire was all a fiction. It was understood to be such by all acquainted with the locality in which the alleged affair occurred. In the first place, Empire City and Dutch Nick's are one, and in the next there is no "great pine forest" nearer than the Sierra Nevada mountains. But it was necessary to publish the story in order to get the fact into the San Francisco papers that the Spring Valley Water Company was "cooking" dividends by borrowing money to declare them on for its stockholders. The only way you can get a fact into a San Francisco journal is to smuggle it in through some great tragedy.

Virginia City Territorial Enterprise
c. November 8, 1863

Letter from Mark Twain

Carson City, November 7, 1863

EDS. ENTERPRISE: This has been a busy week—a notable and a historical week—and the only one which has yet passed over this region, perhaps, whose deeds will make any important stir in the outside world. Some dozens of people in America have heard of Nevada Territory (which they vaguely understand to be in Virginia City, though they have no definite idea as to where Virginia City is) as the place which sends silver bricks to the Sanitary Fund; and some other dozens have heard of Washoe, without exactly knowing whether the name refers to the Northwest Passage or to the source of the Nile—but when it is shouted abroad through the land that a new star has risen on the flag—a new state born to the Union—then the nation will wake up for a moment and ask who we are and where we came from.

They will also ascertain that the new acquisition is called Nevada; they will find out its place on the map, and always recollect afterwards, in a general way, that it is in North America; they will see at a glance that Nevada is not in Virginia City and be surprised at it; they will behold that neither is it in California, and will be unable to comprehend it; they will learn that our soil is alkali flats and our shrubbery sagebrush, and be as wise as they were before; their mouths will water over statistics of our silver bricks, and verily they will believe that God createth silver in that form. This week's work is the first step toward giving the world a knowledge of Nevada, and it is a giant stride, too, for it will provoke earnest inquiry. Immigration will follow, and wild-cat advance.

This Convention of ours is well worth being proud of. There is not another commonwealth in the world, of equal population, perhaps, that could furnish the stuff for its fellow. I doubt if any Constitutional Convention ever officiated at the birth of any State in the Union which could boast of such a large proportion of men of distinguished ability, according to the number of its members, as is the case with ours.

There are thirty-six delegates here, and among them I could point out fifteen who would rank high in any community, and the balance would not be second-rate in most Legislatures. There are men in this body whose reputations are not local, by any means—such as Governor Johnson, Wm. M. Stewart, Judge Bryan, John A. Collins, N. A. H. Ball, General North and James Stark, the tragedian. Such a constellation as that ought to shed living light upon our Constitution. General North is President of the Convention; Governor Johnson is Chairman of the Legislative Committee—one of the most important among the Standing Committees, and one which has to aid in the construction of every department of the Constitution; Mr. Ball occupies his proper place as Chairman of the Committee on Finance, State Debt, etc.; the Judiciary Committee is built of sound timber, and is hard to surpass; it is composed of Messrs. Stewart, Johnson, Larrowe and Bryan.

We shall have a Constitution that we need not be ashamed of, rest assured; but it will not be framed in a week. Every article in it will be well considered and freely debated upon.

And just here I would like to know if it would not be as well to get up a constitutional silver brick or so, and let the Sanitary fund rest a while. It would cost at least ten thousand dollars to put this Convention through in anything approaching a respectable style; yet the sum appropriated by the Legislature for its use was only $3,000, and the scrip for it will not yield $1,500. The new State will have to shoulder the present Territorial debt of $90,000, but it seems to me we might usher her into the world without adding to this an accouchement fee—so to speak—of ten or fifteen thousand more.

Why, the Convention is so poor that it cannot even furnish newspapers for its members to read; kerosene merchants hesitate to afford it light; unfeeling draymen who haul wood to the people, scorn its custom; it elected official reporters, and for two days could negotiate no desks for them to write on; it confers upon them no spittoons, to this day; in fact, there is only one spittoon to every seven members and they furnish their own fine-cut into the bargain; in my opinion there are not inkstands enough to go around, or pens either, for that matter; Col. Youngs, Chairman of the Committee on Ways and Means (to pay expenses), has gone blind and baldheaded, and is degenerating into a melancholy lunatic; this is all on account of his financial troubles; it all comes of his tireless efforts to bullyrag a precarious livelihood for the Convention out of Territorial scrip at forty-one cents on the dollar.

Will ye see him die, when fifty-nine cents would save him? I wish I could move the Convention up to Virginia, that you might see the Delegates worried, and business delayed or brought to a standstill every hour in the day by the eternal emptiness of the Treasury. Then would you grow sick, as I have done, of hearing members caution each other against breeding expense. I begin to think I don't want the Capital at Virginia if this financial distress is always going to haunt us.

Now, I had forgotten until this moment that all these secrets about the poverty of the Convention treasury, and the inoffensive character of Territorial scrip, were revealed to the house yesterday by Colonel Youngs, with a feeling request that the reporters would keep silent upon the subject, lest people abroad should smile at us. I clearly forgot it—but it is too late to mend the matter now.

Hon. Gordon N. Mott is in town, and leaves with his family for San Francisco tomorrow. He proposes to start to Washington by the steamer of the 13th.

Mr. Lemmon's little girl, two years old, had her thigh bone broken in two places this afternoon; she was run over by a wagon. Dr. Tjader set the limb, and the little sufferer is doing as well as could be expected under the circumstances.

I used to hear Governor Johnson frequently mentioned in Virginia as a candidate for the United States Senate from this budding state of ours. He is not a candidate for that or any other office, and will not become one. I make this correction on his own authority, and, therefore, the various senatorial aspirants need not be afraid to give it full credence.

Messrs. Pete Hopkins and A. Curry have compromised with me, and there is no longer any animosity existing on either side. They were a little worried at first, you recollect, about that thing which appeared recently (I think it was in the *Gold Hill News*), concerning an occurrence which has happened in the great pine forest down there at Empire.

We sent our last report to you by our stirring official, Gillespie, Secretary of the Convention. I thought that might account for your not getting it, in case you didn't get it, you know.

The Golden Era
November 17, 1863

Letter from Mark Twain

Carson, November 15, 1863

EDITORS ENTERPRISE: Compiled by our own Reporter! Thus the *Virginia Union* of this morning gobbles up the labors of another man. That "Homographic Record of the Constitutional Convention" was compiled by Mr. Gillespie, Secretary of the Convention, at odd moments snatched from the incessant duties of his position, and unassisted by "our own reporter" or anybody else.

Now this isn't fair, you know. Give the devil his due—by which metaphor I refer to Gillespie, but in an entirely inoffensive manner, I trust; and do not go and give the credit of this work to one who is not entitled to it. I copied that chart myself, and sent it to you yesterday, and I don't see why you couldn't have come out and done the complimentary thing, by claiming its paternity for me. In that case, I should not have mentioned this matter at all. But the main object of the present letter is to furnish you with the revolting details of—

Another Bloody Massacre!

A massacre, in which no less than a thousand human beings were deprived of life without a moment's warning of the terrible fate that was in store for them. This ghastly tragedy was the work of a single individual—a man whose character was gifted with many strong points, among which were great benevolence and generosity, and a kindness of heart which rendered him susceptible of being persuaded to do things which were really, at times, injurious to himself, and which noble trait in his nature made him a very slave to those whom he loved—a man whose disposition was a model of mildness until a fancied wrong drove him mad and impelled him to the commission of this monstrous crime—this wholesale offering of blood to the angry spirit of revenge which rankled in his bosom.

It is said that some of his victims were so gashed, and torn, and mutilated, that they scarcely retained a semblance of human shape. As nearly as I can get at the facts in the case—and I have taken unusual pains in collecting them—the dire misfortune occurred about as follows: It seems that certain enemies ill-treated this man, and in revenge he burned a large amount of property belonging to them. They arrested him, and bound him hand and foot, and brought him down to Lehi, the county seat, for trial. And the Spirit of the Lord came mightily upon him, and the cords that were upon his arms became as flax that was burnt with fire, and his bands loosed from off his hands. And he found a new jawbone of an ass, and put forth his hand and took it, and slew a thousand men there with. When he had finished his terrible tragedy, the desperado, criminal (whose name is Samson), deliberately wiped his bloody weapon upon the leg of his pantaloons, and then tried its edge upon his thumb, as a barber would a razor, simply remarking, "With the jaw-bone of an ass, heaps upon heaps, with the jaw of an ass have I slain a thousand men." He even seemed to reflect with satisfaction upon what he had done, and to derive great comfort from it—as if he would say, "ONLY a mere thousand—Oh, no I ain't on it, I reckon."

I am sorry that it was necessary for me to furnish you with a narrative of this nature, because my efforts in this line have lately been received with some degree of suspicion; yet it is my inexorable duty to keep your readers posted, and I will not be recreant to the trust, even though the very people whom I try to serve upbraid me.

P.S.—Now keep dark, will you? I am hatching a deep plot. I am "laying," as it were, for the editor of that *San Francisco Evening Journal*. The massacre I have related above is all true, but it occurred a good while ago. Do you see my drift? I shall catch that fool. He will look carefully through his Gold Hill and Virginia exchanges, and when he finds nothing in them about Samson killing a thousand men, he will think it is another hoax, and come out on me again, in his feeble way, as he did before. I shall have him foul, then, and I will never let up on him in the world (as we say in Virginia). I expect it will worry him some to find out at last that one Samson actually did kill a thousand men with the jawbone of one of his ancestors, and he never heard of it before.

Virginia City Territorial Enterprise
November 27, 1863

Mark Twain on Artemus Ward, "The Wild Humorist of the Plains"

We understand that Artemus Ward contemplates visiting this region to deliver his lectures, and perhaps make some additions to his big "sho." In his last letter to us he appeared particularly anxious to "sekure a kupple ov horned todes; alsowe, a lizard which it may be persessed of 2 tales, or any comical snaix, and enny sich little unconsidered trifles, as the poets say, which they do not interest the kommun mind. Further, be it nown, that I would like a opportunity for to maik a moddel in wax of a average size wash-owe man, with feet attached, as an kompanion pictur to a waxen figger of a nigger I have sekured, at an large outlaye, whitch it has a unnatural big hed onto it. Could you also manage to gobbel up the skulp of the layte Missus Hopkins? I adore sich foot-prints of atrocity as it were, muchly. I was roominatin' on gittin' a bust of Mark Twain, but I've kwit kontemplatin' the work. They tell me down heer to the Bay that the busts air so kommun it wood only bee an waist of wax too git us kounterfit presentiment." We shall assist Mr. Ward in every possible way about making his Washoe collection and have no doubt but he will pick up many curious things during his sojourn.

Virginia City Territorial Enterprise
November 29, 1863

Review of "Ingomar the Barbarian"

ACT. 1.—Mrs. Claughley appears in the costume of a healthy Greek matron (from Limerick). She urges Parthenia, her daughter, to marry Polydor, and save her father from being sold out by the sheriff—the old man being in debt for assessments.

Scene 2.—Polydor—who is a wealthy, spindle-shanked, stingy old stockbroker—prefers his suit and is refused by the Greek maiden—by the accomplished Greek maiden, we may say, since she speaks English without any perceptible foreign accent.

Scene 3.—The Comanches capture Parthenia's father, old Myron (who is the chief and only blacksmith in his native village) they tear him from his humble cot and carry him away to Reese River. They hold him as a slave. It will cost thirty ounces of silver to get him out of soak.

Scene 4.—Dusty times in the Myron family. Their house is mortgaged—they are without dividends—they cannot "stand the raise."

Parthenia, in this extremity, applies to Polydor. He sneeringly advises her to shove out after her exiled parent herself.

She shoves!

ACT II.—Camp of the Comanches. In the foreground, several of the tribe throwing dice for tickets in Wright's Gift Entertainment. In the background, old Myron packing faggots on a jack. The weary slave weeps—he sighs—he slobbers. Grief lays her heavy hand upon him.

Scene 2.—Comanches on the war-path, headed by the chief, Ingomar. Parthenia arrives and offers to remain as a hostage while old Myron returns home and borrows thirty dollars to pay his ransom with. It was pleasant to note the varieties of dress displayed in the costumes of Ingomar and his comrades. It was also pleasant to observe that in those ancient times the better class of citizens were able to dress in ornamental carriage robes, and even the rank and file indulged in Benkert boots, albeit some of the latter appeared not to have been blacked for several days.

Scene 3.—Parthenia and Ingomar alone in the woods. "Two souls with but a single thought," etc. She tells him that is love. He "can't see it."

Scene 4.—The thing works around about as we expected it would in the first place. Ingomar gets stuck after Parthenia.

Scene 5.—Ingomar declares his love—he attempts to embrace her—she waves him off, gently, but firmly—she remarks, "Not too brash, Ing., not too brash, now!" Ingomar subsides. They finally flee away, and hie them to Parthenia's home.

ACTS III and IV.—Joy! Joy! From the summit of a hill, Parthenia beholds once more the spires and domes of Silver City.

Scene 2.—Silver City. Enter Myron. Tableau! Myron begs for an extension on his note—he has not yet raised the whole ransom, but he is ready to pay two dollars and a half on account.

Scene 3.—Myron tells Ingomar he must shuck himself, and dress like a Christian; he must shave; he must work; he must give up his sword! His rebellious spirit rises. Behold Parthenia tames it with the mightier spirit of Love. Ingomar weakens—he lets down—he is utterly demoralized.

Scene 4.—Enter old Timarch, Chief of Police. He offers Ingomar—but this scene is too noble to be trifled with in burlesque.

Scene 5.—Polydor presents his bill—213 drachmas. Busted again—the old man cannot pay. Ingomar compromises by becoming the slave of Polydor.

Scene 6.—The Comanches again, with Thorne at their head! He asks who enslaved the chief? Ingomar points to Polydor. Lo! Thorne seizes the trembling broker, and snatches him bald-headed!

Scene 7.—Enter the Chief of Police again. He makes a treaty with the Comanches. He gives them a ranch apiece. He decrees that they shall build a town on the American Flat, and appoints great Ingomar to be its Mayor! [Applause by the supes.]

Scene 8.—Grand tableau—Comanches, police, Pi-Utes, and citizens generally—Ingomar and Parthenia hanging together in the centre. The old thing—The old poetical quotation, we mean—They double on it—Ingomar observing "Two souls with but a single Thought," and she slinging in the other line, "Two Hearts that Beat as one." Thus united at last in a fond embrace, they sweetly smiled upon the orchestra and the curtain fell.

Virginia City Territorial Enterprise
c. December 1, 1863

A Tide of Eloquence

Afterwards, Mr. Mark Twain being enthusiastically called upon, arose, and without previous preparation, burst forth in a tide of eloquence so grand, so luminous, so beautiful and so resplendent with the gorgeous fires of genius, that the audience were spellbound by the magic of his words, and gazed in silent wonder in each other's faces as men who felt that they were listening to one gifted with inspiration [Applause.] The proceedings did not end here, but at this point we deemed it best to stop reporting and go to dissipating, as the dread solitude of our position as a sober, rational Christian, in the midst of the driveling and besotted multitude around us, had begun to shroud our spirits with a solemn sadness tinged with fear. At ten o'clock the curtain fell.

San Francisco Daily Morning Call
December 2, 1863

Dispatches by the State Line
(Specially to the Daily Morning Call)
Death - Robbery

CARSON, December 1—Hon. Charles S. Potter, member of the Constitutional Convention, from Washoe County, died at his residence at three o'clock P.M., today. The Convention adjourned over tonight, in consequence.

A teamster was murdered and robbed on the public highway, between Carson and Virginia, today. Our sprightly and efficient officers are on the alert. They calculate to inquire into this thing next week. They are tired of these daily outrages in sight of town, you know.

Virginia City Territorial Enterprise
c. December 6, 1863

Letter from Mark Twain

Carson City, December 5, 1863

EDITOR'S ENTERPRISE: The church in Carson prospereth. A fine edifice will soon be completed here, wherein the gospel may be comfortably preached, and listened to in comfort likewise. A complimentary benefit to this enterprise was given at the theatre last night by Hon. James Stark and Mrs. Cutler, the profits of which amounted to upwards of two hundred dollars. Mrs. Cutler recited several poems, and sang a few choice songs with such grace and excellence as won for her the compliment of repeated and enthusiastic encores. Mr. Stark's readings were well selected and admirably delivered. His recital of the speech of Sergeant Buzfuz, in the great breach of promise case of Bardell vs. Pickwick, was a very miracle of declamation. If all men could read it like him, that speech would live after Cicero's very creditable efforts had been forgotten; yet heretofore I had looked upon that as the tamest of Mr. Dickens' performances.

And just here, I am constrained, in behalf of the community, to do justice to Charley Parker's liberality and good citizenship. He prepared his theatre for this church benefit, put a stove in the green room, and had the house duly cleaned and lighted—all at his own expense. It was a good action, and gracefully and unostentatiously performed.

The Convention will probably complete its labors about Wednesday. The members are growing restive and impatient under this long exile from their private business, and are anxious to finish their work and get back home. Three of the Esmeralda delegation—Messrs. Stark, Conner and Bechtel—being imperatively called away by the necessity of attending to their private affairs, have been granted indefinite leave of absence. These gentlemen have been constantly at their posts, and unremitting in the discharge of their duties, and well deserved this kindness at the hands of the Convention. And between you and me, if there were no ladies in Carson, my estimable old fossil, Colonel Youngs, would ask permission to go home, also. Now, why will a man, when he gets to be a thousand years old, go on hanging around the women, and taking chances on fire and brimstone, instead of joining the church and endeavoring, with humble spirit and contrite heart, to ring in at the eleventh hour, like the thief on the cross? Why will he?

Questions of Privilege

Mr. STERNS rose to a question of privilege again, today, and requested that the reporters would publish his speeches verbatim or not at all. The fact is, they ought to be reported verbatim, but then we work eighteen hours a day, and still have not time to give more than the merest skeletons of the speeches made in the Convention. Johnson and Stewart, and Larrowe, and Bryan, and others, complain not, however, although we condense their remarks fearfully. Even Judge Brosnan's stately eloquence, adorned with beautiful imagery and embellished with classic quotations, hath been reported by us thus tersely: "Mr. Brosnan opposed the motion." Only that, and nothing more. But we had taste enough not to mar a noble speech with the deadly engines of reduction and the third person.

Now, in condensing the following speech the other day, we were necessarily obliged to leave out some of its most salient points, and I acknowledge that my friend Sterns had ample cause for being annoyed at its mutilation. I hope he will find the present report all right, though (albeit the chances are infernally against that result). I have got his style verbatim, whether I have the substance or not.

Mr. Sterns' Speech

The question being on the amendment offered in Committee of the Whole, to Mr. Stewart's proposed substitute for Section 1 of the Article entitled "Taxation," as reported from the Standing Committee:

Mr. STERNS said—Mr. President, I am opposed, I am hostile, I am uncompromisingly against this proposition to tax the mines. I will go further, sir. I will openly assert, sir, that I am not in favor of this proposition. It is wrong, entirely wrong, sir (as the gentleman from Washoe has already said); I fully agree (with the gentleman who has just taken his seat) that it is unjust and unrighteous. I do think, Mr. President, that (as has been suggested by the gentleman from Ormsby) we owe it to our constituents to defeat this pernicious measure. Incorporate it into your Constitution, sir, and (as was eloquently and beautifully set forth in the speech of the gentleman from Storey) the gaunt forms of want, and poverty, and starvation, and despair will shortly walk in the high places of this once happy and beautiful land. Add it to your fundamental law, sir, and (as was stated yesterday by the gentleman from Lander) God will cease to smile upon your labors.

In the language (of my colleague), I entreat you, sir, and gentlemen, inflict not this mighty iniquity upon generations yet unborn! Heed the prayers of the people and be merciful! Ah, sir, the quality of mercy is not strained, so to speak (as has been aptly suggested heretofore), but droppeth like the gentle dew from Heaven, as it were. The gentleman from Douglas has said this law would be unconstitutional, and I cordially agree with him. Therefore, let its course to the ramparts be hurried—let the flames that shook the battle's wreck, shine round it o'er the dead—let it go hence to that undiscovered country from whose bourne no traveler returns (as hath been remarked by the gentleman from Washoe, Mr. Shamp), and in thus guarding and protecting the poor miner, let us endeavor to do unto others as we would that others should do unto us (as was very justly and properly observed by Jesus Christ upon a former occasion).

After which, the Convention not knowing of any good reason why they should not tax the miners, they went to work and taxed them.

Now, that is verbatim, as nearly as I could come at it. I took it from my own mysterious short-hand notes, which are mighty shaky, I am willing to admit; but then, I guarded against inaccuracy by consulting the several authorities quoted in the speech, and from them I have the assurance that my report of Mr. Sterns' comprehensive declamation is eminently correct. I cannot bet on it, though, nevertheless—I cannot possibly bet on it.

I think I have hit upon the right plan, now. It is better to report a member verbatim, occasionally, and keep him pacified, than have him rising to these uncomfortable questions of privilege every now and then. I hope to be able to report Bill Stewart verbatim in the course of a day or two, if he will hold on a spell.

Virginia City Territorial Enterprise
c. December 13, 1863

Letter From Mark Twain

Carson City, December 12, 1863
The Logan Hotel

Such is my destination. Thither I go to recuperate. I take with me a broken spirit, blighted hopes and a busted constitution. Also some gin. I shall return again, after many days, restored to vigorous health; restored to original purity; free from sin, and prepared to accept any lucrative office the people can be induced to force upon me. If elected, I shall donate my salary to charitable institutions. I will finish building this chronic brick church here, and lease a high-priced parson to run it. Also, an exorbitant choir. Everything connected with the church shall be conducted in the bulliest manner.

The Logan Hotel is situated on the banks of Lake Bigler—or Lake Tahoe, which signifieth "grasshopper" in the Digger tongue. I am not going with any of the numerous pleasure parties which go daily to the lake and infest the Logan Hotel. I shall travel like Baxter's hog—in a gang by myself. I am weary of the gay world, and I pine for an hour of solitude.

The hotel is new, handsomely furnished, and commodious; it stands within fifty feet of the water's edge, and commands a view of all the grand scenery thereabout; its table is furnished with the best the market affords, and behold they eat trout there every day; fifteen miles over the new King's Canyon road is all the journey it is necessary to take—after which the worn pilgrim may rest in peace in the bosom of Logan & Stewart. That is as good a thing as I want, as long as I am not married.

No More Mines

A year from now, there will not be a mine left in this Territory. This is an appalling statement, but it is a true one. I guessed it from remarks made by that disreputable old cottonhead, Bill Stewart, who as good as promised me ten feet in the "Justis," and then backed down again when the stock went up to $80 a foot. That was a villainous way to treat me, who have gone on juries for him, and held my grip through all the monstrous fabrications he chose to present in his eloquent sophistry, and then brought in a verdict for him, when it seemed morally certain that Providence would interfere and stop the nefarious business. I said, the last time, that I would never serve on one of Bill Stewart's juries again, until they put a lightning rod on the Court House. I said it, and my word is good. I am not going to take any more chances like that.

But what I commenced to tell about was, that last night, after the Convention adjourned, and the political meeting was called together, Bill Stewart went to work with his characteristic indecent haste (just a parallel case with that Justis affair), to construe the Constitution!—construe and determine the species of the new-laid egg from which is to be hatched our future power and greatness, while the tender thing was warm yet!

Bill Stewart is always construing something—eternally distorting facts and principles. He would climb out of his coffin and construe the burial service. He is a long-legged, bull-headed, whopper-jawed, constructionary monomaniac. Give him a chance to construe the sacred law, and there wouldn't be a damned soul in perdition in a month. I have my own opinion of Bill Stewart, and if it would not appear as if I were a little put out about that Justis (that was an almighty mean thing), I would as soon express it as not.

He construed the Constitution, last night, as I remarked before. He gave the public to understand that the clause providing for the taxation of the mines meant nothing in particular; that he wanted the privilege of construing that section to suit himself; that a mere hole in the ground was not a mine, and it wasn't property (he slung that in because he has a costly well on his premises in Virginia); and that it would be a difficult matter to determine in our courts what does really constitute a mine.

Do you see his drift? Well, I do. He will prove to the satisfaction of the courts that there are only two definite kinds of mine; that one of these is an excavation from which metallic ores or other mineral substances are "dug" (which is the dictionary phrase). Then of course, the miners will know enough to stop "digging" and go to blasting. Bill

Stewart will then show, easily enough, that these fellows' claims are not "mines" according to the dictionary, and consequently they cannot be taxed. He will show that the only other species of "mine" is a "pronominal adjective," and proceed to prove that there is nothing in the Constitution that will permit the State to tax English grammar. He will demonstrate that a mere hole in the ground is not a mine, and is not liable to taxation.

The end will be that a year from now we shall all own in these holes in the ground, but no man will acknowledge that he owns in a "mine"; and about that time custom, and policy, and construction, combined, will have taught us to speak of the staunch old bulwark of the State as "The Great Gould & Curry Hole-in-the Ground." Bill Stewart will put them up to it. In one short year, sir, from this date, I feel within me that Bill Stewart will have succeeded in construing the last vestige of a mine out of this country.

State Printer

This subject worried the Convention some. In the first place, the Standing Committee reported an article providing for the election of a State Printer, whose compensation was to be fixed by law, etc. The members, without even showing the Committee the courtesy of discussing the matter, snubbed them very pointedly, by pitching the bill overboard without offering the semblance of an apology for their conduct. They substituted an article providing for printing State work by contract. That was debated to death, and duly buried with its still-born predecessor. Then they tried a Superintendent of Public Printing. That plan appeared to suit them. They adopted it, and looked upon the work of their hands and pronounced it good.

There the matter rested until last night, when Governor Johnson got up and asked unanimous consent to substitute the original State Printer article for the Superintendent. He pointed out to the Convention that the office of Superintendent would be turned into a mere sinecure, and its incumbent would accomplish no good to the State and behold, without a word of objection, the change was made! Verily, it is vastly better to yield to wisdom at last, than not at all.

School Fund

Speaking of State Printer reminds me that we made a mistake in the report published this morning. We said the school moneys were to be invested only in United States bonds—whereas, the truth is, it was decided that they might be invested in either United States or State bonds.

Hank Monk

A superb gold watch, worth five or six hundred dollars, was presented to Hank Monk, here, night before last. The donors were John S. Henning, Joe Clark, H. H. Raymond, Alex. O'Neil, William Thompson, Jr., John O. Earl, W. M. Lent and three others. The ceremonies were conducted at Frank Ludlow's daguerrean rooms. Judge Turner made the presentation speech, and Judge Hardy replied on behalf of the defendant. Champagne flowed freely. The watch is gorgeously embellished with coaches and horses, and with charms and seals in keeping with the same, and bears for a motto Hank's famous remark to Horace Greeley: "KEEP YOUR SEAT, HORACE—I'LL GET YOU THERE ON TIME!"

"The Old Pah-Utah"

Lovejoy has issued the first number of his paper at Washoe City, and the above is its name. It is as pretty as a sweetheart, and as readable as a love-letter—and in my experience, these similes express a good deal. But why should Lovejoy spell it Pah-Utah? That isn't right—it should be Pi-Uty, or Pi-Ute. I speak by authority. Because I have carefully noted the little speeches of self-gratulation of our noble red brother, and he always delivers himself in this wise: "Pi-Uty boy heepy work—Washoe heep lazy." But if you question his nationality, he remarks, with oppressive dignity: "Me no dam Washoe—me Pi-Ute!" Wherefore, my researches have satisfied me that one of these, or both, is right. Lovejoy ought to know this, even better than me; he came here before May, 1860, and is, consequently, a blooded Pi-Ute, while I am only an ignorant half-breed.

Carson City

Call your Constitutioners home. They do nothing but sing the praises of Carson City, and Carson society, and Carson climate. Hite, and Brosnan, and Youngs, and Sterns, and half the balance of them, are more than half inclined to stay here. It is absurd. Pipe to quarters!

Final Report

The Third House of the Constitutional Convention met in solemn grandeur, at 11 o'clock last night. Tomorrow or next day I shall compile a verbatim report of its proceedings for the forthcoming volume of official reports of the Convention, and if you think you can afford to pay enough for it I will allow you to publish it in advance of that volume.

San Francisco Daily Morning Call
December 11, 1863

Dispatches by the State Line
(Specially to the Daily Morning Call)
Assassination in Carson

CARSON, December 10—Joe Magee was assassinated in the St. Nicholas Saloon, at four o'clock this morning. The gun was fired through the window, from the street. The murderer is not known. It is thought Magee assassinated Jack Williams in Virginia last Winter.

Virginia City Territorial Enterprise
c. December 14, 1863

Nevada State Constitutional Convention; Third House

Carson City, December 13, 1863
Reported in Phonographic Shorthand by Mark Twain

The Third House met in the Hall of the Convention at 11 P. M., Friday, immediately after the final adjournment of the First House.
On motion of Mr. Nightingill, the rules were suspended and the usual prayer dispensed with, on the ground that it was never listened to by the members of the First House, which was composed chiefly of the same gentlemen which constitute the Third, and was consequently merely ornamental and entirely unnecessary.
Mr. Mark Twain was elected President of the Convention, and

Messrs. Small and Hickok appointed to conduct him to the Chair, which they did amid a dense and respectful silence on the part of the house, Mr. Small stepping grandly over the desks, and Mr. Hickok walking under them.

The President addressed the house as follows, taking his remarks down in short-hand as he proceeded.

Gentlemen—This is the proudest moment of my life. I shall always think so. I think so still. I shall ponder over it with unspeakable emotion down to the latest syllable of recorded time. It shall be my earnest endeavor to give entire satisfaction in the high and bully position to which you have elevated me. [Applause.]

The President appointed Mr. Small, Secretary, Mr. Gibson, official reporter, and Mr. Pete Hopkins, Chief Page, and Uncle Billy Patterson, First Assistant Page. These officers came forward and took the following oath:

"We do solemnly affirm that we have never seen a duel, never been connected with a duel, never heard of a duel, never sent or received a challenge, never fought a duel, and don't want to. Furthermore, we will support, protect and defend this constitution which we are about to frame, until we can't rest, and will take our pay in scrip." Mr. Youngs—"Mr. President: I, ah—I—that is—"

The President—"Mr. Youngs, if you have got anything to say, say it; and don't stand there and shake your head and gasp 'I—ah, I—ah,' as you have been in the habit of doing in the former Convention."

Mr. Youngs—"Well, sir, I was only going to say that I liked your inaugural, and I perfectly agree with the sentiments you appeared to express in it, but I didn't rightly understand what—"

The President—"You have been sitting there for thirty days, like a bump on a log, and you never rightly understand anything. Take your seat, sir, you are out of order. You rose for information? Well, you'll not get it—sit down. You will appeal from the decision of the Chair? Take your seat, sir, the Chair will entertain no appeals from its decisions. And I would suggest to you, sir, that you will not be permitted, here, to growl in your seat, and make malicious side remarks in an undertone, for fifteen minutes after you have been called to order, as you have habitually done in the other house."

The President—"The subject before the house is as follows. The Secretary will read:"

Secretary—"A-r, ar,—t-i, ti—arti, c-l-e, cle,—article—"

The President—"What are you trying to do, sir?"

Secretary—"Well, I am only a helpless orphan, and I can't read writing."

The Chair appointed Mr. Hickok to assist Mr. Small, and discharged Mr. Gibson, the official reporter, because he did not know how to write.

 Mr. Youngs—(singing)—"For the lady I love will soon be a bride, with the diadem on her brow-ow-ow."

 President—"Order, you snuffling old granny!"

 Mr. Youngs—"I AM in order, sir."

 The President—"You are not, sir—sit down."

 Mr. Youngs—"I won't, sir! I appeal to—"

 The President—"Take your—seat!"

 Mr. Youngs—"But I insist that Jefferson's Manual—"

 The President—"D—n Jefferson's Manual! The Chair will transact its own business in its own way, sir."

 Mr. Chapin—"Mr. President: I do hope the amendment will not pass. I do beg of gentlemen—I do beseech of gentlemen—that they will examine this matter carefully, and earnestly, and seriously, and with a sincere desire to do the people all the good, and all the justice, and all the benefit it is in their power to do. I do hope, Mr. President—"

 The President—"Now, there YOU go! What are you trying to get through your head?—there's nothing before the house."

 The question being on Section 4, Article 1 (free exercise of religious liberty):

 Mr. Stewart said—"Mr. President: I insist upon it, that if you tax the mines, you impose a burden upon the people which will be heavier than they can bear. And when you tax the poor miner's shafts, and drifts, and bedrock tunnels, you are NOT taxing his property; you are NOT taxing his substance; you are NOT taxing his wealth—no, but you are taxing what may become property some day, or may not; you are taxing the shadow from which the substance may eventually issue or may not; you are taxing the visions of Alnaschar; which may turn to minted gold, or only prove the forerunners of poverty and misfortune; in a word, sir, you are taxing his hopes; taxing the aspirations of his soul; taxing the yearnings of his heart of hearts!

 "Yes, sir, I insist upon it, that if you tax the mines, you will impose a burden upon the people which will be heavier than they can bear. And when you tax the poor miner's shafts, and drifts, and bedrock tunnels, you are NOT taxing his property; you are NOT taxing his substance; you are NOT taxing his wealth—no, but you are taxing what may become property some day, or may not; you are taxing the shadow from which the substance may eventually issue or may not; you are taxing the visions of Alnaschar, which may turn to minted gold, or merely prove the forerunners of poverty and misfortune; in a word, sir, you are taxing his hopes!

taxing the aspirations of his soul!—taxing the yearnings of his heart of hearts! Ah, sir, I do insist upon it that if you tax the mines, you will impose a burden upon the people which will be heavier than they can bear. And when you tax the poor miner's shafts, and drifts, and bed-rock tunnels—"

The President—"Take your seat, Bill Stewart! I am not going to sit here and listen to that same old song over and over again. I have been reporting and re-reporting that infernal speech for the last thirty days, and want you to understand that you can't play it off on this Convention any more. When I want it, I will repeat it myself—I know it by heart, anyhow. You and your bedrock tunnels, and blighted miners' blasted hopes, have gotten to be a sort of nightmare to me, and I won't put up with it any longer. I don't wish to be too hard on your speech, but if you can't add something fresh to it, or say it backwards, or sing it to a new tune, you have simply got to simmer down for awhile."

Mr. Johnson—"Mr. President: I wish it distinctly understood that I am not a candidate for the Senate, or any other office, and have no intention of becoming one. And I wish to call the attention of the Convention to the fact, sir, that outside influences have been brought to bear, here, that—"

The President—"Governor Johnson, there is no necessity of your putting in your shovel here, until you are called upon to make a statement. And if you allude to the engrossing clerk as an outside influence, I must inform you, sir, that his battery has been silenced with Territorial scrip at forty cents on the dollar."

Mr. Sterns—"Mr. President, I cordially agree with the gentleman from Storey county, that if we tax the mines we shall impose a burden upon the people that will be heavier than they can bear. I agree with him, sir, that in taxing the poor miner's shafts, and drifts, and bed-rock tunnels, we would not be taxing his property, or his wealth, or his substance, but only that which may become such at some future day—an Alnascharean vision, which might turn to coin or might only result in disaster and disappointment to the defendant—in a word, sir, I coincide with him in the opinion that it would be equivalent to taxing the hopes of the poor miner—his aspirations—the dear yearnings of his—"

The President—"Yearnings of his grandmother! I'll slam this mallet at the next man that attempts to impose that tiresome old speech on this body. SET DOWN! You have been pretty regular about re-hashing other people's platitudes heretofore, Mr. Sterns, but you have got to be a little original in the Third House. Your sacrilegious lips will be marring the speeches of the Chair, next."

Mr. Ralston—"Mr. President: I have but a word to say, and I do not wish to occupy the attention of the house any longer than I can help; although I could, perhaps, throw more light upon the matter of our eastern boundary than those who have not visited that interesting but comparatively unknown section of our budding commonwealth. It is growing late, and I do not feel as if I had a right to tax the patience—"

    The President—"Tax! Take your seat, sir, take your seat. I will NOT be bullyragged to death with this threadbare subject of taxation. You are out of order, anyhow. How do you suppose anybody can listen in any comfort to your speech, when you are fumbling with your coat all the time you are talking, and trying to button it with your left hand, when you know you can't do it? I have never seen you succeed yet, until just as you got the last word out. And then the moment you sit down, you always unbutton it again. You may speak, hereafter, Mr. Ralston, but I want you to understand that you have got to button your coat before you get up. I do not mean to be kept in hot water all the time by your little oratorical eccentricities."

    Mr. Larrowe—"Mr. President: There are nine mills in Lander County already—let me see—there is Dobson's, five stamp; Thompson's, eight stamp; Johnson's, three stamp—well, I cannot give the names of all of them, but there are nine, sir—NINE splendid, steam-power quartz-mills, disturbing with their ceaseless thunder the dead silence of centuries! Nine noble quartz-mills, sir, cheering with the music of their batteries the desponding hearts of pilgrims from every land!—nine miraculous quartz-mills, sir, from whose steam-pipes and chimneys ascends a grateful incense to the god of Labor and Progress!—nine sceptred and anointed quartz-mills, sir, whose mission it is to establish the power, and the greatness, and the glory of Nevada, and place her high along the—"

    The President—"Now will you just take your seat, and hold your clatter until somebody asks you for your confounded Reese River quartz-mill statistics? What has Reese River got to do with religious freedom?—and what have quartz-mills got to do with it—and what have you to do with it yourself? You are out of order, sir—plant yourself. And moreover, when you get up here to make a speech, I don't want you to yell at me as if you thought I were in San Francisco—I'm not hard of hearing. I don't see why President North didn't tone you down long ago."

    Mr. Larrowe—"I think I am in order, Mr. President. It was a rule in the other Convention that no member could speak when there was no question before the house; but after the question had been announced by the Chair, members could then go on and speak on any subject they pleased—or rather, that was the custom, sir—the ordinary custom."

The President—"Yes, sir, I know it has been the custom for thirty days and thirty nights in the other Convention, but I will let gentlemen know that they can't ring in three-stamp Reese River quartz mills on the third house when I am considering the question of religious liberty—the same being dear to every American heart. Plant yourself, sir—plant yourself. I don't want any more yowling out of you, now."

Mr. Small—"The Secretary would beg leave to state, for the information of the Con—"

The President—"There, now, that's enough of that. You learned that from Gillespie, I won't have any of that kind of nonsense here. When you have got anything to say, talk it right out; and see that you use the personal pronoun 'I,' also, and drop that presumptuous third person. 'The Secretary would beg leave to state!' The devil he would. Now suppose you take a back seat, and wait until somebody asks you to state something. Mr. Chapin, you will please stop catching flies while the Chair is considering the subject of religious toleration."

Mr. Ball—"Mr. President: The Finance Committee, of which I have the honor to be chairman, have arrived at the conclusion that it is a hundred and thirty miles from here to Folsom; that it will take two hundred and thirty miles of railroad iron to build a road that distance, without counting the switches; this would figure up as follows: Bars, 14 feet 3 inches long; weight, 800 pounds; 1,000 bars to the mile, 800,000 pounds; 130,000 bars for the whole distance, weight, 104,000,000 pounds; original cost of the iron, with insurance and transportation to Folsom from St. Louis, via Salt Lake City, added, say three dollars and a half a pound, would mount to a fraction over or under $312,722,239.42. Three hundred and twelve million, seven hundred and twenty-two thousand, two hundred and thirty-nine dollars and forty-two cents, sir. That is the estimate of the Committee, sir, for prime cost of one class of material, without counting labor and other expenses. In view of these facts, sir, it is the opinion of the Committee that we had better not build the road. I did not think it necessary to submit a written report, because—"

The President—"Take your seat, Mr. Ball—take your seat, sir, your evil eye never lights upon this Chair but the spirit moves you to confuse its intellect with some of your villainous algebraical monstrosities. I will not entertain them, sir; I don't know anything about them. You needn't mind bringing in any written reports here—or verbal ones either, unless you can confine yourself to a reasonable number of figures at a time, so that I can understand what you are driving at. No, sir, the Third House will not build the railroad. The other Convention's donation of $3,000,000 in bonds, worth forty cents on the dollar, will buy enough of one of those bars to make a breastpin, and that will have to satisfy this commonwealth for the present. I observe that Messrs. Wasson and Gibson and Noteware and Kennedy have their feet on their desks. The chief page will proceed to remove those relics of ancient conventional barbarism from sight."

Mr. Musser—"Mr. President: To be, or not to be that is the question—"

The President—"No, sir! The question is, shall we tolerate religious indifference in this community; or the rights of conscience; or the right of suffrage; or the freedom of the press; or free speech, or free schools, or free niggers. The Chair trusts it knows what it is about, without any instructions from the members."

Mr. Musser—"But, sir, it was only a quotation from—"

The President—"Well, I don't care, I want you to sit down. The Chair don't consider that you know much about religion anyhow, and consequently the subject will suffer no detriment from your letting it alone. You and Judge Hardy can subside, and study over the preamble until you are wanted."

Mr. Brosnan—"Mr. President, these proceedings have all been irregular, extremely and customarily irregular. I will move, sir, that the question be passed, for the present, and that we take up the next section."

Mr. Mitchell—"I object to that, Mr. President. I move that we go into Committee of the Whole on it."

Mr. Wasson—"I move that it be referred back to the Standing Committee."

Mr. North—"I move that the rules be suspended and the whole article placed upon its final passage."

The President—"Gentlemen, those of you who are in favor of adopting the original proposition, together with the various motions now pending before the house, will signify the same by saying aye."

No one voting in the negative, the chair decided the vote to be unanimous in the affirmative.

The President—"Gentlemen, your proceedings have been exactly similar to those of the convention which preceded you. You have considered a subject which you knew nothing about; spoken on every subject but the one before the house, and voted without knowing what you were voting for or having any idea what would be the general result of your action. I will adjourn the Convention for an hour, on account of my cold, to the end that I may apply the remedy prescribed for it by Dr. Tjader—the same being gin and molasses. The Chief Page is hereby instructed to provide a spoonful of molasses and a gallon of gin, for the use of the President."

Our Carson Dispatch—Second Session
By Telegraph

Third House met after recess, and transacted the following business:

Secretary read Section 15, Legislative Department:

"SECTION 15. The doors of each house shall be kept open during the session."

Kinkead moved to amend by adding the words "and the windows also, if the weather will permit."

Secretary read Section 32, Legislative Department:

"SECTION 32. No law shall be passed authorizing married women to carry on business as sole traders."

On motion of Sterns, construed to mean that married women shall not preach.

Secretary read Section 6, Declaration of Rights:

"SECTION 6. Excessive bail shall not be required, nor excessive fines imposed."

Youngs moved to amend by striking out the word "bair'l" and inserting the word "board." Adopted, unanimously.

SECTION 1. Miscellaneous Provisions, was amended so as to read as follows:

"SECTION 1. The seat of government shall be at Carson, and the Legislature shall hold its session in the plaza during the first six years."

Section added empowering the President of the Third House of the Convention to convene, by proclamation, the Third House of the State Legislature, for the purpose of electing two United States Senators, within thirty days after the Constitution shall have been ratified.

Name of the State changed to "Washoe," in conformity with the law which called the Convention together.

New section added, as follows:

"SECTION. No Sheriff or other officer shall be expected to arrest any assassin or other criminal on strong presumptive evidence, merely, nor any other evidence, unless such assassin or other criminal shall insist upon his privilege of being arrested."

The hour having arrived for the President to take his regular gin and molasses, the Convention adjourned.

Last night, about 12 o'clock—[here the telegraph ceased working—BLOOMER, operator.]

Virginia City Territorial Enterprise
c. December 25, 1863

Local Column

A CHRISTMAS GIFT—"Mr. Twain—compliments of Miss Chase—Christmas, 1863." This handwriting disposed us to suspect treachery, and to regard the box as a deadly infernal machine. It was on this account that we got a stranger to open it. This precaution was unnecessary. The diabolical box had nothing in it but a ghastly, naked, porcelain doll baby. However, we are much obliged—we always had a hankering to have a baby, and now we are satisfied—the mythical "Miss Chase" helped us to the business, and she has our cordial thanks for her share in it.

Virginia City Territorial Enterprise
December 29, 1863

Christmas Presents

CHRISTMAS PRESENTS—We received from Carson, Saturday, a long yellow box, of suspicious appearance, with the following inscription upon it: "Mark Twain, ENTERPRISE Office, Virginia—Free—Politeness Langton's Pioneer Express—Be-hi-me-soi-vin." That last phrase is Greek, and means "Bully for you!" We are not sure that it was written by Mrs. H. F. R., of Carson, and there was no evidence accompanying the box to show that it was. This is what makes us so obstinate in the opinion that it might have been written by somebody else. The box contained a toy rabbit, of the jackass persuasion, gifted with ears of aggravated dimensions, and swathed in sage-brush; an Indian chief—a mere human creation—made of raisins, strung on a skeleton formed of a single knitting-needle, with a solitary fig for a body, and a chicken feather driven into the head of the effigy, to denote its high official character.

One more present remained—the same being a toy watchman's rattle, made of pine and tastefully painted. We are glad to have that rattle now, but when we asked for such a thing at a certain convivial party in Carson, it will be remembered that we meant to bestow it upon another young man who was present, and whose absent mind, we imagined, might be collected together and concentrated by means of such an instrument. We have presented the rabbit to Artemus Ward, to be preserved as a specimen of our resources; the other presents we shall always wear near our heart. The following report of the committee, accompanying the box, has been received, accepted, adopted, and the same referred to the Committee of the Whole People:

Carson City, December 25, 1863.

Mr. MARK TWAIN—Sir: The undersigned has the honor to be selected by the gay company of ladies and gentlemen and boys and girls and Santa Claus, who came in person with Judge Dixson's wolfskin cap, coat, pants and a mask, and sleigh bells around his waist, and dashed in the room just after Mrs. Cutter and two long rows of children had sung a pretty piece, and read a letter from Santa Claus, when that individual immediately dashed into the room to the terror of some of the children, thirty-six in all, and climbed the Christmas tree, all covered with presents, and little lighted candles, and handed down things for everybody, and afterwards danced with the now reconciled children, and then dashed out; after which there was supper and dancing by the ladies and gentlemen; and the school which was thus made to enjoy themselves last night till midnight, was Miss H. K. Clapp and Mrs. Cutter's Seminary, which is one of the best there is, and instructed me to send you these things, which I do by Langton's Express, handed down from the Christmas tree by Santa Claus, marked "Mark Twain," to wit: One rabbit under a sage brush, to represent your design for a seal in the Constitutional Convention; one rattle, presented by a lady of whom you begged for one when you were here last, and a Pi-Ute to be eaten, being a chief with a chicken feather in his hat, composed of a fig for his body and otherwise raisins, sent to you by request of a lady of the medical profession, all of which is submitted by
WILLIAM A. TRINITY, Committee.

Virginia City Territorial Enterprise
December 30, 1863

The Bolters in Convention

AT 7 o'clock last night a large number of citizens met at the Court House for the purpose of selecting sixteen new delegates, which they hoped might prove more acceptable to the State Convention than those elected by the regular County Convention day before yesterday. There appeared to be some discord in this Convention as well as in that which preceded it, but of course the manner in which it was constituted prevented the possibility of anyone's bolting from it in the regular and recognized way. It was a gorgeous sight to behold those two hundred fearless spirits of Storey—those noble human soda-bottles, so to speak, effervescing with the holy gas of pure unselfish patriotism, rising in their might to bust out, as it were, the infamous action of 3,000 voters of Storey County, as done in the County Convention by their chosen representatives. But we are fearfully and wonderfully made, and we glorious Americans will occasionally astonish the God that created us when we get a fair start.

    The proceedings opened with three cheers and a tiger for the stars and stripes.

    Mr. Corson moved that Dr. Minneer be elected chairman of the meetings. Carried.

    Mr. Barclay nominated Wm. H. Davenport and James Phelan as Secretaries. They were elected without opposition.

    The following Vice Presidents were then elected: James Brannon, Dighton Corson, Judge Leconey, J. W. Noyes, Thos. Lynch, Judge Ferris, John A. Collins, A. B. Elliott, E. Bond, W. H. Young, J. S. Black, Thos. G. Taylor, S. A. Kellogg, Judge Frizell, J. H. Heilshorn, P. Quigley, J. T. Sage, John Church, W. R. Warnock and R. H. Rider. [Several of these gentlemen were said to be present.]

    The Chairman reviewed the action of the County Convention, and said it was not satisfactory to the majority of the community; therefore the people had met now to improve upon that action in their sovereign capacity as fountain-head of power in the land. He said the present Convention would nominate sixteen delegates, and hoped they would be accepted by the State Convention in preference to the delegates elected by the late packed Convention.

    [A voice—"Three cheers!" No response.]

    A committee previously and mysteriously appointed immediately brought in a report containing the following names. There was no suspicion of packing about it, however. The report reads as follows:

    Report of the committee appointed by a meeting of citizens held at the Court House on Monday evening, December 29th, to select the names of sixteen citizens to be presented to the mass meeting this evening as suitable persons to represent Storey county in the Union State Convention, to be held at Carson on the 31st inst., beg leave to submit the following names: Dr. Geiger, John Dohle, Thomas Lynch, Captain

White, Joseph Loryea, J. L. Black, George E. Brickett, Thomas Hannah, J. D. Meagher, Augustus Ash.

    Mr. Corson moved that the report be accepted, and the committee discharged. Carried.

    Mr. Fitch was called for and addressed the Convention at great length, re-hashing, adding to and improving his most recent editorials in the *Virginia Union*. He was heard with interest and was frequently applauded.

    As is always his custom, Mr. Brosnan spoke eloquently and feelingly, and was repeatedly and loudly cheered. Public speakers are not given to adhering strictly to the truth as a general thing, but we know Judge Brosnan is. However, he stood up there last night and misrepresented old Nestor—a poor devil who has been dead hundreds and hundreds of years. And Judge Brosnan knew perfectly well that he was departing from the record when he unblushingly abused old Nestor's wardrobe and said he wore a poisoned shirt. Now why couldn't he confine himself to living convention-packers and let dead foreigners alone? That's it—we are down on that kind of thing, you know.

    [Cries, "Hannah! Hannah!" "Gentlemen, wait a moment!" "I call for the adoption of the report before we have any speaking!"]

    However, Mr. Hannah came forward and said that "As had been remarked by both gentlemen who have preceded me," and then went on and made both gentlemen's speeches over again, in such a pleasant way, and with such vehemence of manner that "the people"—that mighty lever being present, and filling very nearly three-fourths of the house—"the people" applauded each familiar argument as it fell upon their ears, and felt really comfortable over it. He touched us very agreeably by speaking of us as "those intelligent reporters who officiated at the late Constitutional Convention." [The word "intelligent" is our own. We had an idea it would make the sentence read better.] Toward the last, Mr. Hannah soared into originality, and touched upon a multitude of subjects on his own hook. Notwithstanding its apparent originality, however, we shall always be haunted by the dreadful suspicion that the fag-end of Tom Hannah's speech was gobbled out of the Babes in the Wood.

    Mr. Brosnan moved that a committee of five be appointed to draft resolutions.

    Mr. Pepper suggested that there was already a question before the house. [A voice "Sit down."]

    The Chairman remarked that there was a question before the house, and proceeded to state it as being on the adoption of the report of the Committee on Nominations.

The house refused to entertain the report in its entirety, and demanded, in great confusion, that the candidates should be voted for separately, which was done, and the following gentlemen elected:

Messrs. Geiger, Dohle, Lynch, White, Black, Hannah, Warnock, Ash, Phillips, G. H. [sic], J. Y. Paul, Doak (?), Frizell, Burke, Knox, Brickett.

Messrs. Loryea and Meagher were voted for and rejected, and confusion grew worse confounded in the meantime.

Mr. Warnock moved the appointment of a Nominating Committee of ten, to present names to the next mass meeting, as candidates for Legislators, Judges, etc. Carried.

The Committee on Resolutions was appointed as follows: Messrs. Brosnan, Frizell, Hannah, Corson, Bond.

The committee created by Mr. Warnock's resolution was then nominated and elected, as follows: Messrs. Warnock, Jas. Campbell, Hannah, Jacob Young, Manning, Lackey, Dimock, Carey, Van Vliet and Flood.

Mr. Corson moved to add five to the committee, and take them from Gold Hill and Flowery. Carried.

The following gentlemen were nominated and elected: Messrs. Phillips, La Flower and Bishop.

[Here great trouble arose about a suggestion that the Convention might possibly be electing people who were opposed to them. It was a wise and bully idea. Mr. James Campbell called at our office after the Convention adjourned, and requested us to remove his name from the nominating committee.]

After which, with remarkable unanimity, the Convention struck off the names of the Gold Hill members from the nominating committee, and left it to the President to fill up with other Gold Hill men.

Mr. Frizell submitted the following names, which he said had been selected by a mass meeting in Gold Hill: Wm. C. Derall, E. R. Burke, Ed. C. Morse, Sam Doak, and J. W. Phillips.

They were unanimously elected.

Chas. H. Knox of Flowery was added to the committee.

The Committee on Resolutions then reported as follows:

Resolved, That as subjects of a Government, yet free, we rejoice at the inestimable right and privilege to publicly assemble and approve or condemn, when the general good requires it, the manner in which our representatives may have discharged the duties assigned them by the suffrages of the people.

2. As the sense of this large assemblage of citizens which may

justly be denominated a spontaneous uprising of an outraged and insulted constituency, that the action of the County Nominating Convention, held in Virginia on the 28th day of December, instant, has been unjust, unfair, arbitrary, and without precedent in the history of conventional legislation.

3. That the resolutions adopted, and the other proceedings had by the said Convention, fail to express the true sentiments of the people of this county, and only proclaim the sentiments of a few interested individuals. Regarding them as such, we unanimously repudiate them, and declare that those resolutions and proceedings ought not to have, and have not, any binding force upon the political action of the free, independent and Union-loving electors of Storey County.

4. That copies of the proceedings of this meeting be transmitted to the members of the ensuing State Nominating Convention, from other counties, accompanied with a respectful request that they will do justice to the great majority of the people of Storey County, and rebuke the odious and unjust system of "packing" conventions by admitting the nominees of this meeting to seats in the Convention, as the true delegates and representatives of the people of Storey.

The resolutions were unanimously adopted.

A County Central Committee was elected, as follows: J. L. Black, Chas. Knox, Jas. Phelan, E. R. Burke, Samuel Doak, T. R. P. Dimock, Thos. Barclay, Dighton Corson, W. D. [sic] Warnock, Jacob Young.

Motion that the delegates elected be instructed to go to Carson tomorrow (Wednesday) and that no proxies be allowed except in extreme cases, and that such extreme cases be attended to by the delegates themselves. Carried.

A motion that the Central Committee meet in the District Court room to-morrow (Wednesday) evening, prevailed.

Also, a motion that the Convention adjourn until next Monday evening—to meet then at the District Court room.

The meeting broke up with cheers for the Convention, the Union, the old flag, and groans for Stewart and Baldwin.

It was a dusty, a very dusty, Convention, and as has been previously remarked in America, we are a great people.

Card

EDS. ENTERPRISE.—The gentleman who reported the proceedings of the Union mass meeting last evening for the ENTERPRISE, unintentionally misquotes. He says Mr. Brosnan slandered the defunct "Nestor." Not so—Mr. B____ made no allusion to that hair brained, crazy old fool, "Nestor," nor to his "wardrobe." But Mr. B____ did mention that other jealous and wicked "cuss," Nessus, and his historical, villainous "shirt."

Now, if that facetious sinner, blunderer and sage-brush painter, "Mark Twain," had thus libelled me, I could forgive him; but to be thus misrepresented (though undesignedly) by the "intelligent" reporter of the ENTERPRISE is, as Mrs. Partington would say, assolutely inseparable.

Virginia, Dec. 30th
C. M. BROSNAN

Virginia City Territorial Enterprise
December 30, 1863

A Gorgeous Swindle

Dr. May, of the International Hotel, has put into our hands the following documents, which will afford an idea of how infinitely mean some people can become when they get a chance. This firm of Read & Co., Bankers, 42 South Third Street, Philadelphia, will do to travel—but not in Washoe, if we understand the peculiar notions of this people. The accompanying letter, circular, and certificate of stock were sent by Read & Co. to Dr. May's nephew, Theodore E. Clapp, Esq., Postmaster at White Pigeon, Michigan.

Through the Doctor, Mr. Clapp had learned a good deal about Washoe, and saw at a glance, of course, that a swindle was on foot which would not only cheat multitudes of the poorest classes of men in the States, but would go far toward destroying confidence in our mines and our citizens if permitted to succeed. He lost no time, therefore, in forwarding the villainous papers to Dr. May, and we are sure the people of the territory are right heartily thankful to him for doing so.

The certificate of stock is a curiosity in the way of unblushing rascality. It does not state how many shares there are in the company, or what a share is represented by. It is a comprehensive arrangement—the company propose to mine all over "Nevada Territory, adjoining California"! They are not partial to any particular mining district. They are going to "carry on" a general "gold and silver mining business"!—the untechnical, leather-headed thieves! The company is "TO BE" organized—at some indefinite period in the future, probably in time for the resurrection. The company is "to be" incorporated "for the purpose of purchasing machinery"—they only organize a company in order to purchase machinery—the inference is, that they calculate to steal the mine. And only to think—a man has only got to peddle forty or fifty of these certificates of stock for Messrs. Read & Co. in order to become fearfully and wonderfully wealthy!—or, as they eloquently put it, "By taking hold now, and assisting to raise the capital stock of this company, you have it within your grasp to place yourself [in] a way to receive a large income annually without spending one cent!"

 Oh, who wouldn't take hold now? Breathes there a man with soul so dead that he wouldn't take hold under such seductive circumstances? Scarcely. Read & Co. want to get money—rather than miss, they will even grab at a paltry two-and-a-half piece thus: "You can send in $2.50 at a time." Two and a half at a time, to buy shares in another Gould & Curry!

 But the coolest, the soothingest, the most refreshingest paragraph (to speak strongly) is that one which is stuck in at the bottom of the circular, with an air about it which mutely says, "it's of no consequence, and scarcely worth mentioning, but then it will do to fill out the page with." The paragraph reads as follows: "N.B.—Subscribers can receive their dividends, as they fall due, at Messrs. Read & Co's Banking House, No. 42 South Third Street, Philadelphia, or have them forwarded by express, of which all will be regularly notified!"

 We imagine we can see a denizen of some obscure western town walking with stately mien to the express office to get his regular monthly dividend; we imagine less fortunate people making way for him, and whispering together, "There goes old Thompson—owns ten shares in the People's Gold and Silver Mining Company—Lord! but he's rich!—he's going after his dividends now." And we imagine we see old Thompson and his regular dividends fail to connect. And finally, we imagine we see the envied Thompson jeered at by his same old neighbors as "the old fool who got taken in by the most palpable humbug of the century."

 Who is "Wm. Heffly, Esq., of San Francisco," who knows it all, and who has calmly waited for three years without once swerving from his purpose of "starting a mining company" as soon as he could become satisfied that quartz-mining was a permanent thing? Cautious scoundrel! You couldn't fool him into going into a highway robbery like the "People's Gold and Silver Mining Company," until he was certain he could make the thing look plausible. But if he wrote those circulars and things, he was never a week in Washoe in his life, because we don't talk about "cap rock" in this country—that's a Pike's Peak phrase; and when we talk about "cap-rock," we never say it pays "$24 to the ton," or any other price; we don't crush wall-rock, as a general thing. There is no "Washoe Mining District" in this Territory, and the President of the People's Company did a bully good thing when he "reserved the right to change the location" of operations whenever he pleased. Mr. Heffly's knowledge of the prices of leading stocks here borders on the marvelous. He says Gould & Curry is worth "$5,000 per share." A "share" is three inches; but Gould & Curry don't sell at $20,000 a foot; he puts Ophir at $2,400 "per share"; now a "share" of Ophir is one inch. All the other prices mentioned by Mr. Heffly are wrong, and never were right at any time, perhaps.

In the items written by Mr. Heffly, and pretended to be clipped from the *Bulletin* and the *Standard*, he uses mining technicalities never uttered either by miners or newspaper men in this part of America. The only true statement in these documents is the one which reads— "Therefore, in subscribing to the capital stock of this company, you are acting on a certainty, and taking no risk whatever." That is eminently so. You are acting on a certainty of being swindled, and so far from there being any risk about that result, it is the deadest "open and shut" thing in the world.

Now this swindle ought to be well ventilated by the newspapers—not that sound businessmen will ever be swindled by it, but the unsuspecting multitude, who yearn to grow suddenly rich, will assuredly have their slender purses drained by it.

Virginia City Territorial Enterprise
c. January 11, 1864

Letter From Mark Twain

Politics

EDITORS ENTERPRISE: Well, how are you and the *News* and the *Bulletin* making out for the Constitution in Storey?

I suppose it will be voted down here. I said so to a Virginia man yesterday. "Well," says he, "that reminds me of a circumstance. A good old practical Dutchman once contributed liberally toward the building of a church. By and by they wanted a lightning rod for it, and they came to the Dutchman again. 'Not a dam cent,' says he, 'not a dam cent! I helps to build a house for the Lord, und if he joose to dunder on it and knock it down, he must do it at his own risk!'

Now in the Constitution, we have placed the Capital here for several years; Carson has always fared well at our hands in the legislature, and finally, we have tacitly consented to say nothing more about the Mint being built in this inconvenient locality. This is the house that has been built for Carson—and now if she chooses to go and dunder on it and knock it down, by the Lord she'll have to take the consequences! The fact is all our bullion is silver, and we don't want the country flooded with silver coin; therefore, we can save the Government a heavy expense, and do the Territory a real kindness, by showing the authorities that we don't need a mint, and don't want one. And as to that Capital, we'll move it up to Storey, where it belongs."

So spake the Virginian. I listened as one having no taxable property and never likely to have; as one being out of office and willing to stay out; as one having no tangible right to take an interest in the Constitution, and consequently not caring a straw whether it carried or not. The man spoke words of wisdom, though. I am aware that the capital could have been removed last session, and from the complexion of the new Territorial Assembly, I suppose it can be done this year. Notwithstanding these things though, and notwithstanding I am a free white male citizen of Storey County, I conjecture that I have a right to my private opinion that Carson is the proper place for the seat of Government and it ought to remain here so long as I don't try to make capital out of that opinion. Nobody has a right to arrest me for being disorderly on such ground as that.

Baggage

Dan, will you send my baggage down here, or have I got to go on borrowing clothes from Pete Hopkins through all eternity?

Young Gillespie

Young Gillespie is down here in my employ. On a small salary. I have got him figuring with the Legislators for extra compensation for the reporters.

The Legislature

The Territorial Legislature will meet here next Tuesday at noon. The rooms used last year in the county buildings have been let by the

County Commissioners for the use of the two Houses, at $500 for the session of forty days, payable in greenbacks. The halls are now being fitted up, and will be ready at the proper time.

House-Warming

All Carson went out to warm Theodore Winters' new house, in Washoe Valley, on Friday evening, and had a pleasant time of it. The house and its furniture together cost $50,000.

Warren Engine Company

The Warren boys brought out their superb machine for practice yesterday. She threw a heavy stream entirely over the tall flag-staff in the Plaza.

Religious

Religious matters are booming along in Carson. Mrs. Wiley, who is an unusually talented vocalist, has been requested to give a concert for the benefit of my old regular chronic brick church, and will probably do so shortly.

The Squares Trial

A jury has finally been empaneled in this murder case, or manslaughter case, or justifiable homicide, or whatever it is, and the trial set for tomorrow.

Marsh Children

Concerning the Marsh troupe, R. G. Marsh sends the following note to Major Dallam, of the *Independent*: "Please insert enclosed corrected advertisement, and make such flourish and announcement as your local feeling will admit of, consistent with a kleer konshuns. Yours till we meat and drink."

The Company will appear at the Carson Theatre on Monday, Tuesday and Wednesday evenings of the present week. Billy O'Neil comes along, too.

Artemus

I received a letter from Artemus Ward, today, dated "Austin, January 1." It has been sloshing around between Virginia and Carson for awhile. I hope there is no impropriety in publishing extracts from a private letter—if there be, I ought not to copy the following paragraph of his:

"I arrived here yesterday morning at 2 o'clock. It is a wild, untamable place, but full of lion-hearted boys. I speak tonight. See small bills. I hope, some time, to see you and Kettle-belly Brown in New York. My grandmother—my sweet grandmother—she, thank God, is too far advanced in life to be affected by your hellish wiles. My aunt—she might fall. But didn't Warren fall, at Bunker Hill? [The old woman's safe. And so is the old girl, for that matter—MARK.] DO not sir, do not, sir, do not flatter yourself that you are the only chastely-humorous writer onto the Pacific slopes. I shall always remember Virginia as a bright spot in my existence, and all others must or rather cannot be, 'as it were.'"

I am glad that old basket-covered jug holds out. I don't know that it does, but I have an impression that way. At least I can't make anything out of that last sentence. But I wish him well, and a safe journey, drunk or sober.

Virginia City Territorial Enterprise
c. January 13, 1864

Legislative Proceedings

House of Representatives

Carson, January 12, 1864

The Constitution pot boils. Gentlemen from the different sections of the Territory—visiting brethren of the Legislature agree in the opinion that the Constitution will carry by a very respectable vote on the 19th. This will have its effect upon Ormsby County, which, strangely enough, considering the advantages she would derive from having the Capital permanently located at Carson, a mint built here, and the number of resident officials increased, has heretofore been opposed to the establishment of a state government.

And speaking of the mint, I have an item of news relating to that subject. Mr. Lockhart, the Indian Agent, has just received a letter from Commissioner Bennet, in which he says he has been informed by Secretary Chase that no further steps will be taken toward building a mint in this region until our state representatives arrive in Washington! This is in consequence of efforts now being made by Mr. Conness to have the mint located at Virginia. The authorities want advice from representatives direct from the people. As I said before, the people of Ormsby will oppose the Constitution.

O, certainly they will! They will if they are sick—or sentimental—or consumptive—or don't know their own interests—or can't see when God Almighty smiles upon them, and don't care anyhow. Now if Ormsby votes against the Constitution, let us clothe ourselves in sackcloth and put ashes on our heads; for in that hour religious liberty will be at an end here—her next step will be to vote against her eternal salvation. However the anti-Constitutional sentiment here is growing weak in the knees.

Most of the members have arrived, and the wheels of government will begin to churn at 12 PM.

Virginia City Territorial Enterprise
c. January 14, 1864

Legislative Proceedings

Before the Legislature begins its labors, I will just mention that the Marsh Troupe will perform in Virginia to-morrow night (Thursday)—at the Opera House of course—for the benefit of Engine Company No. 2. They played here last night—"Toodles," you know. Young George Marsh—whose theatrical costumes are ungainly enough, but not funny—took the part of Toodles, and performed it well—performed it as only cultivated talent, or genius, or which you please, or both, could enable him to do it. Little Jenny Arnot (she with the hideous—I mean affected—voice) appeared as Mrs. Toodles. Jenny is pretty—very pretty; but by the usual sign, common to all those of her sex similarly gifted, I perceive she knows it. Therefore, let us not speak of it. Jenny is smart—but she knows that too, and I grant you it is natural that she should. And behold you, when she does forget herself and make use of her own natural voice, and drop her borrowed one, it is the pleasantest thing in life to see her play.

The other ladies—however, I neglected to preserve a theatre bill, and I do not know what characters they personified. However, one was a handsome sailor boy, and the other was a lovely, confiding girl with auburn hair—the same being stuck after each other. Alexander was gotten up in considerable taste as a ratty old gentleman—the father of one of the stuck—the auburn one, I think. Beatty was one of those dear reformed pirates, who comes in at the finale with a bandaged head and a broken heart, and leans up against the side-scenes and slobbers over his past sins, and is so interesting. Billy O'Neil was so successful in keeping the house in a roar as the Limerick Boy, and especially as the Irish Schoolmaster, that he was frequently driven from his own masterly gravity.

After the performance was over, he said, "Those girls on the front seats knew where the laugh came in, didn't they?" I said they did. I further observed that if there was any place where the laugh didn't come in, those girls on the front seats didn't know it. Wherefore, if so, he had them there. My head was level. I think I am not transcending the limits of truth when I assert that my head was eminently level. I would not flatter Billy O'Neil, yet I cannot help thinking that as "Barney the Baron," night before last, he was the drunkest white man that ever crossed the mountains. George Boulden, assisted by Mr. Alexander, sang "When this Cruel War is Over, as it Were," and was thrice encored.

A circumstance happened to an acquaintance of mine this week, which I promised to say nothing about. A young man from one of the neighboring counties took a good deal of silk dress, with a moderate amount of girl in it, home from the theatre, and on his way back to his constituents he jammed his leg into a suburban post-hole, and remained anchored out there in the dark until considerably after midnight. He wept, and he prayed, and he cussed. He continued to cuss. He cussed himself, and the Board of Aldermen, and the County Commissioners. He even cussed his own relations, and more particularly his grandmother, which was innocent. It seemed a good deal mixed as to whether he was ever going to get loose or not; but the coyotes got to skirmishing around him and grabbing at his independent leg, and made him uncommon lively. Whereat, he put on his strength, and tugged and cussed, and kicked at the coyotes, and cussed again, and tugged, and finally, out he came—but he pulled the post-hole up by the roots in doing of it. It was funny—exceedingly funny. However, I don't mind it; I slept all the same, and just as well.

I have received that carpet-sack of mine at last. It contained two shirts and six empty champagne bottles. Also one garrote collar, with a note from Dan written on it in pencil, accounting for the bottles under the plea that "voluminous baggage maketh a man to be respected." It was an airy and graceful thought, and a credit to his great mind. The shirts were marked respectively "R. M. Daggett" and "Sandy Baldwin," from which I perceive that Dan has been foraging again.

We organized yesterday. "We" is the House of Representatives, you understand. Simmons will make a good Speaker; and, besides, I shall be nearby to volunteer a little of my Third House experience, occasionally. The Council did not expend half an hour in getting very thoroughly and permanently organized. The regular joint committees were appointed to wait on the Governor, and that Body will be produced in Court this morning to testify concerning the condition of the country.

N.B.—The several departments of the law-making power are called Bodies. The Governor is one of them, by law—therefore it is disrespectful to speak of him otherwise than as a Body—a jolly, unctuous, oleaginous old Body. That's it. I do not consider that we are entirely organized yet, either. You see, we are entitled to a Chaplain. The Organic Act vouchsafes unto us the consolations of religion—payable in Greenbacks at three dollars a day. We roped in the Rev. Mr. White, yesterday, and gouged him out of a prayer, for which, of course, we never intend to pay him. We go in for ministers looking to Providence in little matters of this kind. Well, there is no harm in us, and we calculate to run this institution without a Chaplain. In accordance with a motion of Mr. Nightingill, we dispensed with the services of Chaplain in the Third House, and it is a matter of no little pride to me to observe that this Aggregation of Wisdom manifests a disposition, not only in this but in many other respects, to send Jefferson's Manual and the Organic Act to the d—l and take the published proceedings of that Body as its parliamentary gospel—its guide to temporal glory and ultimate salvation. The House will proceed to business now in a few minutes.

Virginia City Territorial Enterprise
c. *January 15, 1864*

Legislative Proceedings

House—Third Day

Carson, Jan. 14

Say—you have got a compositor up there who is too rotten particular, it seems to me. When I spell "devil" in my usual frank and open manner, he puts it "d—l"! Now, Lord love his conceited and accommodating soul, if I choose to use the language of the vulgar, the low-flung and the sinful, and such as will shock the ears of the highly civilized, I don't want him to appoint himself an editorial critic and proceed to tone me down and save me from the consequences of my conduct; that is, unless I pay him for it, which I won't. I expect I could spell "devil' before that fastidious cuss was born.

The Speaker called the House to order at 10 A.M.

Resolutions

Mr. Heaton introduced a concurrent resolution, that when the Legislative Assembly adjourn to-morrow, it is to meet again on Wednesday, 21st, at 12 PM.

A motion to suspend the rules was put to a vote and carried—ayes 15; noes, Messrs. Clagett, Curley, Gillespie, Gove, Hess, Hunter, Jones and Trask.

Mr. Gillespie moved to amend by making the hour 1 P.M.

[More skirmishing about parliamentary usage but the Chair is not in fault.—REPORTER.]

Mr. Fisher offered an amendment, to read "the House of Representatives and Council concurring." [Mr. Fisher got his notion from—well—say inspiration, for instance.—REPORTER.]

Mr. Clagett finally got up and straightened the blasted resolution.

The Speaker made a suggestion concerning the wording of the document. [Half an hour more will get it all right, you know. The parliamentary skirmishing still goes on, with unabated intelligence. This aggregation of wisdom can frame a concurrent resolution, but we must have a reasonable length of time to do it in. I could have furnished all the amendments offered to this document, and all the transmogrifications it has passed through—but then you don't want a column of that kind of information. I don't consider it important.—REP.]

The resolution as infinitely amended and improved, was voted upon at last, and carried—ayes 18, noes 5—Messrs. Clagett, Gillespie, Gove, Hunter and Phillips. [I asked the Clerk what the resolution proposed to do now? And he said he'd be d—d if he knew.—REP.]

Mr. Clagett offered a resolution that the regular daily sessions of the House commence at 10 A.M.

Mr. Fisher moved to insert "except when otherwise ordered."

On a division the motion was lost—14 to 6.

The resolution was then adopted.

Virginia City Territorial Enterprise
c. January 16, 1864

Legislative Proceedings

House—Fourth Day

Carson, Jan. 15

The Committee on Rules for the Government of the House reported yesterday the good old-fashioned and entirely proper rule that members and officers should keep their seats at adjournment until the Speaker had declared the House adjourned and left the Chair. Well, sir, the House debated it and voted it down. I can prove it by the Clerk's Journal. Now, considering that it was a harmless measure, and a customary one, and a mark of respect to the Chair; and considering that it is very seldom enforced, and also, that it was a little disrespectful to the Chair to vote it down, the action of the House in the matter seems somewhat strained.

But I will interrupt you just here, if you please, and suggest to you that it is none of your business, and I want to know what you are putting in your lip about it for? I expect we can attend to our own affairs. And didn't they bullyrag that concurrent resolution yesterday? I reckon not. I do not admire the taste of the lobby members, though, in letting on as if they knew so much more about it, when the House is being rent with the mortal agonies of an effort to adjourn itself over for a week without adjourning the Council at the same time.

The House did not wish to adjourn the Council without being asked to do so by that body, and if the House found it very nearly impossible to word the resolution so as not to adjourn the Council aforesaid, I do not conceive that it was dignified on the part of the lobby members to express by their countenances that they had their own opinions concerning the House. But didn't the House worry that concurrent resolution for a few hours or so? You bet you. However, we had better let "parliamentary usage" alone for the present, until our former knowledge on the knotty subject returns to our memories. Because Providence is not going to put up with this sort of thing much longer, you know. I observe there is no lightning rod on these county buildings.

Virginia City Territorial Enterprise
c. January 19, 1864

Letter from Mark Twain

Miss Clapp's School

By authority of an invitation from Hon. Wm. M. Gillespie, member of the House Committee on Colleges and Common Schools, I accompanied that statesman on an unofficial visit to the excellent school of Miss Clapp and Mrs. Cutler, this afternoon. The air was soft and balmy—the sky was cloudless and serene—the odor of flowers floated upon the idle breeze—the glory of the sun descended like a benediction upon mountain and meadow and plain—the wind blew like the very devil, and the day was generally disagreeable.

The school—however, I will mention first that a charter for an educational institution to be called the Sierra Seminary, was granted to Miss Clapp during the Legislative session of 1861, and a bill will be introduced while the present assembly is in session, asking an appropriation of $20,000 to aid the enterprise. Such a sum of money could not be more judiciously expended, and I doubt not the bill will pass.

The present school is a credit both to the teachers and the town. It now numbers about forty pupils, I should think, and is well and systematically conducted. The exercises this afternoon were of a character not likely to be unfamiliar to the free American citizen who has a fair recollection of how he used to pass his Friday afternoons in the days of his youth. The tactics have undergone some changes, but these variations are not important. In former times a fellow took his place in the luminous spelling class in the full consciousness that if he spelled cat with a "k," or indulged in any other little orthographical eccentricities of a similar nature, he would be degraded to the foot or sent to his seat; whereas, he keeps his place in the ranks now, in such cases, and his punishment is simply to "'bout face."

Johnny Eaves stuck to his first position, today, long after the balance of the class had rounded to, but he subsequently succumbed to the word "nape," which he persisted in ravishing of its final vowel. There was nothing irregular about that. Your rightly constructed schoolboy will spell a multitude of hard words without hesitating once, and then lose his grip and miss fire on the easiest one in the book.

The fashion of reading selections of prose and poetry remains the same; and so does the youthful manner of doing that sort of thing. Some pupils read poetry with graceful ease and correct expression, and others place the rising and falling inflection at measured intervals, as if they had learned the lesson on a "see-saw;" but then they go undulating through a stanza with such an air of unctuous satisfaction, that it is a comfort to be around when they are at it.

"The boy—stoo-dawn—the burning deck—
When-sawl—but him had fled—
The flames—that shook—the battle—zreck—Shone round—him o'er—the dead."

That is the old-fashioned impressive style—stately, slow-moving and solemn. It is in vogue yet among scholars of tender age. It always will be. Ever since Mrs. Hemans wrote that verse, it has suited the pleasure of juveniles to emphasize the word "him," and lay atrocious stress upon that other word "o'er," whether she liked it or not; and I am prepared to believe that they will continue this practice unto the end of time, and with the same indifference to Mrs. Hemans' opinions about it, or any body's else.

They sing in school nowadays, which is an improvement upon the ancient regime; and they don't catch flies and throw spit-balls at the teacher, as they used to do in my time—which is another improvement, in a general way. Neither do the boys and girls keep a sharp look-out on each other's shortcomings and report the same at headquarters, as was a custom of by-gone centuries. And this reminds me of Gov. Nye's last anecdote, fulminated since the delivery of his message, and consequently not to be found in that document. The company were swapping old school reminiscences, and in due season they got to talking about that extinct species of tell-tales that were once to be found in all minor educational establishments, and who never failed to detect and impartially denounce every infraction of the rules that occurred among their mates.

The governor said that he threw a casual glance at a pretty girl on the next bench one day, and she complained to the teacher—which was entirely characteristic, you know. Says she, "Mister Jones, Warren Nye's looking at me." Whereupon, without a suggestion from anybody, up jumped an infamous, lisping, tow-headed young miscreant, and says he, "Yeth, thir, I thee him do it!" I doubt if the old original boy got off that ejaculation with more gusto than the Governor throws into it.

The "compositions" read today were as exactly like the compositions I used to hear read in our school as one baby's nose is exactly like all other babies' noses. I mean the old principal ear-marks were all there: the cutting to the bone of the subject with the very first gash, without any preliminary foolishness in the way of a gorgeous introductory; the inevitable and persevering tautology; the brief, monosyllabic sentences (beginning, as a very general thing, with the pronoun "I"); the penchant for presenting rigid, uncompromising facts for the consideration of the hearer, rather than ornamental fancies; the depending for the success of the composition upon its general merits, without tacking artificial aids to the end of it, in the shape of deductions, or conclusions, or clap-trap climaxes, albeit their absence sometimes imparts to these essays the semblance of having come to an end before they were finished—of arriving at full speed at a jumping-off place and going suddenly overboard, as it were, leaving a sensation such as one feels when he stumbles without previous warning upon that infernal "To be Continued" in the midst of a thrilling magazine story. I know there are other styles of school compositions, but these are the characteristics of the style which I have in my eye at present. I do not know why this one has particularly suggested itself to my mind, unless the literary effort of one of the boys there today left with me an unusually vivid impression. It ran something in this wise:

Composition

"I like horses. Where we lived before we came here, we used to have a cutter and horses. We used to ride in it. I like winter. I like snow.

I used to have a pony all to myself, where I used to live before I came here. Once it drifted a good deal—very deep—and when it stopped I went out and got in it."

That was all. There was no climax to it, except the spasmodic bow which the tautological little student jerked at the school as he closed his labors.

Two remarkably good compositions were read. Miss P.'s was much the best of these—but aside from its marked literary excellence, it possessed another merit which was peculiarly gratifying to my feelings just at that time, because it took the conceit out of young Gillespie as completely as perspiration takes the starch out of a shirt-collar. In his insufferable vanity, that feeble member of the House of Representatives had been assuming imposing attitudes, and beaming upon the pupils with an expression of benignant imbecility which was calculated to inspire them with the conviction that there was only one guest of any consequence in the house. Therefore, it was an unspeakable relief to me to see him forced to shed his dignity.

Concerning the composition, however. After detailing the countless pleasures which had fallen to her lot during the holidays, the authoress finished with a proviso, in substance as follows—I have forgotten the precise language: "But I have no cheerful reminiscences of Christmas. It was dreary, monotonous and insipid to the last degree. Mr. Gillespie called early, and remained the greater part of the day!" You should have seen the blooming Gillespie wilt when that literary bombshell fell in his camp! The charm of the thing lay in the fact that that last naive sentence was the only suggestion offered in the way of accounting for the dismal character of the occasion. However, to my mind it was sufficient—entirely sufficient.

Since writing the above, I have seen the architectural plans and specifications for Miss Clapp and Mrs. Cutler's proposed "Sierra Seminary" building. It will be a handsome two-story edifice, one hundred feet square, and will accommodate forty "boarders" and any number of pupils beside, who may board elsewhere. Constructed of wood, it will cost $12,000; or of stone, $18,000. Miss Clapp has devoted ten acres of ground to the use and benefit of the institution.

I sat down intending to write a dozen pages of variegated news. I have about accomplished the task—all except the "variegated." I have economised in the matter of current news of the day, considerably more than I purposed to do, for every item of that nature remains stored away in my mind in a very unwritten state, and will afford unnecessarily ample material for another letter. It is useless material, though, I suspect, because, inasmuch as I have failed to incorporate it into this, I fear I shall not feel industrious enough to weave out of it another letter until it has become too stale to be interesting. Well, never mind—we must learn to take an absorbing delight in educational gossip; nine-tenths of the revenues of the Territory go into the bottomless gullet of that ravenous school fund, you must bear in mind.

Virginia City Territorial Enterprise
c. *January 21, 1864*

Legislative Proceedings

House—Ninth Day

Carson, January 20

Mr. Dean offered a resolution to employ a copying clerk.

Mr. Gillespie offered an amendment requiring the Engrossing and Enrolling Clerks to do this proposed officer's work. [These two officers are strictly ornamental—have been under wages since the first day of the session—haven't had anything to do, and won't for two weeks yet—and now by the eternal, they want some more useless clerical jewelry to dangle to the Legislature. If the House would discharge its extra scribblers, and let the Chief Clerk hire assistance only when he wants it, it seems to me it would be better.—REP.]

Without considering the appointment of a new jimcrack ornament, and starting his pay six weeks before he goes to work (only thirteen dollars a day), the House adjourned.

Virginia City Territorial Enterprise
c. *January 22, 1864*

Legislative Proceedings—Tenth Day

An officer of the House—Charles Carter, Messenger—is lying at the point of death this morning. He ruptured a blood vessel of the brain, night before last, previous to which time he was in robust health. He was a youth of great promise, and was respected and esteemed by all who knew him. He held the position of Messenger of the House during the session of 1862, and his faithful attention to the duties of the office then was endorsed by his re-election the present session.

The chief portion of the population of Carson spent last night in feasting and dancing at the Warm Springs. Such of them as are out of bed at this hour, declare the occasion to have been one of unmitigated felicity.

The House met at 10 A.M.

Leave of Absence

Mr. Calder asked and obtained leave for one day for Mr. Clagett who was engaged in drafting a bill.

Question of Privilege

Mr. Stewart rose to a question of privilege, and said the ENTERPRISE and Union reporters had been moving Ellen Redman's toll-bridge from its proper position on the Carson Slough to an illegal one on the Humboldt Slough. [I did that. If Ellen Redman don't like it, I can move her little bridge back again—but under protest. I waded that Humboldt Slough once, and I have always had a hankering to see a bridge over it since—MARK.]

Mr. Phillips moved to amend Mr. Gillespie's resolution by striking out that portion which puts the Enrolling and Engrossing Clerks under the sole control of the Chief Clerk. Lost.

A warm debate sprung up on the subject. Mr. Gillespie manfully contended for the justness and expediency of adopting his resolution, and stated several propositions which were eminently correct, to wit: that these subordinate officers ought to be under the control of the Chief Clerk; that they were under the pay of the House, and had been for some time, and yet had nothing to do; and finally, that copying being within the scope of their duties, they ought to be put at it and afforded an opportunity of rendering an equivalent for their salaries.

Messrs. Stewart, Dixson and others were very fearful of discommoding the subordinate clerks, and very anxious to embellish the House with some more fellows calculated to swing a sinecure gracefully. The Chief Clerk stated that Mr. Powell, the Enrolling Clerk, had labored assiduously, from the first, in rendering any and all assistance asked at his hands, but nobody coming forward to say how much Captain Murphy had done, and nobody being supplied with a pile of estimates [sufficient] to portray how much he hadn't done, it became the general impression that Captain Murphy had been considerably more ornamental than useful to the House of Representatives. But I am here only during the courtesy of the House—on my good behavior, as it were—and I am a little afraid that if I say this aggregation of Wisdom elected Captain Murphy more out of regard for his military services than respect for the nasty manner in which he can sling a pen, I shall get notice to quit—MARK.

Mr. Gillespie, on leave, amended his resolution by adding "Provided said clerks shall not be interfered with in the discharge of their respective duties"—and had the resolution not been furnished with this loophole if it had not been thus emasculated, it would not have passed. By a scratch it carried, though, and here are the voters' names:

AYES—Messrs. Calder, Elliott, Gillespie, Gove, Hess, Hunter, McDonald, Nelson, Requa, Trask, Ungar, Speaker—12.

NOES-Messrs. Barclay, Curler, Dean, Dixson, Fisher, Heaton, Jones, Phillips, Stewart, Tennant—10.

Virginia City Territorial Enterprise
c. January 28, 1864

Legislative Proceedings

House—Sixteenth Day

GENERAL ORDERS

The House resolved itself into Committee of the Whole, Mr. Fisher in the chair, upon the unfinished business of the general orders, and occupied the remainder of the forenoon session in the consideration of the Act providing for the appointment of Notaries Public and defining their duties. [This is a most important bill, and if passed will secure clearer and more comprehensible records hereafter. It will leave Storey County twelve notaries in place of the fifteen hundred we have at present, and these twelve will have to be men of solid reputation, since they will have to give heavier bonds than all the fifteen hundred combined do at present; they must give bail in the sum of $5,000 each—$60,000 altogether.]

Mr. Fisher said three would be sufficient for Douglas County—he didn't want all the property there tied up in notary's bonds. Mr. Clagett said there was scarcely a valid deed on the Humboldt records, because the certificates attached to them by ignorant notaries were worthless, and he supposed property worth millions had already been jeopardized in the territory by this kind of officer. He said one really splendid ignoramus out there who forwarded a bond in the sum of $10; had it returned with a notification that it must be increased to $500; he couldn't straddle the blind, and had to give up his commission. Besides, Mr. Clagett said, the passage of this Act would oust from office some twenty-five rabid secessionists in Humboldt County alone! [Sensation.]

If you could just see the official bonds drawn up and sent to the office of the Secretary of the Territory by some of these mentally deaf, dumb and blind notaries, you would wonder, as I do, what they have been and gone and done, that heaven should be down on them so. They never use revenue stamps—they don't subscribe the oath, they—well, they don't do anything that could lay them liable to an accusation of knowing it all, or even any fraction of it.

[Mr. Tennant said some few secesh had been appointed in Lander, but not so many as in Humboldt—they found one secesh in Lander last spring, and Acting-Governor Clemens captured him. I send you a copy of the bill, as they have just finished amending it in the Committee of the Whole, and suggest that you publish it—MARK]

Virginia City Territorial Enterprise
c. January 29, 1864

Legislative Proceedings

House—Seventeenth Day

I delivered that message last night, but I didn't talk loud enough—people in the far end of the hall could not hear me. They said "Louder—louder" occasionally, but I thought that was a way they had—a joke, as it were. I had never talked to a crowd before, and knew none of the tactics of the public speaker. I suppose I spoke loud enough for some houses, but not for that District Court room, which is about seventy-five feet from floor to roof, and has no ceiling. I hope the people will deal as mildly with me, however, as I did with the public officers in the annual message. Some folks heard the entire document, though—there is some comfort in that.

Hon. Mr. Clagett, Speaker Simmons of the inferior House, Hon. Hal Clayton, Speaker of the Third House, Judge Haydon, Dr. Alban, and others whose opinions are entitled to weight said they would travel several miles to hear that message again. It affords me a good deal of satisfaction to mention it. It serves to show that if the audience could have heard me distinctly, they would have appreciated the wisdom thus conferred upon them. They seemed to appreciate what they did hear though, pretty thoroughly. After the first quarter of an hour I ceased to whisper, and became audible. One of these days, when I get time, I will correct, amend and publish the message, in accordance with a resolution of the Third House ordering 300,000 copies in the various languages spoken at the present day.

P.S.—Sandy Baldwin and Theodore Winters heard that message, anyhow, and by thunder they appreciated it, too. They have sent a hundred dollars apiece to San Francisco this morning, to purchase a watch chain for His Excellency Governor Twain. I guess that is a pretty good result for an incipient oratorical slouch like me, isn't it? I don't know that anybody tendered the other Governor a testimonial of any kind.

Virginia City Territorial Enterprise
c. February 1, 1864

Letter from Dayton

[TRAVELING WITH ADOLPH SUTRO—] Eight left Virginia yesterday and came down to Dayton with Mr. Sutro. Time 30 minutes—distance 8 or 9 miles. There is nothing very slow about that kind of travel. We found Dayton the same old place but taking up a good deal more room than it did the last time I saw it, and looking more brisk and lively with its increase of business, and more handsome on account of the beautiful dressed stone buildings with which it is being embellished of late.

Just as we got fairly underway, and were approaching Ball Robert's bridge, Sutro's dog, "Carlo," got to skirmishing around in the extravagant exuberance of his breakfast, and shipped up a fight with six or seven other dogs whom he was entirely unacquainted with, had never met before and probably has no desire to meet again. He waltzed into them right gallantly and right gallantly waltzed out again.

We also left at about this time and trotted briskly across Ball Robert's bridge. I remarked that Ball Robert's bridge was a good one and a credit to that bald gentleman. I said it in a fine burst of humor and more on account of the joke than anything else, but Sutro is insensible to the more delicate touches of American wit, and the effort was entirely lost on him. I don't think Sutro minds a joke of mild character any more than a dead man would. However, I repeated it once or twice without producing any visible effect, and finally derived what comfort I could by laughing at it myself.

Mr. Sutro being a confirmed businessman, replied in a practical and businesslike way. He said the bridge was a good one, and so were all public blessings of a similar nature when entrusted to the hands of private individuals. He said if the county had built the bridge it would have cost an extravagant sum of money, and would have been eternally out of repair. He also said the only way to get public work well and properly done was to let it out by contract.

"For instance," says he, "they have fooled away two or three years trying to capture Richmond, whereas if they had let the job by contract to some sensible businessman, the thing would have been accomplished and forgotten long ago." It was a novel and original idea and I forgot my joke for the next half hour in speculating upon its feasibility . . .

New York Sunday Mercry
February 7, 1864

Doings in Nevada

Our lively correspondent, Mark Twain, sends us his "opinions and reflections" upon recent political movements in Nevada Territory, which will be found interesting.

Carson City, Nevada Territory
January 4, 1864

EDITOR T.T.: The concentrated wisdom of Nevada Territory (known unto and respected by the nations of the earth as "Washoe") assembled in convention at Carson recently, and framed a constitution. It was an excellent piece of work in some respects, but it had one or two unfortunate defects which debarred it from assuming to be an immaculate conception. The chief of these was a clause authorizing the taxing of the mines. The people will not stand that. There are some 30,000 gold and silver mining incorporations here, or mines, or claims, or which you please, or all, if it suits you better. Very little of the kind of property thus represented is improved yet, or "developed" as we call it; it will take two or three years to get it in a developed and paying condition, and will require an enormous outlay of capital to accomplish such a result. And until it does begin to pay dividends, the people will not consent that it shall be burdened and hindered by taxation. Therefore, I am satisfied they will refuse to ratify our new constitution on the 19th inst.

It had an amusing feature in it, also. That was the Great Seal of the State. It had snow-capped mountains in it; and tunnels, and shafts, and pickaxes, and quartz-mills, and pack-trains, and mule-teams. These things were good; what there were of them. And it has railroads in it, and telegraphs, and stars, and suspension bridges, and other romantic fictions foreign to sand and sage-brush. But the richest of it was the motto. It took them thirty days to decide whether it should be *"Volens et Potens"* (which they said meant "Able and Willing") or "The Union Must and Shall be Preserved." Either would have been presumptuous enough, and surpassingly absurd just at present. Because we are not able and willing, thus far, to do a great deal more than locate wild-cat mining claims and reluctantly sell them to confiding strangers at a ruinous sacrifice—of conscience. And if it were left to us to preserve the Union, in case the balance of the country failed in the attempt, I seriously believe we couldn't do it Possibly, we might make it mighty warm for the Confederacy if it came prowling around here, but ultimately we would have to forsake our high trust, and quit preserving the Union. I am confident of it. And I have thought the matter over a good deal, off and on, as we say in Paris.

We have an animal here whose surname is the "jackass rabbit." It is three feet long, has legs like a counting-house stool, ears of monstrous length, and no tail to speak of. It is swifter than a greyhoud, and as meek and harmless as an infant. I might mention, also, that it is as handsome as most infants; however, it would be foreign to the subject, and I do not know that a remark of that kind would be popular in all circles. Let it pass, then—I will say nothing about it, though it would be a great comfort to me to do it, if people would consider the source and overlook it. Well, somebody proposed as a substitute for that pictorial Great Seal, a figure of a jackass-rabbit reposing in the shade of his native sagebrush, with the motto *"Volens* enough, but not so d—d *Potens."* Possibly that had something to do with the rejection of one of the proposed mottoes by the Convention.

State Nominating Convention

We do not fool away much time in this country. As soon as the Constitution was duly framed and ready for ratification or rejection by the people, a convention to nominate candidates for State offices met at

Carson. It finished its labors day before yesterday. The following nominations were made: For Governor, M. N. Mitchell; Lieutenant-Governor, M. S. Thompson; Secretary of State, Orion Clemens; Treasurer, Wm. B. Hickok; Member of Congress, John B. Winters; Superintendent of Public Instruction, Rev. A. F. White.

Now, that ticket will be elected, but the Constitution won't. In that case, what are we to do with these fellows? We cannot let them starve. They are on our hands, and are entitled to our charity and protection. It is different with them from what it is with other people, because, although the Almighty created them, and used to care for and watch over them, no doubt it was long, long ago, and he may not recollect them now. And I think it is our duty to look after them, and see that they do not suffer. Besides, they all owe me something for traducing and vilifying them in the public prints, and thus exciting sympathy for them on the score of persecution, and securing their nomination; and I do not think it right or just that I should be expected to do people favors without being paid for it, merely because those favors failed to produce marketable fruit. No, Sir; I elected those fellows, and I shall take care that I am fairly remunerated for it. Now, if you know any small State, lying around anywhere, that I could get a contract on for the running of it, you will oblige me by mentioning it in your next.

You can say that I have all the machinery on hand necessary to the carrying on of a third-rate State; say, also, that it is comparatively new, portions of it never having been used at all; also, that I will part with it on pretty nearly any terms, as my constitution is prostrated, and I am anxious to go into some other business. And say my various State officers are honest and capable—however, don't say that—just leave that out—let us not jest on a serious matter like this. But you might put in a little advertisement for me in the following shape, for instance. And it would be a real kindness to me if you would be so good as to call attention to it in your editorial columns. You see I am a sort of an orphan, away out here, struggling along on my own hook, as it were. My mother lives in St. Louis. She is sixty years of age, and a member of the Presbyterian Church. She takes no pride in being gay; in fact, she don't rush around much in society, now. However, I do not ask any man's sympathy on that account. I was simply going to offer my little advertisement.

For Sale or Rent

One Governor, entirely new. Attended Sunday-school in his youth, and still remembers it. Never drinks. In other respects, however, his habits are good. As Commander-in-Chief of the Militia, he would be an ornament. Most Governors are.

One Lieutenant-Governor—also new. He has other merits, of minor importance, beside. No objection to going into the country—or elsewhere.

One Secretary of State. An old, experienced hand at the business. Has edited a newspaper, and been Secretary and Governor of Nevada Territory—consequently, is capable; and also consequently, will bear watching; is not bigoted—has no particular set of religious principles—or any other kind.

One small Treasurer—(second-hand). Will make a good officer. Was Treasurer once before, in States. Took excellent care of the funds—has them yet.

One Member of Congress—new, but smart, sometimes called "Old Smarty, from Mud Springs." Has read every newspaper printed in Nevada Territory for two years, and knows all about the war. Would be a good hand to advise the President. Is young, ardent, ambitious, and on it. No objection to traveling, provided his mileage is paid.

One Superintendent of Public Instruction—good as new. Understands all the different systems of teaching, and does not approve of them. It is his laudable boast that he is a self-made man. It has been said of him by his admirers that God Almighty never made such a man. It is probably so. He is the soul of honor, and is willing to take greenbacks at par. No objection to making himself generally useful; can preach, if required.

Also, a large and well-selected assortment of State Legislators, Supreme Judges, Comptrollers, and such gimcracks, handy to have about a State Government, all of which are for sale or rent on the mildest possible terms, as, under present circumstances, they are of no earthly use to the subscriber.

For further particulars, address

MARK TWAIN, Carson, N.T.

Our Constitution Illegal

Now, joking aside, these are all good, honest, capable men, and would reflect credit upon the several positions for which they have been nominated; but then the people are not going to ratify the Constitution; and, consequently, they will never get a chance. I am glad that such is the case. In the Legislature, last year, I was wielding the weapon which, under just such circumstances, is mightier than the sword, at the time that the Act authorizing the calling together of a Convention to form a State Constitution was passed; and I know the secret history of that document. It was reported back from the Committee with a lot of blanks in it (for dates, apportionment, and number of members, amount of money appropriated to defray expenses of the Convention, etc.). Both Houses passed the Bill without filling those blanks; it was duly enrolled, brought back, and signed by the presiding officers of the Legislature, and then transmitted, a worthless, meaningless, and intentionally powerless instrument—to Gov. Nye for his signature—at night. And lo! a miracle. When the bill reached the Governor, there was not a solitary blank in it! Who filled them, is—is a great moral question for instance; but the enrolling clerk did not do it at any rate, since the emendations are in an unknown and atrocious handwriting. Therefore, the bill was a fraud; the convention created by it was a fraud; the fruit of the convention was an illegitimate infant constitution and a dead one at that; a State reared upon such a responsibility would be a fraudulent and impotent institution, and the result would be that we should ultimately be kicked back into a territorial condition again on account of it. Wherefore, when men say, "Let our constitution slide for the present," we say Amen.

Virginia City Territorial Enterprise
February 9, 1864

Letter from Carson City

Concerning Notaries

A strange, strange thing occurred here yesterday, to wit: A MAN APPLIED FOR A NOTARY'S COMMISSION.
Think of it. Ponder over it. He wanted a notarial commission—he said so himself. He was from Storey County. He brought his little peti-

tion along with him. He brought it on two stages. It is voluminous. The county surveyor is chaining it off. Three shifts of clerks will be employed night and day on it, deciphering the signatures and testing their genuineness. They began unrolling the petition at noon, and people of strong mining proclivities at once commenced locating claims on it. We are too late, you know. But then they say the extensions are just as good as the original. I believe you.

Since writing the above, I have discovered that the foregoing does not amount to much as a sensation item, after all. The reason is because there are seventeen hundred and forty-two applications for notaryships already on file in the Governor's office. I was not aware of it, you know. There are also as much as eleven cords of petitions stacked up in his back yard. A watchman stands guard over this combustible material—the back yard is not insured.

Since writing the above, strange events have happened. I started downtown, and had not gone far, when I met a seedy, ornery, ratty, hangdog-looking stranger, who approached me in the most insinuating manner, and said he was glad to see me. He said he had often sighed for an opportunity of becoming acquainted with me—that he had read my effusions (he called them "effusions") with solemn delight, and had yearned to meet the author face-to-face. He said he was Billson—Billson of Lander—I might have heard of him. I told him I had—many a time—which was an infamous falsehood. He said "D—n it, old Quill-driver you must come and take a drink with me"; and says I, "D—n it, old Vermin-ranch, I'll do it." [I had him there.]

We took a drink, and he told the bar-keeper to charge it. After which, he opened a well-filled carpet-sack and took out a shirt-collar and a petition. He then threw the empty carpet-sack aside and unrolled several yards of the petition—"just for a starter," he said. "Now," says he, "Mark, have you got a good deal of influence with Governor?" "Unbounded," says I, with honest pride; "when I go and use my influence with Governor Nye, and tell him it will be a great personal favor to me if he will do so and so, he always says it will be a real pleasure to him—that if it were any other man—any other man in the world—but seeing it's me, he won't." Mr. Billson then remarked that I was the very man; he wanted a little notarial appointment, and he would like me to mention it to the governor. I said I would, and turned away, resolved to damn young Billson's official aspirations with a mild dose of my influence.

I walked about ten steps, and met a cordial man, with the dust of travel upon his garments. He mashed my hands in his, and as I stood straightening the joints back into their places again, says he, "Why darn it, Mark, how well you're looking! Thunder! It's been an age since I saw you. Turn around and let's look at you good. Gad, it's the same old Mark! Well, how've you been—and what have you been doing with yourself lately? Why don't you never come down and see a fellow? Every time I come to town, the old woman's sure to get after me for not bringing you out, as soon as I get back. Why she takes them articles of your'n, and slathers 'em into her old scrap-book, along with deaths and marriages, and receipts for the itch, and the small-pox, and hell knows what all, and if it warn't that you talk too slow to ever make love, dang my cats if I wouldn't be jealous of you. But what's the use fooling away time here?—let's go and gobble a cocktail." This was old Boreas, from Washoe. I went and gobbled a cocktail with him. He mentioned incidentally that he wanted a notaryship, and showed me a good deal of his petition. I said I would use my influence in his behalf, and requested him to call at the governor's office in the morning, and get his commission. He thanked me most heartily, and said he would. [I think I see him doing it.]

I met another stranger before I got to the corner—a pompous little man with a crooked-handled cane and sorrel moustache. Says he, "How do you do, Mr. Twain—how do you do, sir? I am happy to see you, sir—very happy indeed, sir. My name is _____ _____. Pardon me, sir, but I perceive you do not entirely recollect me—I am J. Bidlecome Dusenberry, of Esmeralda, formerly of the city of New York, sir." "Well," says I, "I'm glad to meet you, Dysentery, and—"No, no Dusenberry, sir, Dusenberry!—you—" "Oh, I beg your pardon," says I; "Dusenberry—yes, I understand, now; but it's all the same, you know—Dusenberry, by any other name would—however, I see you have a bale of dry goods—for me, perhaps." He said it was only a little petition, and proceeded to show me a few acres of it, observing casually that he was the candidate in the notarial line—that he had read my lucumbrations (he called it all that) with absorbing interest, and he would like me to use my influence with the governor in his behalf. I assured him his commission would be ready for him as soon as it was signed. He appeared overcome with gratitude, and insisted, and insisted, and insisted, until at last I went and took a drink with him.

On the next corner I met Chief Justice Turner, on his way to the governor's office with a petition. He said, "God bless you, my dear fellow—I'm delighted to see you—" and hurried on, after receiving my solemn promise that he should be a Notary Public if I could secure his appointment. Next I met William Stewart, grinning in his engaging way, and stroking his prodigious whiskers from his nose to his stomach. Sandy Baldwin was with him, and they both had measureless petitions on a dray with the names all signed in their own handwriting. I knew those fellows pretty well and I didn't promise them my influence. I knew if the governor refused to appoint them, they would have an injunction on him in less than twenty-four hours, and stop the issuance of any more notary commissions. I met John B. Winters, next, and Judge North, and Mayor Arick, and Washoe Jim, and John O. Earl, and Ah Foo, and John H. Atchinson, and Hong Wo, and Wells Fargo, and Charley Strong, and Bob Morrow, and Gen. Williams, and seventy-two other prominent citizens of Storey County, with a long pack-train laden with their several petitions. I examined their documents, and promised to use my influence toward procuring notaryships for the whole tribe. I also drank with them.

    I wandered down the street, conversing with every man I met, examining his petition. It became a sort of monomania with me, and I kept it up for two hours with unflagging interest. Finally, I stumbled upon a pensive, travel-worn stranger, leaning against an awning-post. I went up and looked at him. He looked at me. I looked at him again, and again he looked at me. I bent my gaze upon him once more, and says I, "Well?" He looked at me very hard, and says he, "Well—" "Well what?" says I, "Well I would like to examine your petition, if you please."

    He looked very much astonished—I may say amazed. When he had recovered his presence of mind, he says "What the devil do you mean?" I explained to him that I only wanted to glance over his petition for a notaryship. He said he believed I was a lunatic—he didn't like the unhealthy light in my eye, and he didn't want me to come any closer to him. I asked him if he had escaped the epidemic, and he shuddered and said he didn't know of any epidemic. I pointed to the large placard on the wall: "Coaches will leave the Ormsby House punctually every fifteen minutes, for the governor's mansion, for the accommodation of Notorial aspirants, etc., etc.—Schemerhorn, Agent"—and I asked him if he didn't know enough to understand what that meant? I also pointed to the long procession of petition-laden citizens filing up the street toward the governor's house, and asked him if he was not aware that all those fellows were going after notarial commissions—that the balance of the people had already gone, and that he and I had the whole town to ourselves?

    He was astonished again. Then he placed his hand upon his heart, and swore a frightful oath that he had just arrived from over the mountains, and had no petition, and didn't want a notaryship. I gazed upon him a moment in silent rapture, and then clasped him to my breast. After which, I told him it was my turn to treat, by thunder. Whereupon, we entered a deserted saloon, and drank up its contents. We lay upon a billiard table in a torpid condition for many minutes, but at last my exile rose up and muttered in a sepulchral voice, "I feel it—O Heavens, I feel it in me veins!" "Feel what?" says I, alarmed. Says he, "I feel—O me sainted mother!—I feel—feel—a hankering to be a Notary Public!" And he tore down several yards of wall-paper, and fell to writing a petition on it. Poor devil—he had got it at last, and got it bad. I was seized with the fatal distemper a moment afterward. I wrote a petition with frantic haste, appended a copy of the Directory of Nevada Territory to it, and we fled down the deserted streets to the governor's office.

But I must draw the curtain upon these harrowing scenes—the memory of them scorches my brain. Ah, this legislature has much to answer for in cutting down the number of Notaries Public in this territory, with their infernal new law.

Virginia City Territorial Enterprise
February 12, 1864

Letter from Mark Twain

Carson City, February 5, 1864
Winters' New House

EDITORS ENTERPRISE: Theodore Winters' handsome dwelling in Washoe Valley is an eloquent witness in behalf of Mr. Steele's architectural skill. The basement story is built of brick, and the spacious court which surrounds it, and whose columns support the verandah above, is paved with large, old-fashioned tiles. On this floor is the kitchen, dining room, bathroom, bed-chambers for servants, and a commodious storeroom, with shelves laden with all manner of substantials and luxuries for the table.

All these apartments are arranged in the most convenient manner, and are fitted and furnished handsomely and plainly, but expensively. Water pipes are numerous in this part of the house, and the fluid they carry is very pure, and cold and clear. On the next floor above, are two unusually large drawing rooms, richly furnished, and gotten up in every respect with faultless taste which is a remark one is seldom enabled to apply to parlors and drawing-rooms on this coast. The colors in the carpets, curtains, etc., are of a warm and cheerful nature, but there is nothing gaudy about them. The ceilings are decorated with pure, white mouldings of graceful pattern. Two large bed-chambers adjoin the parlors, and are supplied with elaborately carved black walnut four-hundred-dollar bedsteads, similar to those used by Dan and myself in Virginia; the remainder of the furniture of these chambers is correspondingly sumptuous and expensive.

On the floor above are half a dozen comfortable bedrooms for the accommodation of visitors; also a spacious billiard room which will shortly be graced by a table of superb workmanship. The windows of the house are of the "Gothic" style, and set with stained glass; the chandeliers are of bronze; the stair railings of polished black walnut, and the principal doors of some kind of dark-colored wood—mahogany, I suppose. There are two peculiarly pleasant features about this house: the ceilings are high, and the halls of unusual width. The building—above the basement story—is of wood, and strongly and compactly put together. It stands upon tolerably high ground, and from its handsome verandah, Mr. Winters can see every portion of his vast farm. From the stables to the parlors, the house and its belongings is a model of comfort, convenience and substantial elegance; everything is of the best that could be had, and there is no circus flummery visible about the establishment.

I went out there to a party a short time ago, in the night, behind a pair of Cormack's fast horses, with John James. On account of losing the trail of the telegraph poles, we wandered out among the shingle machines in the Sierras, and were delayed several hours. We arrived in time, however, to take a large share in the festivities which were being indulged in by the governor and the Supreme Court and some twenty other guests. The party was given by Messrs. Joe Winters and Pete Hopkins (at Theodore Winters' expense) as a slight testimonial of their regard for the friends they invited to be present. There was nothing to detract from the pleasure of the occasion, except Lovejoy, who detracted most of the wines and liquors from it.

An Excellent School

I expect Mr. Lawlor keeps the best private school in the territory—or the best school of any kind, for that matter. I attended one of his monthly examinations a week ago, or such a matter, with Mr. Clagett, and we arrived at the conclusion that one might acquire a good college education there within the space of six months. Mr. Lawlor's is a little crib of a schoolhouse, papered from door to ceiling with black-boards adorned with impossible mathematical propositions done in white chalk. The effect is bewildering to the stranger, but otherwise he will find the place comfortable enough. When we arrived, the teacher was talking in a rambling way upon a great many subjects, like a member of the

House speaking to a point of order, and three boys were making verbatim reports of his remarks in Graham's phonographic short-hand on the walls of the school-room. These pupils had devoted half an hour to the study and practice of this accomplishment every day for the past four or five months, and the result was a proficiency usually attained only after eighteen months of application. It was amazing.

Mr. Lawlor has so simplified the art of teaching in every department of instruction, that I am confident he could impart a thorough education in a short time to any individual who has as much as a spoonful of brains to work upon. It is in no spirit of extravagance that I set it down here as my serious conviction that Mr. Lawlor could even take one of our Miss Nancy "Meriden" Prosecuting Attorneys and post him up so in a month or two he could tell his own witnesses from those of the defense in nine cases out of ten. Mind, I do not give this as an absolute certainty, but merely as an opinion of mine and one which is open to grave doubts too, I am willing to confess, now when I come to think calmly and dispassionately about it.

No—the truth is, the more I think of it, the more I weaken. I expect I spoke too soon—went off before I was primed, as it were. With your permission, I will take it all back. I know two or three prosecuting attorneys, and I am satisfied the foul density of their intellects would put out any intellectual candle that Mr. Lawlor could lower into them. I do not say that a Higher Power could not miraculously illuminate them. No, I only say I would rather see it first. A man always has more confidence in a thing after he has seen it, you know; at least that is the way with me.

But to proceed with that school. Mr. Clagett invited one of those phonographic boys—Master Barry Ashim—to come and practice his shorthand in the House of Representatives. He accepted the invitation, and in accordance with resolutions offered by Messrs. Clagett and Stewart, he was tendered the compliment of a seat on the floor of the House during the session, and the Sergeant-at-Arms instructed to furnish him with a desk and such stationery as he might require. He has already become a reporter of no small pretensions. There is a class in Mr. Lawlor's school composed of children three months old and upwards, who know the spelling book by heart. If you ask them what the first word is, in any given lesson, they will tell you in a moment, and then go on and spell every word (thirty-five) in the lesson, without once referring to the book or making a mistake. Again, you may mention a word and they will tell you which particular lesson it is in, and what words precede it and follow it. Then, again, you may propound an abstruse grammatical enigma, and the school will solve it in chorus—will tell you what language is correct, and what isn't; and why and wherefore; and quote rules and illustrations until you wish you hadn't said anything. Two or three doses of this kind will convince a man that there are youngsters in this school who know everything about grammar that can be learned, and what is just as important, can explain what they know so that other people can understand it.

But when those fellows get to figuring, let second-rate mathematicians stand from under! For behold, it is their strong suit. They work miracles on a blackboard with a piece of chalk. Witchcraft and sleight-of-hand and all that sort of thing is foolishness to the facility with which they can figure a moral impossibility down to an infallible result. They only require about a dozen figures to do a sum which by all ordinary methods would consume a hundred and fifty. These fellows could cypher a week on a sheet of foolscap. They can find out anything they want to with figures, and they are very quick about it, too. You tell them, for instance, that you were born in such and such a place, on such and such a day of the month, in such and such a year, and they will tell you in an instant how old your grandmother is. I have never seen any banker's clerks who could begin to cypher with those boys. It has been Virginia's unchristian policy to grab everything that was of any account that ever came into the territory—Virginia could do many a worse thing than to grab this school and move it into the shadow of Mount Davidson, teacher and all.

Concerning Undertakers

There is a system of extortion going on here which is absolutely terrific, and I wonder the *Carson Independent* has never ventilated the subject. There seems to be only one undertaker in the town, and he owns the only graveyard in which it is at all high-toned or aristocratic to be buried. Consequently, when a man loses his wife or his child, or his mother, this undertaker makes him sweat for it. I appeal to those whose firesides death has made desolate during the few fatal weeks just past, if I am not speaking the truth. Does not this undertaker take advantage of that unfortunate delicacy which prevents a man from disputing an unjust bill for services rendered in burying the dead, to extort ten-fold more than his labors are worth? I have conversed with a good many citizens on this subject, and they all say the same thing: that they know it is wrong that a man should be unmercifully fleeced under such circumstances, but, according to the solemn etiquette above referred to, he cannot help himself.

All that sounds very absurd to me. I have a human distaste for death, as applied to myself, but I see nothing very solemn about it as applied to anybody—it is more to be dreaded than a birth or a marriage, perhaps, but it is really not as solemn a matter as either of these, when you come to take a rational, practical view of the case. Therefore I would prefer to know that an undertaker's bill was a just one before I paid it; and I would rather see it go clear to the Supreme Court of the United States, if I could afford the luxury, than pay it if it were distinguished for its unjustness.

A great many people in the world do not think as I do about these things. But I care nothing for that. The knowledge that I am right is sufficient for me. This undertaker charges a hundred and fifty dollars for a pine coffin that cost him twenty or thirty, and fifty dollars for a grave that did not cost him ten—and this at a time when his ghastly services are required at least seven times a week. I gather these facts from some of the best citizens of Carson, and I can publish their names at any moment if you want them. What Carson needs is a few more undertakers—there is vacant land enough here for a thousand cemeteries.

Virginia City Territorial Enterprise
c. February 9, 1864

Legislative Proceedings

House—Twenty-Eighth Day

Carson, February 8, 1864

This bill appears—to a man up a tree—to be a bill of sale of Nevada Territory to the California State Telegraph Company. They never print this kind of bill—wherefore I shall have to copy it myself for you. It flashed through the House under a suspension of the rules, before you could wink, they tell me. It provides that Mr. Watson (his other name is the California State Telegraph Company) shall have the exclusive right to connect Star, Unionville, Austin, Virginia, Gold Hill, Carson, etc., etc., with Sacramento and San Francisco, and nobody else shall be permitted to do likewise, for five years after this line is completed, and with a liberal length of time allowed Mr. Watson in which to get ready to begin to commence completing it. To have all the telegraph lines in the hands of one Company, makes it a little binding on newspapers and other people—MARK.

Virginia City Territorial Enterprise
c. February 10, 1864

Legislative Proceedings

House—Twenty-Ninth Day

Carson, February 9

 I see you want the ayes and noes on all important measures. Long ago I got a batch of roll-calls and prepared to post the people concerning the final action of this body upon the various bills presented. But I got tired of it. I found the House too unanimous; they always voted aye, and I discovered that the list of noes was a useless encumbrance to the roll-call. Now when an important measure passes this House, and I neglect the roll-call, that need be no excuse for your doing the same thing; just publish the list of members and say they voted "aye"—you'll be about right.

 The thing is done thus: When a bill is on its final passage, and a member hears his name called, he rouses up and asks what's going on? The Speaker says, by way of information, "Third reading of a bill, sir." The member says, "Oh!—well, I vote aye," and becomes torpid again at once. Now, concerning that infamous telegraph monstrosity, it passed to its third reading in this House on the 4th of February. Messrs. Babcock, Dixson, Gray and Stewart were absent, and had no opportunity of voting aye but all the balance voted affirmatively, of course, as follows: AYES—Messrs. Barclay, Brumfield, Calder, Clagett, Curler, Deane, Elliott, Fisher, Gillespie, Gove, Heaton, Hess, Hunter, Jones, McDonald, Nelson, Phillips, Requa, Tennant, Trask, Ungar and Mr. Speaker.
 NOES—None.

Virginia City Territorial Enterprise
c. February 11, 1864

Legislative Proceedings

House—Tuesday Afternoon

Carson, February 10

The House then went into Committee of the Whole on the special order—Mr. Fisher in the Chair—and took up the first bill on the list. [Some seventy-five ladies have swarmed into the House, and the process of swarming still continues. I have a presentiment that I am to have an exhaustless stream of weak platitudes inflicted upon me by Young Gillespie and other unmarried members—MARK.]

Virginia City Territorial Enterprise
c. February 12, 1864

Legislative Proceedings

House—Thirty-First Day

Carson, February 11

The House met at 10 A.M. Present, 18. Absent, Messrs. Clagett, Dixson, Gillespie, Phillips, Stewart and Ungar.

Questions of Privilege

Mr. Heaton rose to a question of privilege, and said he was reported in the ENTERPRISE as having moved that the Committee of the Whole recommend the rejection of Miss Clapp's Seminary bill. That was a mistake. He said his motion was to refer the bill back to the Standing Committee on Colleges and Common Schools. [I suppose that is true; I do not consider myself responsible for mistakes made when the House is full of beautiful women, who are writing tender notes to me all the time and expecting me to answer them. In cases of this kind, I would just as soon misrepresent a member as any other way—MARK] Mr. Heaton was easy on the reporters, but he was very severe on Mr. Gillespie. He said it would appear from the report that Mr. Gillespie included him among those members who had dodged the issue on the telegraph bill—whereas he was absent from the House, by permission of the Speaker, with the Prison Committee.

The Speaker said there was nothing incorrect about the report—that Mr. Heaton was shielded from Mr. Gillespie's insinuation by a preceding paragraph, which stated the fact that he had been excused from attendance.

Whereupon Jefferson's Manual arose, the same being known on the credit accounts of the several saloons as "Young Gillespie"—and proceeded to waste the time of the House, as usual, in dilating upon some trivial distinction without a difference. [He was after the reporter of the ENTERPRISE, in the first place, but before I could catch his drift, he fell a victim to his old regular "parliamentary usage" dysentery—passed his brains, and became a smiling, sociable, driveling lunatic. Consequently, I failed to find out what I had been doing to young Gillespie, after all—MARK TWAIN.]

House—Afternoon Session

MESSAGE

A message was received from the Council, transmitting the following bills:

Council bill incorporating the Austin Christian Association. [The Speaker was at a loss to know what committee to refer a bill of such an unusual nature to—wherein his head was level. He finally referred it to the Lander delegation, two of the most faithful and consistent supporters of the Devil there are in the House—MARK.]

Council bill for the relief of certain parties. Referred to the Committee on Claims.

At 5 P.M. the House adjourned until 6:30 P.M.

[While I was absent a moment, yesterday, on important business, taking a drink, the House, with its accustomed engaging unanimity, knocked one of my pet bills higher than a kite, without a dissenting voice. I convened the members in extra session last night, and deluged them with blasphemy, after which I entered into a solemn compact with them, whereby, in consideration of their re-instating my bill, I was to make an ample apology for all the mean things I had said about them for passing that infamous, unchristian, infernal telegraph bill the other day. I also promised to apologize for all the mean things that other people had published against them for their depraved action aforesaid. They reinstated my pet today, unanimously, thus fulfilling their contract to the letter, and in conformity with my promise above referred to, I hereby solemnly apologize for their rascally conduct in passing the infamous telegraph bill above mentioned. Under ordinary circumstances, they never would have done such a thing—but upon that occasion I think they had been fraternizing with Clagett and Simmons at the White House, and were under the vicious influence of Humboldt whisky. Consequently, they were not responsible, Sir—they were not responsible, either to anybody on earth or in heaven—MARK TWAIN.]

Virginia City Territorial Enterprise
c. February 13, 1864

Legislative Proceedings

House—Friday Afternoon

Carson, February 12

An Act to amend an Act relating to game and fish. The passage of this bill was also recommended. [It provides that trout shall neither be caught in this Territory, nor exposed for sale, between the first of January and the first of April, under a penalty of $25 for each fish caught, killed or destroyed, or bought, sold or exposed for sale. The Act goes into effect on the first of the coming March, and therefore it would be well to publish it for the information of the people. It is a good law, and calls our lake by its right name Lake Bigler—and rejects the spooney appellation of "Tahoe," which signifieth "grasshopper" in the Digger tongue, and "breech clout" in the Washoe lingo. Bigler is the legitimate name of the Lake, and it will be retained until some name less flat, insipid and spooney than "Tahoe" is invented for it. I am sorry, myself, that it was not called in the first place by some cognomen that could be persuaded to rhyme with something, because, you see, every sentimental cuss who goes up there and becomes pregnant with a poem invariably miscarries because of the unfortunate difficulty I have just mentioned. I speak of the matter lightly, but it is not a frivolous one, for all that. A very beautiful thing was once written by a distinguished English poet about our royal river at home, but the loveliness was all mashed out of it by the stress of weather to which he was obliged to succumb in order to gouge a rhyme out of its name. He had to call it "Mississip"!—MARK.]

Virginia City Territorial Enterprise
c. February 14, 1864

Legislative Proceedings

House—Saturday Afternoon

Carson, February 13

An Act to incorporate the Virginia, Gold Hill, Washoe and Carson railroad.
[More railroads, you observe. The Council killed the Virginia and Dayton Railroad bill the other day. That franchise was well guarded, and the road would have been built. Will this, or any of the others?—REP.]
Mr. Barclay moved to lay the bill on the table. Lost.
The bill then passed by the following vote: [ayes 11, noes 9].

Virginia City Territorial Enterprise
c. February 14, 1864

Letter from Mark Twain

Carson City, February 13, 1864
The Carson Undertaker—Continued

EDITORS ENTERPRISE: The *Independent* takes hold of a wretched public evil and shakes it and bullyrags it in the following determined and spirited manner this morning:
"Our friend, Mark Twain, is such a joker that we cannot tell when he is really in earnest. He says in his last letter to the ENTERPRISE that our undertaker charges exorbitantly for his services—as

much as $150 for a pine coffin, and $50 for a grave and is astonished that the *Independent* has not, ere this, said something about this extortion. As yet we have had no occasion for a coffin or a bit of ground for grave purposes, and therefore know nothing about the price of such things. If any of our citizens think they have been imposed upon in this particular, it is their duty to ventilate the matter. We have heard no complaints."

That first sentence is false, and that clause in the second, which refers to the *Independent*, is false, also. I knew better than to be astonished when I wrote it. Unfortunately for the public of Carson, both propositions in the third sentence are true. Having had no use for a coffin himself, the editor "therefore knows nothing about the price of such things." It is my unsolicited opinion that he knows very little about anything. And anybody who will read his paper calmly and dispassionately for a week will endorse that opinion. And more especially his knowing nothing about Carson, is not surprising; he seldom mentions that town in his paper. If the Second advent were to occur here, you would hear of it first in some other newspaper. He says, "If any of our citizens think they have been imposed upon in this particular, it is their duty to ventilate the latter." It is their duty—the duty of the citizens—to ferret out abuses and correct them, is it? Correct them through your advertising columns and pay for it—is that it? And then turn to your second page and find one of your insipid chalk-milk editorials, defending the abuse and apologizing for the perpetrator of it; or when public sentiment is too well established on the subject, pretending, as in the above case, that you are the only man in the community who don't know anything about it.

Where did you get your notion of the duties of a journalist from? Any editor in the world will say it is your duty to ferret out these abuses, and your duty to correct them. What are you paid for? What use are you to the community? What are you fit for as conductor of a newspaper, if you cannot do these things? Are you paid to know nothing, and keep on writing about it every day? How long do you suppose such a jack-legged newspaper as yours would be supported or tolerated in Carson, if you had a rival no larger than a foolscap sheet, but with something in it, and whose editor would know, or at least have energy enough to find out, whether a neighboring paper abused one of the citizens justly or unjustly?

That paragraph which I have copied, seems to mean one thing, while in reality it means another. Its true translation is, for instance: "Our name is Independent—that is, in different phrase, Opinionless. We have no opinions on any subject—we reside permanently on the fence. In order to have no opinions, it is necessary that we should know nothing—

therefore, if this undertaker is fleecing the people, we will not know it, and then we shall not offend him. We have heard no complaints, and we shall make no inquiries, lest we do hear some."

Now, when I published a sarcasm upon the San Francisco Water Company, and the iniquity of "cooking dividends," some time ago, in the attractive form of a massacre at Dutch Nick's, by an irresponsible crazy man, this lively *Independent* came after me with the spirit of Old Hopkins strong upon him, and launched at me the red bolts of its virtuous wrath for bringing the high mission of journalism into disrepute for leading the citizens of California to believe that the murderous proclivities of this people were more extensive than they really were, or, in other words, creating the impression abroad that we were all lunatics and liable to slay and destroy one another upon the slightest provocation.

I did not reply to that, because I took it to be the fellow's honest opinion; and being his honest opinion, it was his duty to express it, whether it galled me or not. But he has permitted so many greater wrongs to pass unnoticed since then, that I have arrived at the conclusion that he only did it to modify the circulation of the ENTERPRISE hereabouts. I should be sorry to think he did it to procure my discharge. He would not, if he knew I was an orphan. Yet the same eyes that saw a great public wrong in that article on the massacre, willfully see no wrong in this undertaker's impoverishing charges for burying people—charges which are made simply because, from the nature of the service rendered, a man dare not demur to their payment, lest the fact be talked of around town and he be disgraced. Oh, your Independent is a consistent, harmless, non-committal sheet. I never saw a paper of that non-committal name that wasn't. Even the religious papers bearing it give a decided, whole-souled support to neither the Almighty nor the Devil.

The editor of the *Independent* says he don't know anything about this undertaker business. If he would go and report a while for some responsible newspaper, he would learn the knack of finding out things. Now if he wants to know that the undertaker charged three or four prices for a coffin (the late Mr. Nash's) upon one occasion, and then refused to let it go out of his hands, when the funeral was waiting, until it was paid for, although the estate was good for it, being worth $20,000—let him go and ask Jack Harris. If he wants any amount of information, let him inquire of Curry, or Pete Hopkins, or Judge Wright. Stuff! let him ask any man he meets in the street—the matter is as universal a topic of conversation here as is the subject of "feet" in Virginia. But I don't suppose you want to know anything about it. I want to shed one more unsolicited opinion, which is that your *Independent* is the deadest, flattest, [most] worthless thing I know—and I imagine my cold, unsmiling undertaker has his hungry eye upon it.

Mr. Curry says if the people will come forward and take hold of the matter, a city cemetery can be prepared and fenced in a week, and at a trivial cost—a cemetery from which a man can set out for Paradise or perdition just as respectably as he can from the undertaker's private grounds at present. Another undertaker can then be invited to come and take charge of the business. Mr. Curry is right—and no man can move in the matter with greater effect than himself. Let the reform be instituted.

Virginia City Territorial Enterprise
c. February 16, 1864

Legislative Proceedings

House—Thirty-Fifth Day

Carson, February 15

At one o'clock this morning, as Mr. Gray, barkeeper at Bingham's, was leaving the saloon with his cash box in his hand, two men jumped out from the shadow of a door, enveloped him in a blanket, and seized the box. Gray held on to the property until the handle came off, and then, having no pistol, shouted with good enough effect to attract the attention of two foot passengers who had. These gentlemen opened a brisk fire on the retreating highwaymen—sent eight or ten navy balls after them—caused them to observe, plaintively, "O God!" and drop the box. All the dogs in town woke up and barked—they always do on such occasions, but they never bite, and they are opposed to chasing highwaymen—so the same escaped. Mr. Gray recovered the box, of course, which contained about one thousand dollars—MARK.

You have got a mighty responsible delegation here from Storey County. As Mr. Curler remarked the other day, "When you put your finger on that delegation, as a general thing, they ain't there." I believe you. In the face of a notice given last Saturday by Mr. Clagett, of the introduction of a little bill to remove the Capital to Virginia—in the face of it, I say, only one member from Storey, out of eight, was present when the proper time arrived this morning for the introduction of the bill. Mr. Elliott was present—he always is, for that matter, and always awake. It has been a good thing for the whole Territory, on more than one occasion, that he was at his post in this House. One member was present—seven were absent: Messrs. Gillespie, Heaton, Nelson, Phillips, Requa, Ungar and Barclay. Several of these gentlemen arrived an hour after the order for the introduction of bills had been passed. Now if the people of Storey do not want the Capital, it was the duty of these members, since they knew the question was before the House, to be on hand to use their best efforts to kill the bill—and if the people do want the Capital, then it was the duty of those members to be here and do what they could toward securing it.

Above all things, they had no business to be absent at such a time. They knew what was going on, and they knew, moreover, that the fact that they have been pretty regular in their attendance when toll-roads were to be voted on, will indifferently palliate the offense of being absent upon this occasion. Last session Storey offered an immense price for the capital, and nothing in the world could have kept her from getting it but her own delegation. They kept her from it, though. Mr. Burke was absent. His vote, at the proper time, would have moved the Capital—and in the meantime, Mr. Tuttle, of Douglas, was brought from a sick bed to vote no. I suppose this bill will be introduced to-morrow (Tuesday) morning, at 10 o'clock—and I suppose some of the Storey delegation will be absent again. But if you want the roll-call tomorrow, you can have it. I have made a mistake. Mr. Gillespie came in this morning before the introduction of bills, though he was absent at an earlier hour, when the roll was called—MARK.

Virginia City Territorial Enterprise
February 16, 1864

The Removal of the Capital

EDITORS ENTERPRISE: I have just returned from the Capital, where I have been a Legislative spectator for a while. The strongest conviction which the experience of my visit forced upon my mind was that the Capital ought to be removed from Carson City.

I think you would be of my opinion if you could see with your own eyes, and hear with your own ears, the doings of the Legislature for a few days.

My first and best reason for thinking the Capital ought to be removed is, that while it remains in Carson, the Legislative Assembly is beyond the pale of newspaper criticism—beyond its restraining influence, and consequently beyond the jurisdiction of the people, in a manner, since the people are left in ignorance of what their servants are doing, and cannot protest against their acts until it is too late. Your reports of proceedings take up as much room in the city papers as can well be spared, I suppose, and they are ample enough for all intents and purposes—or rather, they would be, if the Virginia newspapers could stay in Carson and criticize these proceedings, and also the members, editorially, occasionally.

A mere skeleton report carries but an indifferent conception of the transactions of a Legislative body to the minds of the people. For instance, in the style and after the manner of one of these synopses: Mr. Stewart gave notice of a bill entitled an Act to audit the claim of D. J. Gasherie. A day or so afterward, we learn that according to former notice, Mr. Stewart introduced his bill. You hear of it again in some committee report. And again, as having been reported "favorably" by a Committee of the Whole. Next, your report says Mr. Stewart's bill passed by so many ayes, and so many noes. The work is done; none of your readers have the slightest idea what Mr. Gasherie's claim was for, and neither does one of them imagine himself even remotely interested in knowing anything about it. Yet the chief portion of your readers, I take it, were very particularly interested in that bill—because they will have to contribute money from their own pockets to pay Mr. Gasherie's claim; and they were further interested, on general principles, because the passage of that bill inflicted a great wrong upon the Territory.

Now, if the Legislature had been in session in Virginia, under the eyes of the press, instead of those of six or seven idle lobby members, I doubt if Mr. Stewart would have introduced the bill; I doubt if the Committee of the Whole would have presumed to consider it; I know the House and the Council would not have passed it. When Mr. Elliott rose in his place and objected that this was a bill to provide payment of a sum out of the Territorial Treasury, amounting to between $1,800 and $1,900, for the maintenance by Sheriff Gasherie, of several Ormsby County paupers, the newspapers would have promptly seconded him in the suggestion that Ormsby County maintain her own paupers, and pay the bill out of her own pocket. And when Mr. Stewart acknowledged the justness of the suggestion, but said Ormsby had bankrupted herself by purchasing a set of fine county buildings, and must therefore beg this favor at the hands of the people of the whole Territory, the newspapers would have known all about it, would have demurred, and the members, with a sense of responsibility thus forced upon them would have intentionally voted no upon the bill, instead of voting aye without really knowing, perhaps, what particular measure was before the House.

Moreover, several other outrageous laws, already passed, could never have been passed in Virginia. Twenty thousand dollars of the people's money have been asked for to build a seminary in Carson City and present it to two of her citizens—a private affair, and no more public in its character than Mr. Chauvel's fencing school here, and no more deserving of a Territorial appropriation of $20,000. Members were not wanting to vote for the measure, and to advocate it strongly. The bill would even have passed, probably, if Messrs. Clagett and Elliott had withheld their earnest opposition to it. Yet a bill to provide for the establishment and maintenance of a public mining college—a polytechnic school—has excited small interest among the members. They forget that a mining education can be best acquired here in the Territory—they forget, also, that the Seminary could offer no inducements of a similar nature, since our citizens, for many years to come, will prefer to educate their daughters at the inexpensive and efficient seminaries of Benicia, San Jose, and Santa Clara.

The Seminary bill was resurrected on Saturday, consolidated with the Polytechnic bill, $30,000 of public money added, and again brought before the Legislature. So—$20,000 for a building, and a tax of 1 percent on $30,000,000 of property, for "sundries." A crowd of young gentlemen and ladies in one building might affect the matter of public morals more than that of public education, I think. The school is not located in the bill, but the Ormsby delegation propose to have it established in Carson. The Governor is to appoint the trustees, and they are to fix upon a location, I believe. A mining school in a town fifteen miles from a mine would be a beneficial thing, in the abstract. Yet this $50,000 bill may pass, after all. So may the act to purchase Mr. Curry's prison for $80,000 more—$130,000 to Carson, by way of compensation for the stream of iniquitous private franchises which has been flowing from one or two members of her delegation during the entire session. Could these bills, unmodified, pass, if the people could be thoroughly posted as to their merits, by the press? I suppose not.

Clagett, Brumfield, Elliott, and two or three other intelligent, industrious and upright members have saved the credit of the Lower House, and protected the interests of the people, in nearly every case where it has been done at all—but they have received no commendation for it; neither have idle members, and members of easy integrity, been censured. It is because the people have been left in the dark as to who they ought to praise and who they ought to blame.

It was urged, last session, that Storey County was disposed to stow away, in her ravenous maw, everything that came in her way. That argument lost her the Capital, by one vote—that argument, and one other, which was a written pledge, on the part of Ormsby County, that if the Capital were permitted to remain in Carson, halls should be furnished for the use of the Legislature, free of charge. Storey County offered to erect capital buildings at her own expense, and move the officers and other governmental appurtenances within her lines, also at her own expense. Let Storey County make that proposition today, and it will be accepted. It is Ormsby County, now that is striving with extraordinary energy to swallow all public benefits—not Storey. And Ormsby has failed to redeem her pledge—for she has charged the Legislature $500 for the use of her courthouse, and after making the contract, is now dissatisfied because the granting of a greater sum is refused her.

Four members of one branch of the Legislature support the Specific Contract bill because it will result to their personal advantage, in sums varying from $1,000 to $4,000. More than that number have supported private franchises on personal pecuniary grounds. One member would vote $20,000 to the Seminary because he would reap an advantage, in dollars and cents, from the passage of the bill. Inasmuch as these statements come from the gentlemen referred to, themselves, they are entitled to full credence. If there could be a merit attached to a wrong motive, I think that merit might be considered to be the small amount of intelligence required to keep from telling about it. But all Legislators are not diplomats. Would it not be well to place the Assembly where the press, and through the press the people, could look after it?

Mr. Clagett gave notice, on Saturday, of an Act to remove the Capital, and the bill will probably be formally introduced today (Monday). If the people of Storey County want the seat of government in their midst, let them signify it promptly and cordially.

A LOOKER-ON

Virginia City Territorial Enterprise
c. February 17, 1864

Legislative Proceedings

House—Thirty-Sixth Day

Carson, February 16, 1864

Mayor Arick, Joe Goodman, George Birdsall, Young Harris, and other solid citizens of Virginia arrived at 3 this morning, having left home at midnight. They came down to see how the Capital question was going. Send a lot more down—the more the merrier, and the greater degree of interest is exhibited. Virginia seldom does things by halves—she generally comes out strong when she takes hold of a question.—MARK.

    Mr. McDonald moved a recess.

    Mr. Clagett hoped the motion would not prevail. He wished to go on with the regular business—introduction of bills etc. [Sensation among opponents to the removal of the Capital.]

    The motion was lost.

    Mr. Clagett moved a call of the House. [Numerous objections.] The motion was carried—ayes 7, noes 5.

    After a moment's delay, Mr. Dixson moved that further proceedings under the call be dispensed with. Lost.

    The absentees, Messrs. Ungar and Curler, were brought forward and excused, and further proceedings under the call were then dispensed with. Mr. Phillips moved a recess. Lost—ayes 9, noes 11.

    Mr. Clagett then, pursuant to previous notice, introduced an Act to locate permanently the Capital of the Territory. [At Virginia—that city to provide suitable buildings for 5 years at her own cost, before October 1, 1864—otherwise the Act to be null and void.]

    The bill was read in answer to numerous calls.

    Mr. Elliott moved that the rules be suspended and the bill engrossed for a third reading.

    Mr. Dixson strenuously objected, and said he couldn't see the object of rushing this bill through with such indecent haste. [Behold the virtuous member from Lander—the heart of the same being in Carson.—MARK.]

    Mr. Ungar moved to refer the bill to the Storey delegation, with instructions to report forthwith.

    Mr. Phillips moved to amend by substituting the Gold Hill portion of the Storey delegation.

    Mr. Clagett hoped the amendments would be rejected and Mr. Elliott's motion agreed to, and in his remarks called attention to the fact that Ormsby County made a written pledge last year that she would furnish free halls to the Legislature from and after that session—but had violated her pledge, inasmuch as those same County Commissioners have charged and received $500 for the halls now being used by the Assembly.

    Mr. Dixson did not want things rushed so—he wanted things printed; he didn't know anything about things, and he wanted time to gain information. He couldn't see what members meant by springing things in this way. [Emotion, indicative of the distress which a Lander member with his heart in Ormsby must naturally feel when he sees an attempt made to ravish Carson against her will.]

Mr. Dixson sat down weeping, and snuffling, and wiping his nose on his coat sleeve. [That's a joke of mine—he had a handkerchief with him.—MARK.]

Mr. Tennant called for the reading of Ormsby's pledge, and Mr. Clagett got it from Mr. Calder, and read it.

Mr. Stewart made an eloquent appeal in behalf of Ormsby County, and moved as a substitute to the three or four motions already before the House, that the bill be referred to a special committee, to consist of one member from each county, with instructions to report tomorrow morning. Carried; on a division—ayes 13, noes 4.

The Speaker appointed the committee as follows: Messrs. Clagett, Stewart, Curler, Dean, Elliott, Gove, McDonald, Tennant and Partridge.

Virginia City Territorial Enterprise
February 1864

Legislative Proceedings

House—Thirty-Seventh Day

CARSON, February 17

[Dallam, of the *Carson Independent*, makes a full and unqualified apology to me this morning—an entire column of it. He says he was not in his right mind at the time, and hardly ever is. Now, when a man comes out like that, and owns up with such pleasant candor, I think I ought to accept his apology. Consequently, we will call it square. It is flattering to me to observe that Dallam's editorials display great ability this morning, and that the paper shows an extraordinary degree of improvement in every respect. A becoming modesty should characterize us all—it is not for me to say who the credit is due to for the improvements mentioned. I only say I am glad to see the *Independent* looking healthy and vigorous again.—MARK.]

Petition

Mr. Stewart presented a petition, signed by most of the responsible citizens of Ormsby, he said, setting forth that it had just come to a knowledge of the fact that the Ormsby Commissioners had pledged free Legislative Halls, and violated that pledge. The petitioners promise that the rent money shall be at once refunded.

Mr. Stewart also presented a communication from the Secretary of the Territory acknowledging the receipt of the full amount of the rent money ($500) as paid over to him by the petitioners yesterday.

Mr. Stewart moved the reference of the two documents to the Special Committee on removal of the Capital.

Mr. McDonald objected that the Committee spoken of were ready now to report, according to instructions. He moved to lay the papers on the table, to be taken up at pleasure. Carried.

Question of Privilege

Mr. Stewart rose to a question of privilege, and spoke at considerable length upon two editorials in the ENTERPRISE in relation to the removal of the capital, and a communication upon the same subject in the same paper, written by one "Looker-On," but whom Mr. Stewart, with ghastly humor and with relentless and malignant irony, persisted in calling "Looker On or Hanger-On, I don't know which!" He said the Gasherie bill for supporting Ormsby County paupers, and which expense the Territory was asked to pay, only amounted to $877, instead of the large amount stated by the writer of the article!

[The amount being less, don't you see, the principle is not the same. Of course. Certainly. Wherefore? Why not? The gentleman's question of privilege was well taken. As long as the paupers did not cost, or propose to cost the Territory much, it was impertinent in a newspaper to mention it. That is the way Mr. Stewart and I look at it—MARK.]

Mr. Stewart said the balance of the money was cash paid out of Mr. Gasherie's own pocket in the catching of Territorial criminals, and of course as anybody would willingly acknowledge, it was the Territory's place to pay it.

Mr. Clagett, from the Special Committee on the removal of the capital, presented a majority report favoring the removal.

Mr. Stewart, from the same committee, presented a minority report recommending the indefinite postponement of the bill.

Mr. Dixson moved the reference of both reports to Committee of the Whole.

Mr. McDonald moved to amend by accepting the majority report. On a division, Mr. Dixson's motion prevailed—13 to 11.

Mr. Clagett called for the reading of the amendments recommended by the majority report, which was done. [Stipulates that Virginia shall also furnish Supreme Court rooms and Clerk's offices for five years—REP.]

Mr. Stewart moved that the Ormsby petition and the communication from the Secretary of the Territory be referred to Committee of the Whole. Carried.

Mr. Barclay moved a reconsideration of the vote by which the bill and the above documents were referred to Committee of the Whole. Lost by the following vote:

AYES—Messrs. Barclay, Clagett, Curler, Elliott, Gillespie, Heaton, McDonald, Nelson, Requa, Tennant, Ungar—11

NOES-Messrs. Brumfield, Calder, Dean, Dixson, Fisher, Gove, Hess, Hunter, Jones, Phillips, Stewart, Trask, Mr. Speaker—13.

Mr. Elliott moved that the Capital Bill be made the special order for tomorrow morning at 11 A.M. Lost by the following vote (required a two-thirds vote to carry):

AYES—Messrs. Barclay, Calder, Clagett, Elliott, Fisher, Gillespie, Heaton, McDonald, Nelson, Phillips, Requa, Tennant, Ungar and Mr. Speaker—14.

NOES—Messrs. Brumfield, Curler, Dean, Dixson, Gove, Hess, Hunter, Jones, Stewart and Trask—10.

Mr. Brumfield moved to change the time to 12 o'clock Saturday night (the moment when the Legislature adjourns finally).

Mr. Clagett opposed the motion.

Lost, by the following vote:

AYES—Messrs. Brumfield, Dean, Dixson, Gove, Hess, Hunter, Jones, Stewart—9.

NOES—Messrs. Barclay, Calder, Clagett, Curler, Elliott, Fisher, Gillespie, Heaton, McDonald, Nelson, Phillips, Requa, Tennant, Trask, Ungar, Mr. Speaker—16.

Mr. Clagett said that in order to stop this frittering away of valuable time, and in order to get a test vote, he would move that the bill be considered engrossed and ordered to a third reading. Carried by the following vote:

AYES—Messrs. Barclay, Brumfield, Calder, Curler, Clagett, Elliott, Fisher, Gillespie, Gove, Heaton, Hunter, Jones, McDonald, Nelson, Phillips, Requa, Stewart, Tennant, Trask, Ungar—20.

NOES—Messrs. Dean, Dixson, Hess, Mr. Speaker—4.

Mr. McDonald moved that the bill be read by title only. Carried.

FINAL PASSAGE OF THE CAPITAL BILL

The bill was accordingly read a third time by title, and finally passed, by the following vote:

AYES—Messrs. Barclay, Calder, Clagett, Curler, Elliott, Gillespie, Heaton, McDonald, Nelson, Requa, Tennant, Ungar and Mr. Speaker—13.

NOES—Messrs. Brumfield, Dean, Dixson, Fisher, Gove, Hess, Hunter, Jones, Phillips, Stewart and Trask—11.

Virginia City Territorial Enterprise
c. *February 19, 1864*

Legislative Proceedings

House—Thirty-Eighth Day

Carson, February 18, 1864

The Capital Question

Mr. Calder, according to previous notice, moved a reconsideration of the vote of yesterday, by which the Capital bill passed. He said his objections had been removed by the bond submitted by Mr. Stewart.

Mr. Clagett spoke at some length on the subject, in demonstration of the fact that a bond could not be drawn under such circumstances that would be valid and binding.

Mr. Brumfield replied rather warmly. In reply to the old argument about newspaper criticism which could be brought to bear on the Legislature if the Capital were in Virginia, he was especially bitter on the *Bulletin*—said he supposed it would be the favorite—that paper which was to have been teeming with mining taxation articles today, but was silent—had been purchased again, doubtless. As for the advantage a community might derive from the presence of the Capital, he couldn't appreciate the proposition; he didn't want the Capital at Virginia; he was going there to live, and he didn't want to be bothered with it. As to buying the Capital with the bond now before the House, neither Ormsby County nor the Legislature had a right to buy and sell the Capital.

After some further debate, Mr. Gillespie moved the previous question, which motion prevailed, and discussion was blockaded.

The motion to reconsider was then put and lost [!—REP.] by the following tie vote [clinching the thing as far as the House is concerned].

AYES—Messrs. Brumfield, Dean, Dixson, Fisher, Gove, Hess, Hunter, Jones, Phillips, Stewart and Trask—11

NOES—Messrs. Calder, Clagett, Curler, Elliott, Gillespie, Heaton, McDonald, Nelson, Tennant, Ungar and Mr. Speaker—11.

ABSENT—Mr. Requa—don't know whether he dodged or not.

DODGED THE ISSUE—Mr. Barclay.

After the above bully proceedings, and on motion of Mr. McDonald, the House took a recess until 2:30 P.M.

Thursday Afternoon

The Sergeant-at-Arms brought in Messrs. Dean, Phillips, Tennant, Jones, Gillespie and Ungar.

Mr. Dean had been talking over family matters. Mr. Phillips had been engineering a lawsuit. Mr. Tennant had been on committee business. Messrs. Jones and Gillespie were playing billiards, and Mr. Ungar's child was sick and he had been playing marbles with her.

Mr. Brumfield moved that Mr. Ungar be granted leave of absence to continue playing marbles with her. [Laughter.]

A motion to fine Mr. Gillespie a box of cigars for engaging in the unholy practice of playing billiards, was lost by a tie vote 10 to 10 [notwithstanding that youth has a remittance at Wells Fargo's from his creditors in Virginia, and which he denied the same—MARK.]

The absentees were all excused.

Virginia City Territorial Enterprise
c. February 20, 1864

Legislative Proceedings

Carson, February 19

Mr. Gillespie moved to reduce the Sergeant-at-Arms' salary to $9 per day, and strike out that portion which gives the reporters $7 per day.

Mr. Barclay said Mr. Gillespie was not so economical when he presented his own bill. Mr. Fisher said he ought to remember the verse,

"The mercy I to others show,
That mercy show to me."

Considering the mercy shown him by the House, his opposition comes with a bad grace from him.

[I feel called upon to observe that Mr. Gillespie got huffy—I would prefer to call it by a milder term, but I cannot conscientiously do so. Mr. Gillespie got huffy.—REP.]

After some further debate, Mr. Gillespie explained that there was no vindictiveness in him—all his motives were dictated from on high—from on high, sir!—[Tremendous applause.] He went on and made further and even more aggravatedly absurd remarks. Mr. Barclay said it was customary to pay the reporters.

Mr. Gillespie's motion in relation to the reporters was lost, by the following vote:

AYES—Messrs. Clagett, Gillespie, Hess, Hunter, Nelson, Phillips, Tennant and Trask—8. NOES—Messrs. Barclay, Brumfield, Calder, Curler, Dean, Dixson, Fisher, Gove, Heaton, Jones, McDonald, Stewart, Ungar and Mr. Speaker—15.

Council—Afternoon Session—Thirty-Ninth Day

Carson, February 19

Removal of the Capital

Mr. Daggett moved that the Capital bill be taken from the table. Mr. Coddington moved that the bill be indefinitely postponed.

Upon the latter's motion a lengthy discussion ensued. Mr. Daggett opposing, and Messrs. Curry, Coddington, Sturtevant, Negus and Hall supporting it.

Mr. Curry presented a communication from certain citizens of Carson City, binding themselves in the sum of $20,000, to furnish suitable halls and rooms for the Legislature and Territorial offices free of cost, provided that the Capital be allowed to remain at Carson City, while Nevada remained a Territory.

At the close of the debate, the motion to indefinitely postpone was carried by the following vote:

AYES—Messrs. Coddington, Curry, Negus, Sturtevant, Waldron, Mr. President.

NOES—Messrs. Daggett, Flagg, Sheldon, Thompson.

Virginia City Territorial Enterprise
c. February 21, 1864

Legislative Proceedings

House—Last Day—Fortieth

Carson, February 20

The Chaplain not being present, Mr. Fisher suggested that the Virginia reporter be requested to officiate in his place.

By courtesy of the House, the Virginia reporter was allowed to explain that he was not on it. [Excused.]

Mr. Phillips moved a call of the House. Carried.

Mr. Gillespie was produced before the bar of the House.

Mr. Brumfield moved, as the heaviest punishment that could be inflicted upon him, that he be denied the comfort of making a single motion for the space of an hour. [Laughter.]

Mr. Barclay moved that he be fined $5, and the same be paid to the Sergeant-at-Arms.

Mr. Phillips moved to amend by contributing the money to the Sanitary Fund.

The motions were lost.

Messrs. Dixson and Hunter were brought in and fined a box of cigars each.

The Sergeant-at-Arms said Mr. Clagett was sick in bed.

The Speaker said he must come anyhow.

Mr. Fisher wanted the editor of the *Independent* sent for. [Laughter.]

The Speaker said he did not think Mr. Clagett needed purging. [Laughter.]

Mr. Heaton came forward and was excused.

Notice

Mr. Stewart gave notice of an act to permanently locate the Capital on the South side of Capt. Pray's saw mill on Lake Tahoe, in Douglas County. [Sensation.]

[But nothing further appears in the record concerning this proposed bill.—H. N. S.]

A Message was received from the Council asking the return of the bill for the removal of the Capital. [Another of those grave Council jokes—REP.]

In view of these portentous symptoms, a call of the House was ordered.

After calling the roll, Mr. Stewart moved that further proceedings under the call be dispensed with.

The Chair decided the motion carried.

A motion to indefinitely postpone the Council message was lost—ayes 9, noes 11.

The motion to comply with the Council's request, carried—ayes 11, noes 8. [Confusion and contention—so to speak. The vote was even taken over again, with the following result:]

AYES—Messrs. Barclay, Calder, Clagett, Elliott, Gillespie, Heaton, McDonald, Nelson, Tennant, Ungar and Mr. Speaker—11.

NOES—Messrs. Brumfield, Curler, Dean, Dixson, Fisher, Gove, Hunter, Jones, Phillips, Stewart and Trask—11.

Mr. Speaker pro tem—Mr. Fisher—decided the motion lost.

Mr. Barclay wished to remind our worthy reporter that he didn't dodge the question this time. [His head is right. I cannot even swear that he dodged it before, with malice aforethought. Good authority says his absence before was unavoidable. I believe it. A man who votes as firmly as Mr. Barclay does for reporters against log-rolling members, would be apt to stick to his points upon all occasions when the same was possible. How's that?—REP.]

Saturday Afternoon

Council bill to amend the Act to prohibit gambling. The bill was read. [The Clerk pronounces the names of all games glibly, and without any perceptible foreign accent—REP.]

Saturday Night

[Mr. Stewart drew his everlasting toll-road on the House again. This has been the old regular result of every five minutes idleness to-day—REP.]

Third House

The institution resolved itself into a respectable body, as expressed in the above heading.

Mr. Thos. Hannah was elected assistant Clerk, and came forward and took the oath.

Mr. Clagett introduced a voluminous bill for the relief of certain citizens of Ormsby County. [It appropriates Curry's Warm Springs—gives it to these parties as a franchise for a swimming school—and—never mind, I will cease reporting and listen to the fun—REP.]

[The *Independent* of this morning touched upon Mr. Clagett's seeming repugnance to the use of the comb. On this hint, Mr. Barclay and other members of the House, had procured a prodigious wooden comb and conferred upon your servant the honor of presenting it—REP.]

Mr. Mark Twain inquired if testimonials were still in order, and received an affirmative reply from the Speaker. He arose in his place and addressed Mr. Clagett as follows—[Never mind publishing it again. I had no speech prepared, and therefore I was obliged to infringe upon etiquette to some extent—that is to say, I had to take Mr. Fisher's speech (apologizing to that gentleman, of course) and read it to Mr. Clagett, merely saying "comb" where the word "cane" occurred, and "legislator" in the place of "parliamentarian," and slinging in a few "as it were," and "so to speaks," etc., to add grace and vigor to the composition. I think I must be a pretty good reader—the audience appeared to admire Fisher's speech more when I delivered it than they did when he delivered it himself.]

Mr. Clagett received the testimonial, and replied felicitously—as he is wont to do. He concluded by saying it was a college practice to give the ugliest student a penknife, with instructions to give it to a man uglier than himself, if he should ever find one. He liked the idea—he thought it his duty to confer the comb upon some person whose hair needed its offices more than his own. [He passed it over to Mr. Hunter, of Washoe. Applause and Laughter.]

Baskets of wine were now brought in, with the compliments of Theodore Winters, President of the Washoe Agricultural, Mining and Mechanical Society, and the House rested awhile to drink health and prosperity to that gentleman.

Shortly after, other baskets were produced, per order, and at the expense of the Speaker, and the operation of drinking was further continued.

Hunter's Memorial

Mr. Hunter, by request, came forward and read a long, solemn, magnificent, hifalutin memorial about the mines, religion, chemistry, social etiquette, agriculture, and other matter proper to a document of this kind. The House applauded tempestuously—and laughed. They laughed immoderately. Why they did it, I cannot imagine, for I never heard an essay like this one before in my life. Now that is honest. Mr. Hunter finally got angry and refused to finish reading the discourse, but when it was explained to him that only lobby members had been laughing all the time he was satisfied, of course. I would like to hear the memorial read in Virginia.

Mr. Stewart, from the special Committee, reported that the Governor had no further communications to make.

Mr. Elliott offered a resolution that the House adjourn sine die at 11:30 P.M.

Mr. McDonald, true to his old regular motion [to adjourn] moved to amend by making the hour 12 P.M. The motion prevailed.

And from this time until midnight, fun ran high.

At 12 P.M. Mr. Speaker declared the House adjourned sine die.

The members went up to the Governor's and had a good time for an hour. The old man is as competent as any that walks, to make an evening pass pleasantly. Wine, music, anecdotes and sentiments composed the programme.

At 2 A.M. the exhilarated members closed the frolic by serenading the Speaker, at the White House.

Virginia City Territorial Enterprise
April 20, 1864

Frightful Accident to Dan De Quille

Our time-honored confrere, Dan, met with a disastrous accident, yesterday, while returning from American City on a vicious Spanish horse, the result of which accident is that at the present writing he is confined to his bed and suffering great bodily pain. He was coming down the road at the rate of a hundred miles an hour (as stated in his will, which he made shortly after the accident) and on turning a sharp corner, he suddenly hove in sight of a horse standing square across the channel; he signaled for the starboard, and put his helm down instantly, but too late, after all; he was swinging to port, and before he could straighten down, he swept like an avalanche against the transom of the strange craft; his larboard knee coming in contact with the rudder-post of the adversary, Dan was wrenched from his saddle and thrown some three hundred yards (according to his own statement, made in his will, above mentioned) alighting upon solid ground, and bursting himself open from the chin to the pit of the stomach. His head was also caved in out of sight, and his hat was afterwards extracted in a bloody and damaged condition from between his lungs; he must have bounced end-for-end after he struck first, because it is evident he received a concussion from the rear that broke his heart; one of his legs was jammed up in his body nearly to his throat, and the other so torn and mutilated that it pulled out when they attempted to lift him into the hearse which we had sent to the scene of the disaster, under the general impression that he might need it; both arms were indiscriminately broken up until they were jointed like a bamboo; the back was considerably fractured and bent into the shape of a rail fence. Aside from these injuries, however, he sustained no other damage. They brought some of him home in the hearse and the balance on a dray. His first remark showed that the powers of his great mind had not been impaired by the accident, nor his profound judgment destroyed—he said he wouldn't have cared a d—n if it had been anybody but himself. He then made his will, after which he set to work with that earnestness and singleness of purpose which have always distinguished him, to abuse the assemblage of anxious hash house proprietors who had called on business, and to repudiate their bills with his customary promptness and impartiality. Dan may have exaggerated the above details in some respects, but he charged us to report them thus, and it is a source of genuine pleasure to us to have the opportunity of doing it. Our noble old friend is recovering fast, and what is left of him will be around the Brewery again today, just as usual.

Virginia City Territorial Enterprise
April 28, 1864

Letter From Mark Twain

Carson City, April 25

EDS. ENTERPRISE: The road from Virginia to Carson—as traveled by Wilson's coaches—is in excellent condition, the same being neither muddy nor very dusty. The stages do not even stop to rest on the chalk hill.

We came by the penitentiary, but I did not consider it worth while to stop at the institution more than a few minutes, inasmuch as I had been in it before. Bob Howland, the Warden, was at his post, and I had sufficient confidence in him to leave him there. He is probably there yet. N.B.—When you journey in this direction, stop at the penitentiary and examine the native silver fish on exhibition there in the aquarium. They are caught in the Warm Springs. They are very like goldfish, only they are longer, and not so wide, and are white instead of yellow, and also differ from goldfish to some extent in the respect that they do not resemble them. This description may sound a little incoherent, but then I have set it down just as I got it from Bob Howland, in whom I have every confidence. Mr. Curry is erecting a handsome stone edifice at the Warm Springs, to be used as a hotel.

I heard in the stage, and also since I arrived here, that an organized effort will shortly be made to rescue Jaynes, the murderer, from the Storey County jail. Whether it be true or not, it will not be amiss to put the officers on their guard with a hint.

The Supreme Court began its session here today, and adjourned over until tomorrow, after hearing arguments for a new trial of Johnson for killing Horace Smith. The ground upon which a new trial is sought, is that some testimony was admitted upon the first trial in the District Court which should have been ruled out. I have spoken with District Attorney Corson on the subject, and he thinks the movement for a rehearing will not succeed. From present appearances, I think Alderman Earl will hold his seat for some time yet (if the sacred ambition to sit in a high place in spite of law and gospel to the contrary shall continue to animate him), as it has already been decided to submit his case, through the District and City Attorneys, to the District Court, and the long session now anticipated for the Supreme Court will doubtless delay his trial for some time. It would have been better, wouldn't it, for the Council to have declared his seat vacant, and allowed him to take legal steps for its restitution himself?

Governor Nye has not yet returned. It is said he will start back to Carson tomorrow.

Acting-Governor Clemens made a requisition upon H. F. Rice, Esq., a day or two since, for offices for the Secretary of the Territory, rent-free, in accordance with the contract entered into by certain citizens during the late session of the Legislature when the subject of removing the Capital to Virginia was agitated. The requisition was duly honored, and in the course of the week, handsome offices will be fitted up in the second story of the north end of the county buildings for the use of the Secretary and his clerks.

Mr. Colburn, or Coleman, or whatever his name is—the young man with a penchant for trying unique experiments, and who was accused of committing a rape on an infant here three years ago—is in trouble again. A young girl who alleges that he seduced her in California some time ago is over here suing him for damages in the Probate Court.

Your carrier here neglects some of his subscribers as often as two or three times a week, sometimes, or else his papers are stolen after he leaves them. Let the matter be attended to—the people hunger after Dan's intellectual rubbish.

The ladies gave a festival here last Friday for the benefit of my chronic brick church. The net proceeds amounted to upwards of $500, and will be applied to furnishing the edifice, which is still in a high state of preservation, and is gradually but surely becoming really ornamental. That is the church for the benefit of which I delivered a Governor's message once, and consequently I still take a religious interest in its welfare. I could sling a strong prayer for its prosperity, occasionally, if I thought it would do any good. However, perhaps it wouldn't—it would certainly be taking chances anyhow.

The ladies are making extraordinary preparations for a grand fancy-dress ball, to come off in the county buildings here on the 5th of May, for the benefit of the great St. Louis Sanitary Fair. The most pecuniary results are anticipated from it, and I imagine, from the interest that is being taken in the matter, the ladies of Gold Hill had better be looking to their laurels, lest the fame of their recent brilliant effort in the Sanitary line be dimmed somewhat by the financial achievements of this forthcoming ball.

The infernal telegraph monopoly saddled upon this Territory by the last Legislature, in the passage of that infamous special Humboldt telegraph bill, and afterwards clinched by a still more rascally enactment on the same occasion, is bearing its fruits, and the people here, as well as at Virginia, are beginning to wince under illegal and exorbitant telegraphic charges. They double the tariff allowed by law, and a man has to submit to the imposition, because he cannot afford the time and trouble of going to law for a trifle of five or ten dollars, notwithstanding the comfort and satisfaction he would derive from worrying the monopolists. The moment that law received the Governor's signature last winter, you will recollect the Telegraph Company doubled their prices for dispatches to and from San Francisco. And that is not the worst they have done, if common report be true. This common report says the telegraph is used by its owners to aid them in stock gambling schemes. I recollect that on the night the jury went out in the Savage and North Potosi case and failed to agree, our San Francisco dispatch failed to come to hand, and the reason assigned was that a dispatch of 3,000 words was being sent from Virginia to San Francisco and the line could not be used for other messages. Now that Telegraph Company may have made money by trading in North Potosi on that occasion, but who is young enough to believe they ever got two dollars and a half for that voluminous imaginary dispatch? That telegraph is a humbug. The Company are allowed to charge $3.50 for the first ten words across the continent, and must submit to a considerable deduction on longer dispatches—but they take the liberty of increasing that rate some thirty-five per cent, and people have to put up with it. Colonel Cradlebaugh tells me that last year, when he was a delegate at Washington from this Territory, they always charged him more for dispatches sent here than if they went through to California. The Government pays the Overland Telegraph Company $40,000 a year, with the understanding that Government messages are to pass over the lines free of charge—but I know of several dispatches of this character that were not permitted to leave the telegraph offices until they were paid for. It is properly the District Attorney's business to look after these telegraphic speculators, and that officer ought to be reminded of the fact. The next Grand Jury here will endeavor to make it interesting to the Telegraph Company.

  Gillespie's monument—the ratty old Agricultural Fair shanty—still rears its ghastly form in the plaza, and serves to remind me of that statesman's extraordinary career in the House of Representatives. It consisted in saving to his country the usual but extravagant sum of eight or ten dollars a day extra pay to Legislative reporters, and in making a speech in favor of the Sierra Seminary bill which had the effect of killing that really worthy measure. All through the session Gillespie was mighty handy about smashing the life out of any little incipient law that he chose to befriend, with one of his calamitous speeches. His vote was patent, too; his "nay" invariably passed a bill, and his "aye" was the deadest thing! [My language may be unrefined, but it has the virtue of being uncommonly strong.] But that monument in the plaza looks as hungry as Gillespie does himself, and much more unsightly, and I look for one of them to eat the other some day, if they ever get close enough together.

I depart for Silver Mountain in the Esmeralda stage at 7 o'clock tomorrow morning. It is the early bird that catches the worm, but I would not get up at that time in the morning for a thousand worms, if I were not obliged to.

Virginia City Territorial Enterprise
May 1, 1864

Washoe "Information Wanted"

Springfield, MO., April 12

"DEAR SIR—My object in writing to you is to have you give me a full history of Nevada: What is the character of its climate? What are the productions of the earth? Is it healthy? What diseases do they die of mostly? Do you think it would be advisable for a man who can make a living in Missouri to emigrate to that part of the country? There are several of us who would emigrate there in the spring if we could ascertain to a certainty that it is a much better country than this. I suppose you know Joel H. Smith? He used to live here; he lives in Nevada now; they say he owns considerable in a mine there. Hoping to hear from you soon, etc., I remain yours, truly,

WILLIAM _____.

DEAREST WILLIAM—Pardon my familiarity—but that name touchingly reminds me of the loved and lost, whose name was similar. I have taken the contract to answer your letter, and although we are now strangers, I feel we shall cease to be so if we ever become acquainted with each other. The thought is worthy of attention, William. I will now respond to your several propositions in the order in which you have fulminated them.

Your object in writing is to have me give you a full history of Nevada. The flattering confidence you repose in me, William, is only equalled by the modesty of your request. I could detail the history of Nevada in five hundred pages octavo, but as you have never done me any harm, I will spare you, though it will be apparent to everybody that I would be justified in taking advantage of you if I were a mind to do it.

However, I will condense. Nevada was discovered many years ago by the Mormons, and was called Carson County. It only became Nevada in 1861, by act of Congress. There is a popular tradition that God Almighty created it; but when you come to see it, William, you will think differently. Do not let that discourage you, though. The country looks something like a singed cat, owing to the scarcity of shrubbery, and also resembles that animal in the respect that it has more merits than its personal appearance would seem to indicate. The Grosch brothers found the first silver lead here in 1857. They also founded Silver City, I believe. (Observe the subtle joke, William.)

But the "history" of Nevada which you demand properly begins with the discovery of the Comstock lead, which event happened nearly five years ago. The opinion now prevailing in the East that the Comstock is on the Gould & Curry is erroneous; on the contrary, the Gould & Curry is on the Comstock. Please make the correction, William. Signify to your friends, also, that all the mines here do not pay dividends as yet; you may make this statement with the utmost unyielding inflexibility—it will not be contradicted from this quarter. The population of this Territory is about 35,000, one half of which number reside in the united cities of Virginia and Gold Hill. However, I will discontinue this history for the present, lest I get you too deeply interested in this distant land and cause you to neglect your family or your religion. But I will address you again upon the subject next year. In the meantime, allow me to answer your inquiry as to the character of our climate.

It has no character to speak of, William, and alas! in this respect it resembles many, ah, too many chambermaids in this wretched, wretched world. Sometimes we have the seasons in their regular order, and then again we have winter all the summer and summer all winter. Consequently, we have never yet come across an almanac that would just exactly fit this latitude. It is mighty regular about not raining, though, William. It will start in here in November and rain about four, and sometimes as much as seven days on a stretch; after that, you may loan out your umbrella for twelve months, with the serene confidence which a Christian feels in four aces. Sometimes the winter begins in November and winds up in June; and sometimes there is a bare suspicion of winter in March and April, and summer all the balance of the year. But as a general thing, William, the climate is good, what there is of it.

What are the productions of the earth? You mean in Nevada, of course. On our ranches here, anything can be raised that can be produced on the fertile fields of Missouri. But ranches are very scattering—as scattering, perhaps, as lawyers in heaven. Nevada, for the most part, is a barren waste of sand, embellished with melancholy sage-brush, and fenced in with snow clad mountains. But these ghastly features were the salvation of the land, William, for no rightly constituted American would have ever come here if the place had been easy of access, and none of our pioneers would have stayed after they got here if they had not felt satisfied that they could not find a smaller chance for making a living anywhere else. Such is man, William, as he crops out in America.

"Is it healthy?" Yes, I think it is as healthy here as it is in any part of the West. But never permit a question of that kind to vegetate in your brain, William, because as long as providence has an eye on you, you will not be likely to die until your time comes.

"What diseases do they die of mostly?" Well, they used to die of conical balls and cold steel, mostly, but here lately erysipelas and the intoxicating bowl have got the bulge on those things, as was very justly remarked by Mr. Rising last Sunday. I will observe, for your information, William, that Mr. Rising is our Episcopal minister, and has done as much as any man among us to redeem this community from its pristine state of semi-barbarism. We are afflicted with all the diseases incident to the same latitude in the States, I believe, with one or two added and half a dozen subtracted on account of our superior altitude. However, the doctors are about as successful here, both in killing and curing, as they are anywhere.

Now, as to whether it would be advisable for a man who can make a living in Missouri to emigrate to Nevada, I confess I am somewhat mixed. If you are not content in your present condition, it naturally follows that you would be entirely satisfied if you could make either more or less than a living. You would exult in the cheerful exhilaration always produced by a change. Well, you can find your opportunity here, where, if you retain your health, and are sober and industrious, you will inevitably make more than a living, and if you don't you won't. You can rely upon this statement, William. It contemplates any line of business except the selling of tracts. You cannot sell tracts here, William; the people take no interest in tracts; the very best efforts in the tract line—even with pictures on them—have met with no encouragement here. Besides, the newspapers have been interfering; a man gets his regular text or so from the Scriptures in his paper, along with the stock sales and the war news, every day, now. If you are in the tract business, William, take no chances on Washoe; but you can succeed at anything else here.

"I suppose you know Joel H. Smith?" Well—the fact is—I believe I don't. Now isn't that singular? Isn't it very singular? And he owns "considerable" in a mine here, too. Happy man. Actually owns in a mine here in Nevada Territory, and I never even heard of him. Strange—strange—do you know, William, it is the strangest thing that ever happened to me? And then he not only owns in a mine, but owns "considerable;" that is the strangest part about it—how a man could own considerable in a mine in Washoe and I not know anything about it. He is a lucky dog, though. But I strongly suspect that you have made a mistake in the name; I am confident you have; you mean John Smith—I know you do; I know it from the fact that he owns considerable in a mine here, because I sold him the property at a ruinous sacrifice on the very day he arrived here from over the plains. That man will be rich one of these days. I am just as well satisfied of it as I am of any precisely similar instance of the kind that has come under my notice. I said as much to him yesterday, and he said he was satisfied of it, also. But he did not say it with that air of triumphant exultation which a heart like mine so delights to behold in one to whom I have endeavored to be a benefactor in a small way. He looked pensive a while, but, finally, says he, "Do you know, I think I'd a been a rich man long ago if they'd ever found the d—d ledge?" That was my idea about it. I always thought, and I still think, that if they ever do find that ledge, his chances will be better than they are now. I guess Smith will be all right one of these centuries, if he keeps up his assessments—he is a young man yet.

Now, William, I have taken a liking to you, and I would like to sell you "considerable" in a mine in Washoe. I think I could get you a commanding interest in the "Union," Gold Hill, on easy terms. It is just the same as the "Yellow Jacket," which is one of the richest mines in the Territory. The title was in dispute between the two companies some two years ago, but that is all settled now. Let me hear from you on the subject. Greenbacks at par is as good a thing as I want. But seriously, William, don't you ever invest in a mining stock which you don't know anything about; beware of John Smith's experience.

You hope to hear from me soon? Very good. I shall also hope to hear from you soon, about that little matter above referred to. Now, William, ponder this epistle well; never mind the sarcasm, here and there, and the nonsense, but reflect upon the plain facts set forth, because they are facts, and are meant to be so understood and believed.

Remember me affectionately to your friends and relations, and especially to your venerable grandmother, with whom I have not the pleasure to be acquainted—but that is of no consequence, you know. I have been in your town many a time, and all the towns of the neighboring counties—the hotel keepers will recollect me vividly. Remember me to them—I bear them no animosity.

> Yours, affectionately,
> MARK TWAIN.

Virginia City Territorial Enterprise
May 24, 1864

Personal Correspondence

[I]
Enterprise Office
Saturday, May 21, 1864

JAMES LAIRD, ESQ.—Sir: In your paper of the present date appeared two anonymous articles, in which a series of insults were leveled at the writer of an editorial in Thursday's ENTERPRISE, headed "How is it?—How it is." I wrote that editorial.

Some time since it was stated in the *Virginia Union* that its proprietors were alone responsible for all articles published in its columns. You being the proper person, by seniority, to apply to in cases of this kind, I demand of you a public retraction of the insulting articles I have mentioned, or satisfaction. I require an immediate answer to this note. The bearer of this—Mr. Stephen Gillis—will receive any communication you may see fit to make.
SAM. L. CLEMENS

[II]
Office of the Virginia Daily Union
Virginia, May 21, 1864

SAMUEL CLEMENS, ESQ.—Mr. James Laird has just handed me your note of this date. Permit me to say that I am the author of the Article appearing in this morning's *Union*. I am responsible for it. I have nothing to retract. Respectfully,
J. W. WILMINGTON

[III]
Enterprise Office,
Saturday Evening, May 21, 1864

JAMES LAIRD, ESQ.—Sir:—I wrote you a note this afternoon demanding a published retraction of insults that appeared in two Articles in the *Union* of this morning—or satisfaction. I have since received what purports to be a reply, written by a person who signs himself "J. W. Wilmington," in which he assumes the authorship and responsibility of one of said infamous articles. Mr. Wilmington is a person entirely unknown to me in the matter, and has nothing to do with it. In the columns of your paper you have declared your own responsibility for all articles appearing in it, and any farther attempt to make a catspaw of any other individual and thus shirk a responsibility that you had previously assumed will show that you are a cowardly sneak. I now peremptorily demand of you the satisfaction due to a gentleman—without alternative.
SAM. L. CLEMENS

[IV]
Office of the Virginia Daily Union
Virginia, Saturday evening, May 21st, 1864

SAM'L. CLEMENS, ESQ:—Your note of this evening is received. To the first portion of it I will briefly reply, that Mr. J. W. Wilmington, the avowed author of the article to which you object, is a gentleman now in the employ of the *Union* office. He formerly was one of the proprietors of the *Cincinnati Enquirer*. He was Captain of a Company in the Sixth Ohio Regiment, and fought at Shiloh. His responsibility and character can be vouched for to your abundant satisfaction.

For all editorials appearing in the *Union*, the proprietors are personally responsible; for communications, they hold themselves ready, when properly called upon, either to give the name and address of the author, or failing that, to be themselves responsible.

The editorial in the ENTERPRISE headed "How is it?" out of which this controversy grew, was an attack made upon the printers of the *Union*. It was replied to by a *Union* printer, and a representative of the printers, who in a communication denounced the writer of that article as a liar, a poltroon and a puppy. You announce yourself as the writer of the article which provoked this communication, and demand "satisfaction"—which satisfaction the writer informs you, over his own signature, he is quite ready to afford. I have no right, under the rulings of the code you have invoked, to step in and assume Mr. Wilmington's position, nor would he allow me to do so. You demand of me, in your last letter, the satisfaction due to a gentleman, and couple the demand with offensive remarks. When you have earned the right to the title by complying with the usual custom, I shall be most happy to afford you any satisfaction you desire at any time and in any place. In short, Mr. Wilmington has a prior claim upon your attention. When he is through with you, I shall be at your service. If you decline to meet him after challenging him, you will prove yourself to be what he has charged you with being: "a liar, a poltroon and a puppy," and as such, cannot of course be entitled to the consideration of a gentleman.

    Respectfully,
    JAMES L. LAIRD

[V]
Enterprise Office, Virginia City
May 21, 1864—9 o'clock, P.M.

    JAMES L. LAIRD, ESQ.—Sir: Your reply to my last note in which I peremptorily demanded satisfaction of you, without alternative—is just received, and to my utter astonishment you still endeavor to shield your craven carcass behind the person of an individual who in spite of your introduction is entirely unknown to me, and upon whose shoulders you cannot throw the whole responsibility. You acknowledge and reaffirm in this note that "For all editorials appearing in the *Union*, the proprietors are personally responsible." Now, sir, had there appeared no editorial on the subject endorsing and reiterating the slanderous and disgraceful insults heaped upon me in the "communication," I would have simply called upon you and demanded the name of its author, and upon your answer would have depended my farther action. But the "Editorial" alluded to was equally vile and slanderous as the "communication," and being an "Editorial" would naturally have more weight in the minds of readers. It was the following undignified and abominably insulting slander appearing in your "Editorial" headed "The 'How is it' issue," that occasioned my sending you first an alternative and then a peremptory challenge:

    "Never before in a long period of newspaper intercourse—never before in any contact with a contemporary, however unprincipled he might have been, have we found an opponent in statement or in discussion, who had no gentlemanly sense of professional propriety, who conveyed in every word, and in every purpose of all his words, such a groveling disregard for truth, decency and courtesy as to seem to court the distinction, only, of being understood as a vulgar liar. Meeting one who prefers falsehood; whose instincts are all toward falsehood; whose thought is falsification; whose aim is vilification through insincere professions of honesty; one whose only merit is thus described, and who evidently desires to be thus known, the obstacles presented are entirely insurmountable, and whoever would touch them fully, should expect to be abominably defiled."—*Union*, May 21

You assume in your last note, that I "have challenged Mr. Wilmington," and that he has informed me "over his own signature" that he is quite ready to afford me "satisfaction." Both assumptions are utterly false. I have twice challenged you, and you have twice attempted to shirk the responsibility. Mr. W's note could not possibly be an answer to my demand of satisfaction from you; and besides, his note simply avowed authorship of a certain "communication" that appeared simultaneously with your libelous "editorial," and states that its author had "nothing to retract." For your gratification, however, I will remark that Mr. Wilmington's case will be attended to in due time by a distant acquaintance of his who is not willing to see him suffer in obscurity. In the meantime, if you do not wish yourself posted as a coward, you will at once accept my peremptory challenge, which I now reiterate.
SAM. L. CLEMENS

[VI]
Office Territorial Enterprise
Virginia, May 21, 1864

J. W. WILMINGTON—Sir: You are, perhaps, far from those who are wont to advise and care for you, else you would see the policy of minding your own business and letting that of other people alone. Under these circumstances, therefore, I take the liberty of suggesting that you are getting out of your sphere. A contemptible ass and coward like yourself should only meddle in the affairs of gentlemen when called upon to do so. I approve and endorse the course of my principal in this matter, and if your sensitive disposition is aroused by any proceeding of his, I have only to say that I can be found at the ENTERPRISE office, and always at your service.
S. E. GILLIS

[To the above, Mr. Wilmington gave a verbal reply to Mr. Millard—the gentleman through whom the note was conveyed to him—stating that he had no quarrel with Mr. Gillis; that he had written his communication only in defense of the craft, and did not desire a quarrel with a member of that craft; he showed Mr. G's note to Mr. Millard, who read it, but made no comments upon it.]

[VII]
Office of the Virginia Daily Union,
Monday Morning, May 23, 1864

SAMUEL CLEMENS, ESQ.:—In reply to your lengthy communication, I have only to say that in your note opening this correspondence, you demanded satisfaction for a communication in the *Union* which branded the writer of an article in the ENTERPRISE as a liar, a poltroon and a puppy. You declare yourself to be the writer of the ENTERPRISE article, and the avowed author of the *Union* communication stands ready to afford satisfaction. Any attempt to evade a meeting with him and force one upon me will utterly fail, as I have no right under the rulings of the code, to meet or hold any communication with you in this connection. The threat of being posted as a coward cannot have the slightest effect upon the position I have assumed in the matter. If you think this correspondence reflects credit upon you, I advise you by all means to publish it; in the meantime you must excuse me from receiving any more long epistles from you. JAMES L. LAIRD

I denounce Mr. Laird as an unmitigated liar, because he says I published an editorial in which I attacked the printers employed on the *Union*, whereas there is nothing in that editorial which can be so construed. Moreover, he is a liar on general principles, and from natural instinct. I denounce him as an abject coward, because it has been stated in his paper that its proprietors are responsible for all articles appearing in its columns, yet he backs down from that position; because he acknowledges the "code," but will not live up to it; because he says himself that he is responsible for all "editorials," and then backs down from that also; and because he insults me in his note marked "IV," and yet refuses to fight me. Finally, he is a fool, because he cannot understand that a publisher is bound to stand responsible for any and all articles printed by him, whether he wants to do it or not.

Virginia City Territorial Enterprise
May 24, 1864

"Miscegenation"

We published a rumor, the other day, that the moneys collected at the Carson Fancy Dress Ball were to be diverted from the Sanitary Fund and sent forward to aid a "miscegenation" or some other sort of Society in the East. We also stated that the rumor was a hoax. And it was—we were perfectly right. However, four ladies are offended. We cannot quarrel with ladies—the very thought of such a thing is repulsive; neither can we consent to offend them even unwittingly—without being sorry for the misfortune, and seeking their forgiveness, which is a kindness we hope they will not refuse. We intended no harm, as they would understand easily enough if they knew the history of this offense of ours, but we must suppress that history, since it would rather be amusing than otherwise, and the amusement would be at our expense. We have no love for that kind of amusement—and the same trait belongs to human nature generally. One lady complained that we should at least have answered the note they sent us. It is true. There is small excuse for our neglect of a common politeness like that, yet we venture to apologize for it, and will still hope for pardon, just the same. We have noticed one thing in this whole business—and also in many an instance which has gone before it—and that is, that we resemble the majority of our species in the respect that we are very apt to get entirely in the wrong, even when there is no seeming necessity for it; but to offset this vice, we claim one of the virtues of our species, which is that we are ready to repair such wrongs when we discover them.

Virginia City Territorial Enterprise
c. June 17, 1864

"Mark Twain" in the Metropolis

To a Christian who has toiled months and months in Washoe; whose hair bristles from a bed of sand, and whose soul is caked with a cement of alkali dust; whose nostrils know no perfume but the rank odor of sage-brush—and whose eyes know no landscape but barren mountains and desolate plains; where the winds blow, and the sun blisters, and the broken spirit of the contrite heart finds joy and peace only in Limburger cheese and lager beer—unto such a Christian, verily the Occidental Hotel is Heaven on the half shell. He may even secretly consider it to be Heaven on the entire shell, but his religion teaches a sound Washoe Christian that it would be sacrilege to say it.

Here you are expected to breakfast on salmon, fried oysters and other substantials from 6 till half-past 12; you are required to lunch on cold fowl and so forth, from half-past 12 until 3; you are obliged to skirmish through a dinner comprising such edibles as the world produces, and keep it up, from 3 until half-past 7; you are then compelled to lay siege to the tea-table from half-past 7 until 9 o'clock, at which hour, if you refuse to move upon the supper works and destroy oysters gotten up in all kinds of seductive styles until 12 o'clock, the landlord will certainly be offended, and you might as well move your trunk to some other establishment. [It is a pleasure to me to observe, incidentally, that I am on good terms with the landlord yet.]

Why don't you send Dan down into the Gould & Curry mine, to see whether it has petered out or not, and if so, when it will be likely to peter in again. The extraordinary decline of that stock has given rise to the wildest surmises in the way of accounting for it, but among the lot there is harm in but one, which is the expressed belief on the part of a few that the bottom has fallen out of the mine. Gould & Curry is climbing again, however.

It has been many a day since San Francisco has seen livelier times in her theatrical department than at present. Large audiences are to be found nightly at the Opera House, the Metropolitan, the Academy of Music, the American, the New Idea, and even the Museum, which is not as good a one as Barnum's. The Circus company, also, played a lucrative engagement, but they are gone on their travels now. The graceful, charming, clipper-built Ella Zoyara was very popular.

Miss Caroline Richings has played during the past fortnight at Maguire's Opera House to large and fashionable audiences, and has delighted them beyond measure with her sweet singing. It sounds improbable, perhaps, but the statement is true, nevertheless.

You will hear of the Metropolitan, now, from every visitor to Washoe. It opened under the management of the new lessees, Miss Annette Ince and Julia Dean Hayne, with a company who are as nearly all stars as it was possible to make it. For instance—Annette Ince, Emily Jordan, Mrs. Judah, Julia Dean Hayne, James H. Taylor, Frank Lawlor,

Harry Courtaine and Fred. Franks (my favorite Washoe tragedian, whose name they have put in small letters in the programme, when it deserves to be in capitals—because, whatever part they give him to play, don't he always play it well? and does he not possess the first virtue of a comedian, which is to do humorous things with grave decorum and without seeming to know that they are funny?)

The birds, and the flowers, and the Chinamen, and the winds, and the sunshine, and all things that go to make life happy, are present in San Francisco today, just as they are all days in the year. Therefore, one would expect to hear these things spoken of, and gratefully, and disagreeable matters of little consequence allowed to pass without comment. I say, one would suppose that. But don't you deceive yourself—anyone who supposes anything of the kind, supposes an absurdity. The multitude of pleasant things by which the people of San Francisco are surrounded are not talked of at all. No—they damn the wind, and they damn the dust, and they give all their attention to damning them well, and to all eternity. The blasted winds and the infernal dust—these alone form the eternal topics of conversation, and a mighty absurd topic it seems to one just out of Washoe. There isn't enough wind here to keep breath in my body, or dust enough to keep sand in my craw. But it is human nature to find fault—to overlook that which is pleasant to the eye, and seek after that which is distasteful to it. You take a stranger into the Bank Exchange and show him the magnificent picture of Sampson and Delilah, and what is the first object he notices?—Sampson's fine face and flaming eye? or the noble beauty of his form? or the lovely, half-nude Delilah? or the muscular Philistine behind Sampson, who is furtively admiring her charms? or the perfectly counterfeited folds of the rich drapery below her knees? or the symmetry and truth to nature of Sampson's left foot? No, sir, the first thing that catches his eye is the scissors on the floor at Delilah's feet, and the first thing he says, "Them scissors is too modern—there warn't no scissors like that in them days, by a d—d sight!"

The Californian
October 1, 1864

A Notable Conundrum

    The Fair continues, just the same. It is a nice place to hunt for people in. I have hunted for a friend there for as much as two hours of an evening, and at the end of that time found the hunting just as good as it was when I commenced.
    If the projectors of this noble Fair never receive a dollar or even a kindly word of thanks for the labor of their hands, the sweat of their brows and the wear and tear of brain it has cost them to plan their work and perfect it, a consciousness of the incalculable good they have conferred upon the community must still give them a placid satisfaction more precious than money or sounding compliments. They have been the means of bringing many a pair of loving hearts together that could not get together anywhere else on account of parents and other obstructions. When you see a young lady standing by the sanitary scarecrow which mutely appeals to the public for quarters and swallows them, you may know by the expectant look upon her face that a young man is going to happen along there presently; and, if you have my luck, you will notice by that look still remaining upon her face that you are not the young man she is expecting. They court a good deal at the Fair, and the young fellows are always exchanging notes with the girls. For this purpose the business cards scattered about the place are found very convenient. I picked up one last night which was printed on both sides, but had been interlined in pencil, by somebody's Arabella, until one could not read it without feeling dizzy. It ran about in this wise—though the interlineations were not in parentheses in the original:
    "John Smith, (My Dearest and Sweetest:) Soap Boiler and Candle Factor; (If you love me, if you love) Bar Soap, Castile Soap and Soft Soap, peculiarly suitable for (your Arabella, fly to the) Pacific coast, because of its non-liability to be affected by the climate. Those who may have kitchen refuse to sell, can leave orders, and our soap-fat carts will visit the (Art Gallery. I will be in front of the big mirror in an hour from now, and will go with you to the) corner designated. For the very best Soap and Candles the market affords, apply at the (Academy of Music. And from there, O joy! how my heart thrills with rapture at the prospect! with souls surcharged with bliss, we will wander forth to the) Soap Fac-

tory, or to the office, which is located on the (moon-lit beach,) corner of Jackson street, near the milk ranch. (From Arabella, who sends kisses to her darling) John Smith, Pioneer Soap Boiler and Candle Factor."

    Sweethearts usually treasure up these little affectionate billets, and that this one was lost in the Pavilion, seemed proof to me that its contents were rather distracting to the mind of the young man who received it. He never would have lost it if he had not felt unsettled about something. I think it is likely he got mixed, so to speak, as to whether he was the lucky party, or whether it was the soap-boiler. However, I have possession of her extraordinary document now, and this is to inform Arabella that, in the hope that I may answer for the other young man, and do to fill a void or so in her aching heart, I am drifting about, in an unsettled way, on the lookout for her—sometimes on the Pacific Coast, sometimes at the Art Gallery, sometimes at the soap factory, and occasionally at the moonlit beach and the milk ranch. If she happen to visit either of those places shortly, and will have the goodness to wait a little while, she can calculate on my drifting around in the course of an hour or so.

    I cannot say that all visitors to the Fair go there to make love, though I have my suspicions that a good many of them do. Numbers go there to look at the machinery and misunderstand it, and still greater numbers, perhaps, go to criticize the pictures. There is a handsome portrait in the Art Gallery of a pensive young girl. Last night it fell under the critical eye of a connoisseur from Arkansas. She examined it in silence for many minutes, and then she blew her nose calmly, and, says she, "I like it—it is so sad and thinkful."

    Somebody knocked Weller's bust down from its shelf at the Fair, the other night, and destroyed it. It was wrong to do it, but it gave rise to a very able pun by a young person who has had much experience in such things, and was only indifferently proud of it. He said it was Weller enough when it was a bust, but just the reverse when it was busted. Explanation: He meant that it looked like Weller in the first place, but it did not after it was smashed to pieces. He also meant that it was well enough to leave it alone and not destroy it. The Author of this fine joke is among us yet, and I can bring him around if you would like to look at him. One would expect him to be haughty and ostentatious, but you would be surprised to see how simple and unpretending he is and how willing to take a drink.

    But I have been playing the noble game of "Muggins." In that game, if you make a mistake of any kind, however trivial it may be, you are pronounced a muggins by the whole company, with great unanimity and enthusiasm. If you play the right card in the wrong place, you are a muggins; no matter how you play, in nine cases out of ten you are a muggins. They inform you of it with a shout which has no expression in it of regret. I have played this fine game all the evening, and although I knew little about it at first, I got to be quite a muggins at last. I played it very successfully on a policeman as I went home. I had forgotten my night-key and was climbing in at the window. When he clapped his hand on my shoulder, I smiled upon him and, says I, "Muggins!" with much vivacity. Says he, "How so?" and I said, "Because I live here, and you play the wrong card when you arrest me for entering my own house." I thought it was rather neat. But then there was nobody at home to identify me, and I had to go all the way to the station-house with him and give bail to appear and answer to a charge of burglary. As I turned to depart says he "Muggins!" I thought that was rather neat also.

But the conundrum I have alluded to in the heading of this article, was the best thing of the kind that has ever fallen under my notice. It was projected by a young man who has hardly any education at all, and whose opportunities have been very meagre, even from his childhood up. It was this: "Why was Napoleon when he crossed the Alps, like the Sanitary cheese at the Mechanics' Fair?"

It was very good for a young man just starting in life; don't you think so? He has gone away now to Sacramento. Probably we shall never see him more. He did not state what the answer was.

The Californian
October 8, 1864

Concerning The Answer To That Conundrum

I went out, several days ago, to see the whale—I speak in the singular number, because there was only one whale on the beach at that time. The day was excessively warm, and my comrade was an invalid; consequently we travelled slowly, and conversed about distressing diseases and such other matters as I thought would be likely to interest a sick man and make him feel cheerful. Instead of commenting on the mild scenery we found on the route, we spoke of the ravages of the cholera in the happy days of our boyhood; instead of talking about the warm weather, we reveled in bilious fever reminiscences; instead of boasting of the extraordinary swiftness of our horse, as most persons similarly situated would have done, we chatted gaily of consumption; and when we caught a glimpse of long white lines of waves rolling in silently upon the distant shore, our hearts were gladdened and our stomachs turned by fond memories of sea-sickness. It was a nice comfortable journey, and I could not have enjoyed it more if I had been sick myself.

When we got to the Cliff House we were disappointed. I had always heard there was such a grand view to be seen there of the majestic ocean, with its white billows stretching far away until it met and mingled with the bending sky; with here and there a stately ship upon its surface, ploughing through plains of sunshine and deserts of shadow cast from the clouds above; and, near at hand, piles of picturesque rocks, splashed with angry surf and garrisoned by drunken, sprawling sea-lions and elegant, long-legged pelicans.

It was a bitter disappointment. There was nothing in sight but an ordinary counter, and behind it a long row of bottles with Old Bourbon, and Old Rye, and Old Tom, and the old, old story of man's falter and woman's fall in them. Nothing in the world to be seen but these things. We stayed there an hour and a half, and took observations from different points of view, but the general result was the same—nothing but bottles and a bar. They keep a field-glass there, for the accommodation of those who wish to see the sights, and we looked at the bottles through that, but it did not help the matter any to speak of; we turned it end for end, but instead of increasing the view it diminished it. If it had not been fashionable, I would not have engaged in this trivial amusement; I say trivial, because, notwithstanding they said everybody used the glass, I still consider it trivial amusement, and very undignified, to sit staring at a row of gin bottles through an opera-glass. Finally, we tried a common glass tumbler, and found that it answered just as well, on account of the close proximity of the scenery, and did not seem quite so stupid. We continued to use it, and the more we got accustomed to it, the better we liked it. Although tame enough at first, the effects eventually became really extraordinary. The single row of bottles doubled, and then trebled itself, and finally became a sort of dissolving view of inconceivable beauty and confusion. When Johnny first looked through the tumbler, he said: "It is rather a splendid display, isn't it?" and an hour afterwards he said: "Thas so -'s a sp-(ic!)-splennid 'splay!" and set his glass down with sufficient decision to break it.

We went out, then, and saw a sign marked "CHICKEN SHOOTING," and we sat down and waited a long time, but finally we got weary and discouraged, and my comrade said that perhaps it was no use—maybe the chicken was not going to shoot that day. We did not mind the disappointment so much, but the hiccups were so distressing. I am subject to them when I go abroad.

We left the hotel, then, and drove along the level beach, drowsily admiring the terraced surf, and listening to the tidings it was bringing from other lands in the mysterious language of its ceaseless roar, until we hove in sight of the stranded whale. We thought it was a cliff, an isolated hill, an island—anything but a fish, capable of being cut up and stowed away in a ship. Its proportions were magnified a thousand-fold beyond any conception we had previously formed of them. We felt that we could not complain of a disappointment in regard to the whale, at any rate. But we were not prepared to see a magnified mastodon, also; yet there seemed to be one towering high above the beach not far from the whale. We drove a hundred yards further—it was nothing but a horse.

Then the light of inspiration dawned upon me, and I knew what I would do if I kept the hotel, and the whale belonged to me. I would not permit any one to approach nearer than six or eight hundred yards to the show, because at that distance the light mists, or the peculiar atmosphere, or something, exaggerates it into a monster of colossal size. It grows smaller as you go towards it. When we got pretty close to it, the island shrunk into a fish—a very large one for a sardine, it is true, but a very small one for a whale—and the mastodon dwindled down to a Cayuse pony. Distance had been lending immensity to the view. We were disappointed again somewhat; but see how things are regulated! The very source of our disappointment was a blessing to us. As it was, there was just as much smell as two of us could stand; and if the fish had been larger there would have been more, wouldn't there? and where could we have got assistance on that lonely beach to help us smell it? Ah! it was the great law of compensation—the great law that regulates Nature's heedless agents, and sees that when they make a mistake, they shall at the self-same moment prevent that mistake from working evil consequences. Behold, the same gust of wind that blows a lady's dress aside, and exposes her ankle, fills your eyes so full of sand that you can't see it. Marvelous are the works of Nature!

The whale was not a long one, physically speaking—say thirty-five feet—but he smelt much longer; he smelt as much as a mile and a half longer, I should say, for we traveled about that distance beyond him before we ceased to detect his fragrance in the atmosphere. My comrade said he did not admire to smell a whale; and I adopt his sentiments while I scorn his language. A whale does not smell like magnolia, nor yet like heliotrope or "Balm of a Thousand Flowers," I do now know, but I should judge that it smells more like a thousand pole-cats.

With these few remarks I will now proceed to unfold a conundrum which I consider one of the finest that has ever emanated from the human mind. My invalid comrade produced it while we were driving along slowly in the open country this side of the Ocean House. I think it was just where we crossed the aqueduct of the Spring Valley Water Company, though I will not be certain; it might have been a little to the east of it, or maybe a little to the west, but at any rate it was in the immediate vicinity of it. I remember the time, though, very distinctly, for I was looking at my watch at the moment he commenced speaking, and it was a quarter of a minute after 3 o'clock—I made a memorandum of it afterward in my note-book which I will show you if you will remind me of it when I visit the CALIFORNIAN office. The sun was shining very brightly, but a light breeze was blowing from the sea, which rendered the weather pleasanter than it had been for several hours previously, and as it blew the dust in the same direction in which we were traveling, we experienced no inconvenience from it, although, as a general thing, I do not enjoy dust. It was under these circumstances that my invalid comrade, young John William Skae, who is in the quartz-milling business in Virginia City now, but was born in the state of Pennsylvania, where his parents, and in fact most of his relatives, still reside, except one of his brothers, who is in the army, and his aunt, who married a minister of the gospel and is living out West, sometimes having an improving season in the vineyard and sometimes chased around considerable by the bushwhackers, who cannot abide preachers, and who stir them up impartially, just the same as they do those who have not yet got religion; and also except his first cousin, James Peterson, who is a skirmisher and is with the parson—he goes through the camp-meetings and skirmishes for raw converts, whom he brings to the front and puts them in the corral, or the mourner's bench, as they call it in that section, so that the parson can exhort them more handy—it was under these circumstances, as I was saying, that young Skae, who had been ruminating in dead silence for a long time, turned toward me with an unwholesome glare in his eye, at a quarter of a minute after 3 o'clock, while we were in the vicinity of the aqueduct of the Spring Valley Water Company, and notwithstanding the light breeze that was blowing and the filmy dust that was drifting about us, says he: "Why is a whale like a certain bird which has blue feathers and is mostly found in the West, where he is considered a good bird though not remarkable? It is, because he is the Kingfisher—(the king fish, sir.)"

    There was no house nearby, except an old shed that had been used by some workmen, but I took him to that and did what I could for him; his whole nervous system seemed prostrated; he only raised his head once, and asked in a feeble voice, but with an expression of ineffable satisfaction in it—"How's that?" I knew he did not want medicine—if anything could save him, it would be rest and quiet. Therefore, I removed the horses to a distance, and then went down the road, and by representing the case fairly and openly to all passengers, I got them to drive by him slowly so that they would make no noise to excite him. My efforts were successful; his pulse was at two hundred and ninety when I put him in the shed, and only forty-two when I took him out.

Now I thought that conundrum would have done honor to the finest mind among us, and I think it especially good for an invalid from Pennsylvania. How does it strike you? It is circumscribed in its action, though, and is applicable only to men; you could not say "Because it is the king fish, madam," without marring the effect of the joke by rendering the point in a manner obscure.

Some friends of mine of great powers and high intellectual culture, and who naturally take an interest in conundrums, besought me to procure the answer to that one about Napoleon and the Sanitary cheese, and publish it. I have written to the author of it, and he informs me that he and his mother, who is a woman of extraordinary sagacity and a profound thinker, are ciphering at it night and day, and they confidently expect to have the answer ready in time for your next week's issue. From what I can understand, they are making very encouraging progress; they have already found out why Napoleon was like the cheese, but thus far they have not been able to ascertain in what respect the cheese resembles Napoleon.

The Californian
October 15, 1864

Still Further Concerning That Conundrum

In accordance with your desire, I went to the Academy of Music on Monday evening, to take notes and prepare myself to write a careful critique upon the opera of the Crown Diamonds. That you considered me able to acquit myself creditably in this exalted sphere of literary labor was gratifying to me, and I should even have felt flattered by it had I not known that I was so competent to perform the task well, that to set it for me could not be regarded as a flattering concession, but, on the contrary, only a just and deserved recognition of merit.

Now, to throw disguise aside and speak openly, I have long yearned for an opportunity to write an operatic diagnostical and analytical dissertation for you. I feel the importance of carefully—digested newspaper criticism in matters of this kind—for I am aware that by it the dramatic and musical tastes of a community are moulded, cultivated and irrevocably fixed—that by it these tastes are vitiated and debased, or elevated and ennobled, according to the refinement or vulgarity, and the competency or incompetency of the writers to whom this department of the public training is entrusted. If you would see around you a people who are filled with the keenest appreciation of perfection in musical execution and dramatic delineation, and painfully sensitive to the slightest departures from the true standard of art in these things, you must employ upon your newspapers critics capable of discriminating between merit and demerit, and alike fearless in praising the one and condemning the other. Such a person—although it may be in some degree immodest in me to say so—I claim to be. You will not be surprised, then, to know that I read your boshy criticisms on the opera with the most exquisite anguish—and not only yours, but those which I find in every paper in San Francisco.

You do nothing but sing one everlasting song of praise; when an artist, by diligence and talent, makes an effort of transcendent excellence, behold, instead of receiving marked and cordial attention, both artist and effort sink from sight, and are lost in the general slough of slimy praise in which it is your pleasure to cause the whole company, good, bad and indifferent, to wallow once a week. With this brief but very liberal and hearty expression of sentiment, I will drop the subject and leave you alone for the present, for it behooves me now to set you a model in criticism.

The opera of the Crown Diamonds was put upon the stage in creditable shape on Monday evening, although I noticed that the curtains of the "Queen of Portugal's" drawing-room were not as gorgeous as they might have been, and that the furniture had a second-hand air about it, of having seen service in the preceding reign. The acting and the vocalization, however, were in the main good. I was particularly charmed by the able manner in which Signor Bellindo Alphonso Cellini, the accomplished basso-relievo furniture-scout and sofa-shifter, performed his part. I have before observed that this rising young artist gave evidence of the rarest genius in his peculiar department of operatic business, and have been annoyed at noticing with what studied care a venomous and profligate press have suppressed his name and suffered his sublimest efforts to pass unnoticed and unglorified. Shame upon such grovelling envy and malice! But, with all your neglect, you have failed to crush the spirit of the gifted furniture-scout, or seduce from him the affectionate encouragement and appreciation of the people. The moment he stepped upon the stage on Monday evening, to carry out the bandit chieftain's valise, the upper circles, with one accord, shouted, "Supe! supe!" and greeted him with warm and generous applause. It was a princely triumph for Bellindo; he told me afterwards it was the proudest moment of his life.

I watched Alphonso during the entire performance and was never so well pleased with him before, although I have admired him from the first. In the second act, when the eyes of the whole audience were upon him—when his every movement was the subject of anxiety and suspense—when everything depended upon his nerve and self-possession, and the slightest symptom of hesitation or lack of confidence would have been fatal—he stood erect in front of the cave, looking calmly and unflinchingly down upon the camp-stool for several moments, as one who has made up his mind to do his great work or perish in the attempt, and then seized it and bore it in triumph to the foot-lights! It was a sublime spectacle. There was not a dry eye in the house. In that moment, not even the most envious and uncharitable among the noble youth's detractors would have had the hardihood to say he was not endowed with a lofty genius.

Again, in the scene where the Prime Minister's nephew is imploring the female bandit to fly to the carriage and escape impending wrath, and when dismay and confusion ruled the hour, how quiet, how unmoved, how grandly indifferent was Bellindo in the midst of it all! - what solidity of expression lay upon his countenance! While all save himself were unnerved by despair, he serenely put forth his finger and mashed to a shapeless pulp a mosquito that loitered upon the wall, yet betrayed no sign of agitation the while. Was there nothing in this lofty contempt for the dangers which surrounded him that marked the actor destined hereafter to imperishable renown?

Possibly upon that occasion when it was necessary for Alphonso to remove two chairs and a table during the shifting of the scenes, he performed his part with undue precipitation; with the table upside down upon his head, and grasping the corners with hands burdened with the chairs, he appeared to some extent undignified when he galloped across the stage. Generally his conception of his part is excellent, but in this case I am satisfied he threw into it an enthusiasm not required and also not warranted by the circumstances. I think that careful study and reflection will convince him that I am right, and that the author of the opera intended that in this particular instance the furniture should be carried out with impressive solemnity. That he had this in view is evidenced by the slow and stately measure of the music played by the orchestra at that juncture.

But the crowning glory of Cellini's performance that evening was the placing of a chair for the Queen of Portugal to sit down in after she had become fatigued by earnestly and elaborately abusing the Prime

Minister for losing the Crown Diamonds. He did not grab the chair by the hind leg and shove it awkwardly at her Majesty; he did not seize it by the seat and thrust it ungracefully toward her; he did not handle it as though he was undecided about the strict line of his duty or ignorant of the proper manner of performing it. He did none of these things. With a coolness and confidence that evinced the most perfect conception and the most consummate knowledge of his part, he came gently forward and laid hold of that chair from behind, set it in its proper place with a movement replete with grace, and then leaned upon the back of it, resting his chin upon his hand, and in this position smiled a smile of transfigured sweetness upon the audience over the Queen of Portugal's head. There shone the inspired actor! and the people saw and acknowledged him; they waited respectfully for Miss Richings to finish her song, and then with one impulse they poured forth upon him a sweeping tempest of applause.

At the end of the piece the idolized furniture-scout and sofa-skirmisher was called before the curtain by an enthusiastic shouting and clapping of hands, but he was thrust aside, as usual, and other artists (who chose to consider the compliment as intended for themselves) swept bowing and smirking along the footlights and received it. I swelled with indignation, but I summoned my fortitude and resisted the pressure successfully. I am still intact.

Take it altogether, the Crown Diamonds was really a creditable performance. I feel that I would not be doing my whole duty if I closed this critique without speaking of Miss Caroline Richings, Miss Jenny Kempton, Mr. Hill, Mr. Seguin and Mr. Peakes, all of whom did fair justice to their several parts, and deserve a passing notice. With study, perseverance and attention, I have no doubt these vocalists will in time achieve a gratifying success in their profession.

I believe I have nothing further to say. I will call around, tomorrow, after you have had time to read, digest and pass your judgment upon my criticism, and, if agreeable, I will hire out to you for some years in that line.

Mark Twain.

P. S. - No answer to that conundrum this week. On account of over-exertion on it the old woman has got to having fits here lately. However, it will be forthcoming yet, when she runs out of them, if she don't die in the meantime, and I trust she will not. We may as well prepare ourselves for the worst, though, for it is not to be disguised that they are shaking her up mighty lively.

The Californian
October 22, 1864

Whereas

LOVE'S BAKERY! I am satisfied I have found the place now that I have been looking for all this time. I cannot describe to you the sensation of mingled astonishment, gladness, hope, doubt, anxiety, and balmy, blissful emotion that suffused my being and quivered in a succession of streaky thrills down my backbone, as I stood on the corner of Third and Minna streets, last Tuesday, and stared, spell-bound, at those extraordinary words, painted in large, plain letters on a neighboring window-curtain—"LOVE'S BAKERY." "God bless my soul!" said I, "will wonders never cease? - are there to be no limits to man's spirit of invention?-is he to invade the very realms of the immortal, and presume to guide and control the great passions, the impalpable essences, that have hitherto dwelt in the secret chambers of the soul, sacred from all save divine intrusion?"

I read and re-read that remarkable sign with constantly-increasing wonder and interest. There was nothing extraordinary in the appearance of the establishment, and even if it had possessed anything of a supernatural air, it must necessarily have been neutralized by the worldly and substantial look of a pyramid of excellent bread that stood in the window—a sign very inconsistent, it seemed to me, with the character of a place devoted to the high and holy employment of instilling the passion of love into the human heart, although it was certainly in keeping with the atrocious taste which was capable of conferring upon a vice-royalty of heaven itself such an execrable name as "Love's Bakery." Why not Love's Bower, or the Temple of Love, or the Palace of Cupid?—anything—anything in the world would have been less repulsive than such hideous vulgarity of nomenclature as "Love's Bakery."

The place seemed very complete, and well supplied with every facility for carrying on the business of creating love successfully. In a window of the second story was a large tin cage with a parrot in it, and near it was a sign bearing the inscription, "Preparatory School for Young Ladies"—that is, of course, a school where they are taught certain things necessary to prepare them for the bakery down below. Not far off is also a "Preparatory School for Young Gentlemen," which is doubtless connected with Love's Bakery too. I saw none of the pupils of either of the schools, but my imagination dwelt upon them with a deep and friendly interest. How irksome, I thought, must this course of instruction be to these tender hearts, so impatient to be baked into a state of perfect love!

Greatly moved by the singular circumstances which surrounded me, I fell into a profound and pleasing reverie. Here, I thought, they take a couple of hopeful hearts in the rough, and work them up, with spices and shortening and sweetening enough to last for a lifetime, and turn them out well kneaded together, baked to a turn, and ready for matrimony, and without having been obliged to undergo a long and harrowing courtship, with the desperate chances attendant thereon, of persevering rivals, unwilling parents, inevitable love-quarrels, and all that sort of thing.

Here, I thought, they will bake you up a couple in moderate circumstances, at short notice and at a cheap rate, and turn them out in good enough shape for the money, perhaps, but nevertheless burnt with the fire of jealousy on one side, and flabby and "duffy" with lukewarmness and indifference on the other, and spotted all over with the salaeratus stains of a predisposition to make the conjugal cake bitter and unpalatable for all time to come.

Or they will take an excessively patrician pair, charge them a dozen prices, and deliver them to order in a week, all plastered over with the ghostly vines and flowers of blighted fancies, hopes and yearnings, wrought in chilly ice-work.

Or, perhaps, they will take a brace of youthful, tender hearts and dish them up in no time, into crisp, delicate "lady-fingers," tempting to contemplate, and suggestive of that serene after-dinner happiness and sociability that come when the gross substantials have been swept from the board and are forgotten in soft dalliance with pastry and ices and sparkling Moselle.

Or maybe they will take two flinty old hearts that have harbored selfishness, envy and all uncharitableness in solitude for half a century, and after a fortnight's roasting, turn them out the hardest kind of hardtack, invulnerable to all softening influences for evermore.

Here was a revolution far more extended, and destined to be attended by more momentous consequences to the nations of the earth, than any ever projected or accomplished by the greatest of the world's military heroes! Love, the master passion of the human heart, which, since the morning of the creation had shaped the destinies of emperors and beggars alike, and had ruled all men as with a rod of iron, was to be hurled from the seat of power in a single instant, as it were, and brought into subjection to the will of an inspired, a sublimely-gifted baker! By some mysterious magic, by some strange and awful invention, the divine emotion was to be confined within set bounds and limits, controlled, weighed, measured, and doled out to God's creatures in quantities and qualities to suit the purchaser, like vulgar beer and candles!

And in times to come, I thought, the afflicted lover, instead of reading Heuston & Hastings' omnipresent sign and gathering no comfort from it, will read "GO TO LOVE'S BAKERY!" on the dead-walls and telegraph poles, and be saved.

Now I might never have published to the world my discovery of this manufactory of the human affections in a populous thoroughfare of San Francisco, if it had not occurred to me that some account of it would serve as a peculiarly fitting introductory to a story of love and misfortune, which it falls to my lot to relate. And yet even Love's Bakery could afford no help to the sufferers of whom I shall speak, for they do not lack affection for each other, but are the victims of an accumulation of distressing circumstances against which the efforts of that august agent would be powerless.

The facts in the following case came to me by letter from a young lady who lives in the beautiful city of San Jose; she is perfectly unknown to me, and simply signs herself "Aurelia Maria," which may possibly be a fictitious name. But no matter, the poor girl is almost heart-broken by the misfortunes she has undergone, and so confused by the conflicting counsels of misguided friends and insidious enemies, that she does not know what course to pursue in order to extricate herself from the web of difficulties in which she seems almost hopelessly involved. In this dilemma she turns to me for help, and supplicates for my guidance and instruction with a moving eloquence that would touch the heart of a statue. Hear her sad story:

She says that when she was sixteen years old she met and loved, with all the devotion of a passionate nature, a young man from New Jersey, named Williamson Breckinridge Caruthers, who was some six years her senior. They were engaged, with the free consent of their friends and relatives, and for a time it seemed as if their career was destined to be characterized by an immunity from sorrow beyond the usual lot of humanity. But at last the tide of fortune turned; young Caruthers became infected with smallpox of the most virulent type, and when he recovered from his illness his face was pitted like a waffle-mould, and his comeliness gone forever. Aurelia thought to break off the engagement at first, but pity for her unfortunate lover caused her to postpone the marriage-day for a season, and give him another trial. The very day before the wedding was to have taken place, Breckinridge, while absorbed in watching the flight of a balloon, walked into a well and fractured one of his legs, and it had to be taken off above the knee. Again Aurelia was moved to break the engagement, but again love triumphed, and she set the day forward and gave him another chance to reform. And again misfortune overtook the unhappy youth. He lost one arm by the premature discharge of a Fourth-of-July cannon, and within three months he got the other pulled out by a carding-machine. Aurelia's heart was almost crushed by these latter calamities. She could not but be deeply grieved to see her lover passing from her by piecemeal, feeling, as she did, that he could not last forever under this disastrous process of reduction, yet knowing of no way to stop its dreadful career, and in her tearful despair she almost regretted, like brokers who hold on and lose, that she had not taken him at first, before he had suffered such an alarming depreciation. Still, her brave soul bore her up, and she resolved to bear with her friend's unnatural disposition yet a little longer. Again the wedding-day approached, and again disappointment overshadowed it; Caruthers fell ill with the erysipelas, and lost the use of one of his eyes entirely. The friends and relatives of the bride, considering that she had already put up with more than could reasonably be expected of her, now came forward and insisted that the match should be broken off, but after wavering awhile, Aurelia, with a generous spirit which did her credit, said she had reflected calmly upon the matter, and could not discover that Breckinridge was to blame. So she extended the time once more, and he broke his other leg. It was a sad day for the poor girl when she saw the surgeons reverently bearing away the sack whose uses she had learned by previous experience, and her heart told her the bitter truth that some more of her lover was gone. She felt that the field of her affections was growing more and more circumscribed every day, but once more she frowned down her relatives and renewed her betrothal. Shortly before the time set for the nuptials another disaster occurred. There was but one man scalped by the Owens River Indians last year. That man was Williamson Breckinridge Caruthers, of New Jersey. He was hurrying home with happiness in his heart, when he lost his hair forever, and in that hour of bitterness he almost cursed the mistaken mercy that had spared his head.

    At last Aurelia is in serious perplexity as to what she ought to do. She still loves her Breckinridge, she writes, with truly womanly feeling - she still loves what is left of him - but her parents are bitterly opposed to the match, because he has no property and is disabled from working, and she has not sufficient means to support both comfortably. "Now, what should she do?" she asks with painful and anxious solicitude.

It is a delicate question; it is one which involves the life-long happiness of a woman, and that of nearly two-thirds of a man, and I feel that it would be assuming too great a responsibility to do more than make a mere suggestion in the case. How would it do to build to him? If Aurelia can afford the expense, let her furnish her mutilated lover with wooden arms and wooden legs, and a glass eye and a wig, and give him another show; give him ninety days, without grace, and if he does not break his neck in the meantime, marry him and take the chances. It does not seem to me that there is much risk, any way, Aurelia, because if he sticks to his singular propensity for damaging himself every time he sees a good opportunity, his next experiment is bound to finish him, and then you are safe, married or single. If married, the wooden legs and such other valuables as he may possess revert to the widow, and you see you sustain no actual loss save the cherished fragment of a noble but most unfortunate husband, who honestly strove to do right, but whose extraordinary instincts were against him. Try it, Maria. I have thought the matter over carefully and well, and it is the only chance I see for you. It would have been a happy conceit on the part of Caruthers if he had started with his neck and broken that first; but since he has seen fit to choose a different policy and string himself out as long as possible, I do not think we ought to upbraid him for it if he has enjoyed it. We must do the best we can under the circumstances and try not to feel exasperated at him.

The Californian
October 29, 1864

A Touching Story of George Washington's Boyhood

If it please your neighbor to break the sacred calm of night with the snorting of an unholy trombone, it is your duty to put up with his wretched music and your privilege to pity him for the unhappy instinct that moves him to delight in such discordant sounds. I did not always think thus: this consideration for musical amateurs was born of certain disagreeable personal experiences that once followed the development of a like instinct in myself. Now this infidel over the way, who is learning to play on the trombone, and the slowness of whose progress is almost miraculous, goes on with his harrowing work every night, uncurled by me, but tenderly pitied. Ten years ago, for the same offense, I would have set fire to his house. At that time I was a prey to an amateur violinist for two or three weeks, and the sufferings I endured at his hands are inconceivable. He played "Old Dan Tucker," and he never played anything else; but he performed that so badly that he could throw me into fits with it if I were awake, or into a nightmare if I were asleep. As long as he confined himself to "Dan Tucker," though, I bore with him and abstained from violence; but when he projected a fresh outrage, and tried to do "Sweet Home," I went over and burnt him out. My next assailant was a wretch who felt a call to play the clarinet. He only played the scale, however, with his distressing instrument, and I let him run the length of his tether, also; but finally, when he branched out into a ghastly tune, I felt my reason deserting me under the exquisite torture, and I sallied forth and burnt him out likewise. During the next two years I burned out an amateur cornet player, a bugler, a bassoon-sophomore, and a barbarian whose talents ran in the base-drum line.

    I would certainly have scorched this trombone man if he had moved into my neighborhood in those days. But as I said before, I leave him to his own destruction now, because I have had experience as an amateur myself, and I feel nothing but compassion for that kind of people. Besides, I have learned that there lies dormant in the souls of all men a penchant for some particular musical instrument, and an unsuspected yearning to learn to play on it, that are bound to wake up and demand attention some day. Therefore, you who rail at such as disturb your slumbers with unsuccessful and demoralizing attempts to subjugate a fiddle, beware! for sooner or later your own time will come. It is customary and popular to curse these amateurs when they wrench you out of a pleasant dream at night with a peculiarly diabolical note; but seeing that we are all made alike, and must all develop a distorted talent for music in the fullness of time, it is not right. I am charitable to my trombone maniac; in a moment of inspiration he fetches a snort, sometimes, that brings me to a sitting posture in bed, broad awake and weltering in a cold perspiration. Perhaps my first thought is, that there has been an earthquake; perhaps I hear the trombone, and my next thought is, that suicide and the silence of the grave would be a happy release from this nightly agony; perhaps the old instinct comes strong upon me to go after my matches; but my first cool, collected thought is, that the trombone man's destiny is upon him, and he is working it out in suffering and tribulation; and I banish from me the unworthy instinct that would prompt me to burn him out.

    After a long immunity from the dreadful insanity that moves a man to become a musician in defiance of the will of God that he should confine himself to sawing wood, I finally fell a victim to the instrument they call the accordion. At this day I hate that contrivance as fervently as any man can, but at the time I speak of I suddenly acquired a disgusting and idolatrous affection for it. I got one of powerful capacity, and learned to play "Auld Lang Syne" on it. It seems to me, now, that I must have been gifted with a sort of inspiration to be enabled, in the state of ignorance in which I then was, to select out of the whole range of musical composition the one solitary tune that sounds vilest and most distressing on the accordion. I do not suppose there is another tune in the world with which I could have inflicted so much anguish upon my race as I did with that one during my short musical career.

After I had been playing "Lang Syne" about a week, I had the vanity to think I could improve the original melody, and I set about adding some little flourishes and variations to it, but with rather indifferent success, I suppose, as it brought my landlady into my presence with an expression about her of being opposed to such desperate enterprises. Said she, "Do you know any other tune but that, Mr. Twain?" I told her, meekly, that I did not. "Well, then," said she, "stick to it just as it is; don't put any variations to it, because it's rough enough on the boarders the way it is now."

The fact is, it was something more than simply "rough enough" on them; it was altogether too rough; half of them left, and the other half would have followed, but Mrs. Jones saved them by discharging me from the premises.

I only stayed one night at my next lodging-house. Mrs. Smith was after me early in the morning. She said, "You can go, sir; I don't want you here; I have had one of your kind before—a poor lunatic, that played the banjo and danced breakdowns, and jarred the glass all out of the windows. You kept me awake all night, and if you was to do it again, I'd take and mash that thing over your head!" I could see that this woman took no delight in music, and I moved to Mrs. Brown's.

For three nights in succession I gave my new neighbors "Auld Lang Syne," plain and unadulterated, save by a few discords that rather improved the general effect than otherwise. But the very first time I tried the variations the boarders mutinied. I never did find anybody that would stand those variations. I was very well satisfied with my efforts in that house, however, and I left it without any regrets; I drove one boarder as mad as a March hare, and another one tried to scalp his mother. I reflected, though, that if I could only have been allowed to give this latter just one more touch of the variations, he would have finished the old woman.

I went to board at Mrs. Murphy's, an Italian lady of many excellent qualities. The very first time I struck up the variations, a haggard, care-worn, cadaverous old man walked into my room and stood beaming upon me a smile of ineffable happiness. Then he placed his hand upon my head, and looking devoutly aloft, he said with feeling unction, and in a voice trembling with emotion, "God bless you, young man! God bless you! for you have done that for me which is beyond all praise. For years I have suffered from an incurable disease, and knowing my doom was sealed and that I must die, I have striven with all my power to resign myself to my fate, but in vain—the love of life was too strong within me. But Heaven bless you, my benefactor! for since I heard you play that tune and those variations, I do not want to live any longer—I am entirely resigned—I am willing to die—in fact, I am anxious to die." And then the old man fell upon my neck and wept a flood of happy tears. I was surprised at these things; but I could not help feeling a little proud at what I had done, nor could I help giving the old gentleman a parting blast in the way of some peculiarly lacerating variations as he went out at the door. They doubled him up like a jack-knife, and the next time he left his bed of pain and suffering he was all right, in a metallic coffin.

    My passion for the accordion finally spent itself and died out, and I was glad when I found myself free from its unwholesome influence. While the fever was upon me, I was a living, breathing calamity wherever I went, and desolation and disaster followed in my wake. I bred discord in families, I crushed the spirits of the light-hearted, I drove the melancholy to despair, I hurried invalids to premature dissolution, and I fear me I disturbed the very dead in their graves. I did incalculable harm, and inflicted untold suffering upon my race with my execrable music; and yet to atone for it all, I did but one single blessed act, in making that weary old man willing to go to his long home.

    Still, I derived some little benefit from that accordion; for while I continued to practice on it, I never had to pay any board—landlords were always willing to compromise, on my leaving before the month was up.

    Now, I had two objects in view in writing the foregoing, one of which was to try and reconcile people to those poor unfortunates who feel that they have a genius for music, and who drive their neighbors crazy every night in trying to develop and cultivate it; and the other was to introduce an admirable story about Little George Washington, who could Not Lie, and the Cherry-Tree—or the Apple-Tree—I have forgotten now which, although it was told me only yesterday. And writing such a long and elaborate introductory has caused me to forget the story itself; but it was very touching.

The Californian
November 5, 1864

Daniel In The Lion's Den—And Out Again All Right

Some people are not particular about what sort of company they keep. I am one of that kind. Now for several days I have been visiting the Board of Brokers, and associating with brokers, and drinking with them, and swapping lies with them, and being as familiar and sociable with them as I would with the most respectable people in the world. I do this because I consider that a broker goes according to the instincts that are in him, and means no harm, and fulfils his mission according to his lights, and has a right to live, and be happy in a general way, and be protected by the law to some extent, just the same as a better man. I consider that brokers come into the world with souls—I am satisfied they do; and if they wear them out in the course of a long career of stock-jobbing, have they not a right to come in at the eleventh hour and get themselves half-soled, like old boots, and be saved at last? Certainly—the father of the tribe did that, and do we say anything against Barabbas for it today? No! we concede his right to do it; we admire his mature judgment in selling out of a worked-out mine of iniquity and investing in righteousness, and no man denies, or even doubts, the validity of the transaction. Other people may think as they please, and I suppose I am entitled to the same privilege; therefore, notwithstanding what others may believe, I am of the opinion that a broker can be saved. Mind, I do not say that a broker will be saved, or even that is uncommon likely that such a thing will happen—I only say that Lazarus was raised from the dead, the five thousand were fed with twelve loaves of bread, the water was turned into wine, the Israelites crossed the Red Sea dry-shod, and a broker can be saved. True, the angel that accomplishes the task may require all eternity to rest himself in, but has that got anything to do with the establishment of the proposition? Does it invalidate it? does it detract from it? I think not. I am aware that this enthusiastic and maybe highly-colored vindication of the brokers may lay me open to suspicion of bribery, but I care not; I am a native of Washoe, and I will stand by anybody that stands by Washoe.

The place where stocks are daily bought and sold is called by interested parties the Hall of the San Francisco Board of Brokers, but by the impartial and disinterested the Den of the Forty Thieves; the latter name is regarded as the most poetic, but the former is considered the most polite. The large room is well stocked with small desks, arranged in semi-circular ranks like the seats of an amphitheatre, and behind these sit the brokers. The portly president, with his gavel of office in his hand, an abundance of whiskers and moustaches on his face, spectacles on nose, an expression of energy and decision on his countenance and an open plaza on his head, sits, with his three clerks, in a pulpit at the head of the hall, flanked on either hand by two large cases, with glass doors, containing mineralogical specimens from Washoe and California mines—the emblems of the traffic. Facing the president, at the opposite end of the hall, is a blackboard, whereon is written in accusing capitals, "John Smith delinquent to John Jones, $1,550; William Brown delinquent to Jonas White, $475!" You might think brokers wouldn't mind that, maybe, but they do; a delinquent loses caste, and that touches his fine moral sensibilities—and he is suspended from active membership for the time being, and even expelled if his delinquency savors of blundering and ungraceful rascality—a thing which the Board cannot abide—and this inflicts exquisite pain upon the delicate nerves and tissues of his pocket, now when a seat in the Den is worth twelve or fifteen hundred dollars, and in brisker times even three thousand.

The session of the Board being duly opened, the roll is rapidly called, the members present responding, and the absentees being noted by the clerks for fines:

"Ackerman, (Here!) Adams, Atchison, (Here!) Babcock, Bocock, (Here!) Badger, Blitzen, Bulger, Buncombe, (Here!) Caxton, (Here!) Cobbler, Crowder, Clutterback, (Here!) Dashaway, Dilson, Dodson, Dummy (Here!)"—and so on, the place becoming lively and animated, and the members sharpening their pencils, disposing their printed stock-lists before them, and getting ready for a sowing of unrighteousness and a harvest of sin.

In a few moments the roll-call was finished, the pencils all sharpened, and the brokers prepared for business—some with a leg thrown negligently over the arms of their chairs, some tilted back comfortably with their knees against their desks, some sitting half upright and glaring at the President, hungry for the contention to begin—but not a rascal of them tapping his teeth with his pencil—only dreamy, absent-minded people do that.

Then the President called "Ophir!" and after some bidding and counter-bidding, "Gould and Curry!" and a Babel arose—an infernal din and clatter of all kinds and tones of voices, inextricably jumbled together like original chaos, and above it all the following observation by the

President pealed out clearly and distinctly, and with a rapidity of enunciation that was amazing:

"Fift'naitassfrwahn fift'nseftfive bifferwahn fift'naitfive botherty!"

I said I believed I would go home. My broker friend who had procured my admission to the Board asked why I wanted to go so soon, and I was obliged to acknowledge to him that I was very unfamiliar with the Kanaka language, and could not understand it at all unless a man spoke it exceedingly slow and deliberately.

"Oh," said he, "sit still; that isn't Kanaka; it's English, but he talks so fast and runs one word into another; it is easy SOLD! to understand when you GIVE FIFTEEN-NINETY BUYER TEN NO DEPOSIT! come to get used to it. He always talks so, and sometimes he says THAT'S MINE! JIGGERS SOLD ON SLADDERY'S BID! his words so fast that even some of the members cannot comprehend them readily. Now what he said then was NO SIR! I DIDN'T SAY BUYER THIRTY, I SAID REGULAR WAY! 'Fifteen-eighty, (meaning fifteen hundred and eighty dollars) asked for one, (one foot) fifteen-seventy-five bid for one, fifteen-eighty-five buyer thirty,' (thirty days' time on the payment,) 'TWASN'T MY BID, IT WAS SWIGGINS TO BABCOCK! and he was repeating the bids and offers of the members after them as fast as they were made. I'LL TAKE IT, CASH!"

I felt relieved, but not enlightened. My broker's explanation had got so many strange and incomprehensible interpolations sandwiched into it that I began to look around for a suitable person to translate that for me also, when it occurred to me that those interpolations were bids, offers, etc., which he had been throwing out to the assembled brokers while he was talking to me. It was all clear, then, so I have put his side-remarks in small capitals so that they may be clear to the reader likewise, and show that they have no connection with the subject matter of my friend's discourse.

And all this time, the clatter of voices had been going on. And while the storm of ejaculations hurtled about their heads, these brokers sat calmly in their several easy attitudes, but when a sale was made—when, in answer to some particularly liberal bid, somebody sung out "Sold!" down came legs from the arms of chairs, down came knees propped against desks, forward shot the heads of the whole tribe with one accord, and away went the long ranks of pencils dancing over the paper! The sale duly recorded by all, the heads, the legs and the knees came up again, and the negligent attitudes were resumes once more.

The din moderated now, somewhat, and for a while only a random and desultory fire was kept up as the President drifted down the stock-list, calling at intervals, "Savage!" "Uncle Sam!" "Chollar!" "Potosi!" "Hale and Norcross!" "Imperial!" "Sierra Nevada!" "Daney!" the monotony being broken and the uncomfortable attitudes demolished, now and then, by a lucky chance-shot that went to the mark and made a sale. But when the old gentleman called "Burning Moscow!" you should have seen the fiends wake up! you should have heard the racket! you should have been there to behold the metaphorical bull in the China shop! The President's voice and his mallet went into active service, then, and mingled their noise with the clamors of the mob. The members thus:

"Sell ten forty-five cash!" "Give forty-three for ten, regular way!" "Give forty-one cash for any part fifty!" "Twenty thirty-eight seller sixty!" "Give forty-four for ten buyer thirty!" "Sold!" (Down with your legs again, forward with your heads, and out with your pencils!) "Sell ten forty-three cash!" "Sold!" Then from every part of the house a din like this: "Ten more!" "Sold!" "Ten more!" "SOLD!" "Ten more!" "Sold!" "Ten more!" "Sold!" "Ten"

President (rap with his gavel)—Silence! Orfuplease (order if you please) gentlemen! Higgins ten to Smithers - Dodson ten to Snodgrass -

Billson - "No, sir! Billson ten to Snodgrass! It was me that sold 'em, sir!"

Dodson - "I didn't sell, sir, I bought - Jiggers ten to Dodson!"

President - "Billson ten to Snodgrass - Jiggers ten to Dodson - Slushbuster ten to Bladders - Simpson ten to Blivens - Guttersnipe ten to Hogwash - aw-right! go on!"

And they did go on, hotter and heavier than ever. And as they yelled their terms, the President repeated after them—the words flowing in a continuous stream from his mouth with inconceivable rapidity, and melting and mingling together like bottle-glass and cinders after a conflagration:

"Fortwahnasscash fortray bidbortenn fortsix botherty fortsevnoffsetherty fortfourbiffertenn - (smash! with the gavel) whasthat? - aw right! fortfive offranparfortbotherty nodeposit fortfivenaf botherty bid fortsix biglerway!"

Which, translated, means: "Forty-one asked, cash; forty-three bid, buyer ten; forty-six, buyer thirty; forty-seven offered, seller thirty; forty-four bid for ten - (pause) - What's that? All right - forty-five offered for any part of forty, buyer thirty, no deposit; forty-five and a half, buyer thirty, bid; forty-six bid, regular way!"

And I found out that a "Bull" is a broker who raises the market-price of a stock by every means in his power, and a "Bear" is one who depresses it; that "cash" means that the stock must be delivered and paid for immediately—that is, before the banks close; that "regular way" means that delivery of the stock and payment must be made within two days; that it is the seller who "offers" stock, and the buyer who "bids" for it; that "buyer ten, thirty," or whatever the specified number may be, signifies the number of days the purchaser is allowed in which to call for the stock, receive it and pay for it, and it implies also that he must deposit in somebody's hands a fifth part of the price of the stock purchased, to be forfeited to the seller in case the full payment is not made within the time set—full payment must be made, though, notwithstanding the forfeit, or the broker loses his seat if the seller makes complaint to the Board within forty-eight hours after the occurrence of the delinquency; that when the words "no deposit" are added to "buyer thirty," they imply that the twenty per cent deposit is not to be made, of course; that "seller thirty" means that any time the seller chooses, during the thirty days, he can present the stock to the buyer and demand payment—the seller generally selling at a figure below the market rate, in the hope that before his time is up a depression may occur that will enable him to pick up the stock at half price and deliver it—and the buyer taking chances on a great advance, within the month, that will accrue to his profit. Think of one of these adventurous "seller thirty's" "selling short," at thirty dollars a foot, several feet of a stock that was all corralled and withdrawn from the market within a fortnight and went to about fifteen hundred! It is not worthwhile to mention names—I suppose you remember the circumstance.

But I digress. Sometimes on the "second call" of stocks—that is, after the list has been gone through with in regular order, and the members are privileged to call up any stock they please—strategy is driven to the utmost limit by the friends of some pet wildcat or other, to effect sales of it to disinterested parties. The seller "offers" at a high figure, and the "bidder" responds with a low one; then the former comes warily down a dollar at a time, and the latter approaches him from below at about the same rate; they come nearer and nearer, skirmish a little in close proximity, get to a point where another bid or another offer would commit the parties to a sale, and then in the imminence of the impending event the seller hesitates a second and is silent. But behold! as has been said of Woman, "The Broker that hesitates is lost!" The nervous and impatient President can brook no silence, no delay, and calls out: "Awstock?" (Any other stock?) Somebody yells "Burning Moscow!" and the tender wildcat, almost born, miscarries. Or perhaps the skirmishers fight shyly up to each other, counter and cross-counter, feint and parry, back and fill, and finally clinch a sale in the center—the bidder is bitten, a smile flits from face to face, down come the legs, forward the ranks of heads, the pencils charge on the stock-lists, and the neat transaction is recorded with a rare gusto.

But twelve pages of foolscap are warning me to cut this thrilling sketch short, notwithstanding it is only half finished. However, I cannot leave the subject without saying I was agreeably disappointed in those brokers; I expected to see a set of villains with the signs of total depravity hung out all over them, but now I am satisfied there is some good in them; that they are not entirely and irredeemably bad; and I have been told by a friend, whose judgment I respect, that they are not any more unprincipled than they look. This was said by a man who would scorn to stoop to flattery. At the same time, though, as I scanned the faces assembled in that hall, I could not help imagining I could see old St. Peter admitting that band of Bulls and Bears into Paradise—see him standing by the half-open gate with his ponderous key pressed thoughtfully against his nose, and his head canted critically to one side, as he looks after them tramping down the gold-paved avenue, and mutters to himself: "Well, you're a nice lot, any way! Humph! I think you'll find it sort of lonesome in heaven, for if my judgment is sound, you'll not find a good many of your stripe in there!"

The Californian
November 19, 1864

A Full And Reliable Account
Of The Extraordinary Meteoric Shower Of Last Saturday Night

I found the following paragraph in the morning papers of the 11th inst.:

VIRGINIA, November 10. - Astronomers anticipate a recurrence this year of the November meteoric shower of 1833. The mornings from the 11th to the 15th are all likely to show an unusual number of meteors, especially from the 12th to the 14th. The best time of observation is from half-past one o'clock, A.M., onward. The radiant point is the constellation Leo. Observers in California, Nevada and the Pacific Coast generally, are requested to report their observations to Professor Silliman, Jr., San Francisco, for the American Journal of Science, where they will be published for the good of science.
    B. SILLIMAN, JR.

PROF. B. SILLIMAN, JR. -Dear Sir: In accordance with the above request, which you so politely extended to all "observers," I took copious notes of the amazing meteoric phenomena of last Saturday night, and I now hasten to make my report to you for publication in the American Journal of Science "for the good of science."

I began my observations early in the evening, previously providing myself with the very best apparatus I could find wherewith to facilitate my labors. I got a telescopic glass tumbler, and two costly decanters, (containing eau de vie and Veuve Cliquot to wash out the instrument with whenever it should become clouded), and seated myself in my window, very nearly under the constellation Leo. I then poured about a gill of liquid from each decanter into the telescopic tumbler and slowly elevated it to an angle of about ninety degrees. I did not see anything. The second trial was also a failure, but I had faith in that wash, and I washed out the instrument again. And just here let me suggest to you, Professor, that you can always depend on that mixture; rightly compounded, I expect it is the most powerful aid to human eyesight ever invented; assisted by it I have known a man to see two drinks on the counter before him when in reality there was but one—and so strong was the deception that I have known that man to get drunk on thirteen of these duplicate drinks when he was naturally gauged for twenty-six.

Very well; after I had washed out my glass the third time, three or four stars, of about the nineteenth magnitude, I should judge, shot from the zenith and fell in the general direction of Oakland. During the fourth wash, and while I had one eye sighted on Venus and the other one closed in blissful repose, that planet fell upon the roof of the Russ House and bounced off into Bush street; immediately afterward, Jupiter fell and knocked a watchman's eye out—at least I think it was that star, because I saw the watchman clap his hand to his eye and say "By Jupiter!" The assertion was positive, and made without hesitation, as if he had the most perfect confidence in the accuracy of his judgment; but at the same time it is possible that he might have been mistaken, and that the damage was not done by Jupiter after all. I maintain, though, that the chances are all in favor of his being correct, because I have noticed that policemen usually know as much about stars as anybody, and take more interest in them than most people.

Up to this time the wind had been north by northeast half west, and I noticed an uncommon dryness in the atmosphere, but it was less marked after I applied the fifth wash. My barometer never having had any experience in falling stars, got hopelessly tangled in trying to get the run of things, and after waltzing frantically between "stormy" and "falling weather" for awhile without being able to make up its mind, it finally became thoroughly demoralized and threw up its commission. My thermometer did not indicate anything; I noted this extraordinary phenomenon, of course, but at the same time I reasoned—and, I think, with considerable sagacity—that it was less owing to the singular condition of the atmosphere than to the fact that there was no quicksilver in the instrument. About this time a magnificent spectacle dazzled my vision—the whole constellation of the Great Menken came flaming out of the heavens like a vast spray of gas-jets, and shed a glory abroad over the universe as it fell! [N.B. I have used the term "Great Menken" because I regard it as a more modest expression than the Great Bear, and consequently better suited to the columns of THE CALIFORNIAN, which goes among families, you understand—but when you come to transfer my report to the Journal of Science, Professor, you are at liberty to change it if you like.]

I applied the sixth wash. A sprinkle of sparkling fragments ensued—fragments of some beautiful world that had been broken up and cast out of the blue firmament—and then a radiance of noonday flared out of the zenith, and Mercury, the winged symbol of Progress, came sweeping down like a banished sun, and catching in the folds of the flag that floats from the tall staff in the Plaza, remained blazing in the centre of its dim constellation of stars! "Lo, a miracle! the thirty-sixth star furnished from the imperial diadem of heaven! while yet no welcome comes from the old home in the Orient, behold the STATE OF NEVADA is recognized by God!" says I, and seized my telescope, filled her to the brim and washed her out again! The divinity student in the next room came in at this juncture and protested against my swearing with so much spirit, and I had some difficulty in making him understand that I had only made use of a gorgeous metaphor, and that there was really no profanity intended in it.

About this time the wind changed and quite a shower of stars fell, lasting about twenty minutes; a lull ensued, and then came several terrific discharges of thunder and lightning, and how it poured! You couldn't see the other side of the street for the hurtling tempest of stars! I got my umbrella—which I had previously provided along with my other apparatus—and started down the street. Of course there was plenty of light, although the street lamps were not lit (you let that sagacious gas company alone, Professor, to make a good thing out of it when the almanac advertises anything of this kind. I put in these parentheses to signify a complicated wink—you understand?) I met Charles Kean, and

I expect he was drunk; I drifted down the pavement, tacking from one side of it to the other, and trying to give him a wide berth, but it was no use; he would run into me, and he did—he brought up square against me and fell. "Down goes another star," I observed and stopped a moment to make a note of it.

The meteoric storm abated gradually, and finally ceased, but by that time the stars had cut my umbrella nearly all to pieces, and there were a dozen or more sticking in it when I lowered it. It was the most furious deluge I ever saw, while it lasted. Pretty soon I heard a great huzzaing in the distance, and immediately afterward I noticed a brilliant meteor streaming athwart the heavens with a train of fire of incredible length appended to it. It swept the sky in a graceful curve, and after I had watched its splendid career a few seconds and was in the act of making the proper entry in my note-book, it descended and struck me such a stunning thump in the pit of the stomach that I was groveling in the dust before I rightly knew what the matter was. When I recovered consciousness, I remarked "Down went a couple of us then," and made a note of it. I saved the remains of this most remarkable meteor, and I transmit them to you with this report, to be preserved in the National Astronomical Museum. They consist of a fragment of a torn and jagged cylinder the size of your wrist, composed of a substance strongly resembling the pasteboard of this world; to this is attached a slender stick some six feet long, which has something of the appearance of the pine wood so well known to the commerce of this earth, but of such a supernatural fineness of texture, of course, as to enable one to detect its celestial origin at once. There is food here for philosophic contemplation, and a series of interesting volumes might be written upon a question which I conceive to be of the utmost importance to Science, viz.: Do they cultivate pines in Paradise? And if it be satisfactorily demonstrated that they do cultivate pines in Paradise, may we not reasonably surmise that they cultivate cabbages there also? O, sublime thought! O, beautiful dream! The scientific world may well stand speechless and awe-stricken in the presence of these tremendous questions! But may we not hope that the learned German who has devoted half his valuable life to determining what materials a butterfly's wing is made of, and to writing unstinted books upon the subject, will devote the balance of it to profound investigation of the celestial cabbage question? And is it too much to hope that that other benefactor of our race who has proven in his thirteen inspired volumes that it is exceedingly mixed as to whether the extraordinary bird called the Phoenix ever really existed or not, will lend his assistance to the important work and turn out a few tomes upon the subject, wherewith to enrich our scientific literature? My dear sir, this matter is worthy of the noblest effort; for we know by the past experience of learned men, that whosoever shall either definitely settle this cabbage question, or indefinitely unsettle it with arguments and reasonings and deductions freighted with that odor of stately and incomprehensible wisdom which is so overpowering to the aspiring student and so dazzling and bewildering to the world at large, will be clothed with titles of dignity by our colleges, and receive medals of gold from the Kings and Presidents of the earth.

    As I was meandering down the street, pondering over the matters treated of in the preceding paragraph, I ran against another man, and he squared off for a fight. I squared off, also, and dashed out with my left, but he dodged and "cross-countered." [I have since learned that he was educated at the Olympic Club.] That is to say, he ducked his head to one side and avoided my blow, and at the same time he let go with his right and caved the side of my head in. At this moment I beheld the most magnificent discharge of stars that had occurred during the whole evening. I estimated the number to be in the neighborhood of fifteen hundred thousand. I beg that you will state it at that figure in the Journal of Science, Professor, and throw in a compliment about my wasting no opportunity that seemed to promise anything for the good of the cause. It might help me along with your kind of men if I should conclude to tackle science for a regular business, you know. You see they have elected a new governor over there in Nevada, and consequently I am not as much Governor of the Third House there as I was. It was a very comfortable berth; I had a salary of $60,000 a year when I could collect it.

    While my stranger and myself were staggering under the two terrific blows which we had exchanged—and especially myself, on account of the peculiar nature of the "cross-counter" as above described—a singular star dropped in our midst which I would have liked well to possess, because of its quaint appearance, and because I had never seen anything like it mentioned in Mr. Dick's astronomy. It emitted a mild silvery lustre, and bore upon its face some characters which, in the fervor of my astronomical enthusiasm, I imagined spelt "Police - 18," but of course this was an absurd delusion. I only mention it to show to what lengths scientific zeal will sometimes carry a novice. This marvellous meteor was already in the possession of another enthusiast, and he would not part with it.

    On my way home, I met young John William Skae—the inimitable punster of Virginia City, and formerly of Pennsylvania, perhaps you know him? –and I knew from his distraught and pensive air that he was building a joke. I was anxious not to intrude any excitement upon him, which might have the effect of bringing the half-finished edifice down about my ears, but my very caution precipitated the catastrophe I was trying to avert. Said I, "Are you out looking for meteors, too?" His eye instantly lighted with a devilish satisfaction, and says he: "Well, sorter; I'm looking for my Susan—going to meteor by moonlight alone; O Heavens! why this sudden pang, this bursting brain! save me, save me or I perish!"

But I didn't save him—I let him drop; and I deserted him and left him moaning there in the gutter. A man cannot serve me that way twice and expect me to stand by him and chafe his temples and blow his nose and sandpaper his legs and fetch him round again. I would let him perish like an outcast first, and deny him Christian burial afterwards. That Skae has always been following me around trying to make me low-spirited with his dismal jokes, but since that time he caught me out in the lonely moor on the Cliff House road, and intimidated me into listening to that execrable pun on the Kingfisher, I have avoided him as I would a pestilence.

I will now close my report, Professor. If you had not just happened to print that assurance in your little notice that these things should be published in the American Journal of Science, "for the good of Science," I expect it never would have occurred to me to make any meteorological observations at all; but you see that remark corralled me. It has been the dearest wish of my life to do something for the good of Science and see it in print in such a paper as the one you mention, and when I saw this excellent opportunity presented, I thought it was now or never with me. It is a pity that the astonishing drawings which accompany this report cannot be published in the CALIFORNIAN; it could not be helped, though: the artist who was to have engraved them was not healthy, and he only took one look at them and then went out in the back yard and destroyed himself. But you can print them in the Journal of Science, anyhow, just the same; get an artist whose sensibilities have been toned down by chiseling melancholy devices on tombstones all his life, and let him do them up for you. He would probably survive the job.

Works by Mark Twain

Source: *The Official Web Site of Mark Twain*
http://www.cmgww.com/historic/twain/about/writings.htm

(1867) Advice for Little Girls (fiction)
(1867) The Celebrated Jumping Frog of Calaveras County (fiction)
(1868) General Washington's Negro Body-Servant (fiction)
(1868) My Late Senatorial Secretaryship (fiction)
(1869) The Innocents Abroad (non-fiction travel)
(1870-71) Memoranda (monthly column for The Galaxy magazine)
(1871) Mark Twain's Autobiography and First Romance (fiction)
(1872) Roughing It (non-fiction)
(1873) The Gilded Age: A Tale of Today (fiction)
(1875) Sketches New and Old (fictional stories)
(1876) Old Times on the Mississippi (non-fiction)
(1876) The Adventures of Tom Sawyer (fiction)
(1877) A True Story and the Recent Carnival of Crime (stories)
(1878) Punch, Brothers, Punch! and other Sketches (stories)
(1880) A Tramp Abroad (non-fiction travel)
(1880) 1601: Conversation, as it was by the Social Fireside, in the Time of the Tudors (fiction)
(1882) The Prince and the Pauper (fiction)
(1883) Life on the Mississippi (non-fiction)
(1884) Adventures of Huckleberry Finn (fiction)
(1889) A Connecticut Yankee in King Arthur's Court (fiction)
(1892) The American Claimant (fiction)
(1892) Merry Tales (fictional stories)
(1893) The £1,000,000 Bank Note and Other New Stories (stories)
(1894) Tom Sawyer Abroad (fiction)
(1894) Pudd'n'head Wilson (fiction)
(1896) Tom Sawyer, Detective (fiction)
(1896) Personal Recollections of Joan of Arc (fiction)
(1897) How to Tell a Story and other Essays (non-fiction essays)
(1897) Following the Equator (non-fiction travel)
(1900) The Man That Corrupted Hadleyburg (fiction)

(1901) Edmund Burke on Croker and Tammany (political satire)
(1902) A Double Barrelled Detective Story (fiction)
(1904) A Dog's Tale (fiction)
(1905) King Leopold's Soliloquy (political satire)
(1905) The War Prayer (fiction)
(1906) The $30,000 Bequest and Other Stories (fiction)
(1906) What Is Man? (essay)
(1907) Christian Science (non-fiction)
(1907) A Horse's Tale (fiction)
(1907) Is Shakespeare Dead? (non-fiction)
(1909) Captain Stormfield's Visit to Heaven (fiction)
(1909) Letters from the Earth (fiction, posthumous)
(1910) Queen Victoria's Jubilee (non-fiction, posthumous)
(1924) Mark Twain's Autobiography (non-fiction, posthumous)
(1935) Mark Twain's Notebook (posthumous)

Sources/Internet Sites

Hathitrust Digital Library
http://www.hathitrust.org/

Mark Twain in the Virginia City Territorial Enterprise
http://www.twainquotes.com/teindex.html

Mark Twain Project Online
http://www.marktwainproject.org

Internet Archive
https://archive.org/

Unz.org
http://www.unz.org/

Further Reading

Beebe, Lucius. *Comstock Commotion.* Stanford, CA: Stanford University Press, 1954.

Branch, Edgar, ed. *Clemens of the "Call": Mark Twain in San Francisco.* Berkeley, CA: University of California Press, 1969.

Branch, Edgar, ed. *Mark Twain's Letters, Volume I: 1853 - 1866.* Berkeley, CA: University of California Press, 1988.

Caron, James. *Mark Twain: Unsanctified Newspaper Reporter.* University of Missouri Press, 2011.

De Quille, Dan. *History of the Big Bonanza: An Authentic Account of the Biscovery, History, and Working of the World Renowned Comstock Silver Lode of Virginia City, Nevada.* Los Angeles, CA: Peruse Press, 2013

Jake Highton. *Nevada Newspaper Days: A History of Journalism in the Silver State.* Stockton: Heritage West Books, 1990.

Lewis, Oscar. *The Life and Times of the Virginia City "Territorial Enterprise": Being Reminiscences of Five Distinguished Comstock Journalists.* Ashland, OR: ewis Osborne, 1971.

Lingenfelter, Richard E. and Karen Rix Gash. *The Newspapers of Nevada: A History and Bibliography, 1854-1979.* Reno, NV: University of Nevada Press, 1984.

Smith, Harriet Elinor, ed. *The Autobiography of Mark Twain: The Complete and Authoritative Edition.* Berkeley, CA: University of California Press, 2010.

Smith Henry Nash, ed. *Mark Twain of the "Enterprise": Newspaper Articles and Other Documents.* Berkeley, CA: University of California Press, 1957.

Tarnoff, Ben. *The Bohemians: Mark Twain and the San Francisco Writers Who Reinvented American Literature.* New York: Penguin Books, 2015.

Twain, Mark. *Early Tales and Sketches, 1851 - 1864.* University of California Press, 1979.

Williams, George. *Mark Twain: His Life in Virginia City.* Riverside, CA: Tree by the River Publications, 1986.

from The Archive

Theodore Roosevelt
Wilderness, Vol. 1
ISBN: 978-0-9907137-1-5
List Price: $24.95

In the western territories a young Theodore Roosevelt found inspiring loneliness and a hunter's paradise. Out here TR enjoyed tough physical challenges and a pleasing distance from the half-formed men of the East, who grasped so desperately for money and power. As the "open season" on buffalo, antelope, mountain goat and white-tailed deer brought these species close to extinction, however, he began to understand the meaning and value of conservation-a progression expressed eloquently in the articles he penned for Century, The Outlook, Outing, Forest and Stream and other journals. This volume is the first of two offering Roosevelt's complete and unabridged articles on the great western outdoors which inspired one of his most important legacies: the preservation of vast swaths of America's frontier in its natural state. Presented in chronological order, the articles reveal TR's personal progression from dedicated hunter and rancher to determined environmentalist, who came to understand the threat to western flora and fauna from unchecked development and decimating "recreational" sports. The collection includes writings on ranching and the cowboy life that appeared in contemporary juvenile magazines, including Youth's Companion and St. Nicholas.

Richard Harding Davis
The Great War Reporter: Journalism 1914 - 1916
ISBN: 978-0-9907137-4-6
List Price: $24.95

A skilled foreign correspondent with a wide public following, Richard Harding Davis represented a new generation of adventurous journalists, for whom no battle zone, revolution or political turmoil posed too great a danger for the pursuit of news. By the time of World War I, Davis was a literary star for hundreds of evocative articles written from the front lines as well as his (now-forgotten) novels and plays. Dispatched to France, he covered the major early battles of the war, the brutal occupation of Belgian cities, the horrors of trench warfare, the war-time escapades of American civilians and officers, and his own arrest by the Germans on a capital charge of espionage. This collection of newspaper and magazine reports, complete and unabridged, offers the reader a front page seat to the compelling events of the Great War, and newspaper reporting as done with literary skill, social conscience and a flair for the dramatic.

Nellie Bly
Undercover: Reporting for *The New York World* **1887-1894**
ISBN: 978-0-9907137-2-2
List Price: $24.95
Nellie Bly's convincing disguises gained her admission to oppressive sweatshops, underground gambling parlors, illicit adoption agencies and creepy mesmerists' parlors, all in the service of sensational headlines and the steadily rising circulation numbers boasted by the New York World. This fascinating collection of original, unabridged articles—compiled for the first time since their original publication--traces Bly's brief yet astounding career as an undercover journalist.

Lincoln Steffens
The System: Journalism 1897 - 1920
ISBN: 978-0-9907137-3-9
List Price: $24.95

The "muckraker" Lincoln Steffens dug deep into business criminality and political corruption in a powerful series of articles written for McClure's magazine. Establishment newspapers and "System" politicians dismissed his work as just another example of the decrepit modern journalism that could never pass for genuine writing. But Steffens' dogged quest for truth and justice set the bar high for investigative journalists in print, television and the Internet who follow in his footsteps. This new collection from The Archive includes the author's detailed and dramatic pieces on the civic troubles in Chicago, Minneapolis, St. Louis, Philadelphia, Rhode Island, Wisconsin, New Jersey, Ohio, and New York. In addition, The System includes early pieces Steffens wrote on architecture and the newspaper business, three pen portraits of his friend Theodore Roosevelt, and eyewitness descriptions of the social turmoil in early Soviet Russia.

Stephen Crane
Journorealism: The War with Spain, 1898

On February 15, 1898, a massive explosion destroyed the USS Maine in Havana's harbor, killing hundreds of American sailors and raising dark suspicions in the minds of many that Spain, Cuba's colonial master, had committed a dastardly act of sabotage. Within hours, William Randolph Hearst brought out a spectacular edition of the *New York Journal* that roused the masses, and the government, to the Spanish-American War. *Blackwood's* magazine offered a young American journalist 60 English pounds to report directly from the battle zones in Cuba or wherever he may find them.

Struggling with debts and in poor health, Stephen Crane accepted without hesitation and set out from New York. Although *The Red Badge of Courage*, his powerful novel of Civil War fear and heroism, had found a wide audience, Crane was earning poor reviews and derisively small advances for his articles and short stories. Journalism seemed his true calling and the medium in which he found the widest readership. In his articles for *Blackwood's*, the *New York Journal* and the *New York Tribune* Crane strived for simple realism, unadulterated by the discursive, distracting Victorian-era prose that, in his opinion, was strangling American writers.

As a journalist Crane was anything but a simple observer. He sought out the drama in all situations, and relied on the conflict and turmoil of war to transform dry reporting into compelling and very human story. This new approach to newspaper work left a lasting impression on the public and on other young writers, including the adventurer Jack London and an eager World War I volunteer, Ernest Hemingway, whose own approach to war, writing and life became a conscious imitation of Stephen Crane.

Journorealism: The War with Spain collects 45 of Crane's articles, complete and unabridged, as they appeared in leading newspapers in the United States and Britain. This collection, the first of four volumes in The Archive's unique Stephen Crane series, represents a complete primary-source chronicle of the Spanish-American War as created by a writer of the first rank, who helped bring about an important transformation in American literature as the century turned.

Ray Stannard Bker
Afflicting the Comfortable
A journalist of wide-ranging interests, Ray Stannard Baker covered urban crime rackets, business corruption, political shenanigans, and the often-violent struggles of union leaders for the right to organize and negotiate for wage-earners. After joining *McClure's* magazine, he came to national prominence as a "muckraker" (in Theodore Roosevelt's derisive term), a writer who investigated high-level misdeeds and who took seriously the journalist's duty to "comfort the afflicted, and afflict the comfortable." The Archive's three-volume collection of Baker's journalism, scheduled for publication in 2017, will be the first reference source to offer students, historians, and teachers a comprehensive collection of Baker's work, unabridged and reproduced as it first appeared in the pages of *Outlook*, *McClure's*, *Harper's Weekly*, and *Frank Leslie's Illustrated Weekly*.

Ida Tarbell
Busting a Trust: The Standard Oil Stories
Growing up in northwestern Pennsylvania, Ida Tarbell experienced first-hand the great oil boom. Her father was a successful small-scale refiner; the market for crude oil and refined kerosene grew steadily, and the family attained a comfortable middle-class life. Then, in 1872, Mr. Tarbell and hundreds of other refiners, drillers and transporters suffered the total loss of their markets, and livelihoods, to the South Improvement price-fixing scheme and the brilliant, underhanded business tactics of a Cleveland upstart named John D. Rockefeller. Although her family had fallen on hard times, Tarbell completed studies at Allegheny College and moved on to teaching and journalism. A curiosity for history inspired her long biographies of Lincoln and Napoleon in *McClure's*, but a single contemporary drew her as a fit subject: a man whose oil trust now had national attention for its ruthless, some said unfair and probably illegal business practices.

Tarbell's investigation of Standard Oil and John D. Rockefeller ran for 19 long and detailed installments over a period of nearly two years. The articles did not stop at the revelation of Rockefeller's monopolies and price-fixing, his underhanded machinations against competitors, or his manipulation of the oil markets. In its later installments *The History of the Standard Oil Company* became a damning character study without parallel in American journalism, a look at the dark side of business and the corrosive effects of ambition and greed. This new edition of Tarbell's absorbing investigation includes all of the original installments in the series, unabridged, unedited and formatted as they originally appeared in the pages of *McClure's*.

www.ingramcontent.com/pod-product-compliance
Lightning Source LLC
Chambersburg PA
CBHW021121300426
44113CB00006B/234